Counterfeit Sauerkraut
& The Weekend Teeth

JON DAWSON

A nun was just arrested for robbing liquor store in Boston; charged with being habitual felon.

AMERICAN HIKERS CONFIRM THEY ARE
FULL-BLOWN MORONS
SEPT. 27, 2011

If you're like me, national TV news is at best a minor background irritant — sort of like a gnat that isn't in your face, but just knowing it's there is grating nonetheless.

Even if you've caught just a smidge of national TV news as of late, you've probably heard about the trials and tribulations of two Americans — Josh Fattal and Shane Bauer — who, along with their friend Sarah Shourd, accidentally crossed the Iranian border while hiking. Fattal and Bauer were released last week after being imprisoned for 781 days; Shourd was released in 2010.

I caught a few seconds of the press conference Bauer and Fattal held upon their return, and while they spoke passionately about their ordeal, they never addressed one key issue: What in the hell were they doing near the Iranian border in the first place? Are there no hiking trails in the bourgeois United States of America? Had these three stooges already hiked every foot of the Appalachian Trail?

Maybe the Grand Canyon just made too much sense.

Just out of curiosity, I cranked up the Internet and typed "United States hiking trail" into the Google search engine. Within less than a second, 64,200,000 results were plopped in front of my blue Sinatra-esque eyeballs.

With a high-speed Internet connection, it would have taken 781 days to investigate each search result. The fact that Fattal, Bauer and Shourd couldn't be satisfied with a nice walk down the Cumberland Gap is one thing; the fact they decided the primo spot was near the Iranian border confirms they are all full-blown morons.

While the media and apparently most of the population is happy about the return of Dumb and Dumber, I — for one — am a little ambivalent. Why? Because Bauer and Shourd are engaged; not to power the U.S.S. Enterprise through a meteor shower, but to get MARRIED.

That's right — two of the most ignorant (pronounced 'ig-nant') people in the United States are going to marry, and most likely will produce another generation of stupid children. If the collective stupidity of these two gene pools is allowed to creep into the American mainstream, we'll have a problem on our hands that'll make the deficit look like being a nickel short at a strip club.

You could wrap these unfortunate offspring in fluorescent orange bubble wrap and they'd still poke an eye out why trying to operate a spoon.

If going for a stroll in the Armpit of The Universe wasn't enough to prove these wits dim, then take a gander at this statement Bauer made upon his return:

From the Associated Press — "... Sarah, Josh and I oppose U.S. policies towards Iran which perpetuate this hostility."

Now I'm against meaningless jingoism as much as the next guy, but if the U.S. Government — as flawed as it is — had just had a hand in negotiating the freedom of my person from an Iranian prison, I think Emily Post would back me up in saying it would be prudent to wait a couple of days before TRASHING THE VERY PEOPLE THAT GOT YOU OUT OF AN IRANIAN PRISON!

I can't figure out if these people are more pompous or stupid; to paraphrase Jerry Clower, maybe they're just educated beyond their intelligence.

Bauer and Fattal's bail was a combined $1 million. Whoever coughed up the dough has so far remained anonymous, but if the mystery millionaire is reading, I have a plea of my own. I have a wife, a couple of kids and a dog. I don't have the time, financial resources or desire to go for a hike near the Iranian border.

Heck, I'm lucky if I can find time to veg out on the couch for a few minutes on a Sunday.

This job I'm forced to turn up for every day is really harshing my mellow and $1 million would allow me to quit and focus on my true goal in life, which is to someday have nothing to do. Sure, I might walk down the path to my mailbox to see if Victoria's Secret has sent out another catalog filled with half-nekkid women, but that would be about it.

I hearby declare that if you, kind sir or madam, could see fit to award me $1 million, I nor any of my offspring or kin will fill a backpack with oyster crackers and go hiking near Mahmoud Aquavelva's house in Iran. A few of my friends would probably try it, but they think Iran was a hit for Flock of Seagulls in 1982, so I think we're safe on all fronts.

Just think it over.

I'm not sure, but I don't believe Peter Falk ever made an adult film.

LOCAL STORE ACCUSED OF SELLING
ANIMAL PORNOGRAPHY
SEPT. 29, 2011

A La Grange woman says her local grocery store is selling products she deems vulgar

"I'm no prude," says Paulette Burroughs, 39, of La Grange. "But something I saw in that store was way over the line."

Burroughs said she made the discovery Monday afternoon while planning a "Dancing with the Stars" viewing party at her home.

"We had a real good time, except for when old Nancy Grace decided to turn one of her sweater puppies loose," Burroughs said. "That thing looked like it'd been eatin' lemons all day."

While Burroughs was gathering chips, dip and wrist restraints for her party, she started to notice a few items in the store that she'd never noticed before.

"At the end of one aisle there was a giant bag of 'adult' dog food," Burroughs said. "I covered my grandson's eyes and moved in to get a closer look."

Burroughs recalled the package said the contents were "suitable for mature dogs" and that there was a naked photo of a dog on the front of the package.

"I ain't never in my life," Burroughs said.

When contacted by The Free Press, the manager of (censored by Freedom Communications) said he was not aware of any pornographic materials being sold in his store.

"There was an incident involving 'Ben & Jerry's Monkey Butt' ice cream that ended up in court," said store manager James Hetfield. "But that was more of a case of PETA harassment than anything else. Apparently there was a rumor going around that 'Ben and Jerry's Monkey Butt" ice cream contained meat from monkeys that were smuggled into the country illegally, which is false. All of the monkey meat used in that ice cream is supplied by The Marlin Perkins Chimp Farm of Jupiter, Fla."

In a phone interview with The Free Press, Marlin Perkins III — grandson of Mutual of Omaha's Wild Kingdom host Marlin Perkins — said most people have a hard time believing his grandfather would start a business whose sole purpose is to raise monkeys that will eventually be used to spice up ice cream made by a couple of hippies.

"The truth of the matter is Grandpa Marlin hated monkeys, chimps, baboons — the whole lot of 'em," Perkins said as he threw darts at a King Kong poster. "He'd go out to film these animal specials, and more often than not, one of those banana swillers would bite him right in the back seat. That's why he eventually started sending Jim Fowler down to do the dirty work while he sat in the helicopter."

Perkins III said his grandfather suffered such carnage to his backside that he was eventually relegated to the studio.

"His rear end was so uneven that he started sliding out of the helicopter," a tearful Perkins recalled. "Everybody thought he was drunk, but his butt was crooked."

For his part, Perkins III is glad "Ben & Jerry's Monkey Butt" has become a success.

"Every time a tub of that ice cream is sold, I feel like I'm retrieving a little bit of Grandpa's hind end," Perkins said. "I hope wherever he is now he's sitting comfortably."

LA GRANGE WOMAN GIVES OUT MEDS
IN LIEU OF CANDY
NOV. 1, 2011

You can never be too careful with your children — especially at Halloween. Short of bubble-wrapping them every time they walk out the door, it's always better to be safe than sorry.

There was always that kid in school who swore up and down that Halloween was his favorite holiday — and he really needed to be punched. First off, even the worst toy left by Santa was more impressive than the best candy garnered from the richest neighborhoods in town. Secondly, Christmas meant parole from school; Halloween meant a couple of hours sweating your face off behind a toxic mask held on by a rubber band that could slice through a trailer hitch.

A few of my colleagues at the time would be dropped off in a neighborhood with little to no parental supervision. At the time, this practice seemed like bad parenting, but looking back on it now, it may have been an attempt to ditch these heathen children.

It was common knowledge at the time that Paulette Burroughs, 39, of La Grange, would start handing out horse tranquilizers when she ran out of candy. Oddly, Paulette never owned a horse, but rumor has it one of her Halloween visitors — now a 38-year-old man living in the woods behind the old Piggly Wiggly building in La Grange — ate what he thought was a Sweet Tart and had a complete psychological breakdown.

Luckily, he's still wearing the Incredible Hulk uniform he had on in 1983, so the fact he's outgrown it isn't a problem.

My parents only took me to the houses of family and friends, which is a tradition I've continued with both of my tax deductions. I've spent too much time and energy keeping them alive for some nutjob to get them all goofed up on happy juice via a tainted Three Musketeers bar. Just to be safe, I eat half of each piece of candy before the kids get ahold of it.

You may think it's cruel offering children half-eaten candy, but it's given both of them a greater appreciation for vegetables.

Having two tax deductions to traipse around on Oct. 31 means I don't have to spend any money on Halloween candy. When I was a kid, the

Creech's up the road would leave a GIANT bowl of candy on their front porch as they were busy taking their sons Chris and Tony trick-or-treating. I guess I could follow their example and do the same thing, but my vicious guard dog Lucy would probably eat all the candy and anyone who tried to take it from her.

One year, she ate a Butterfinger and ended up holding a family of four hostage on the porch until I was able to talk her down with a bag of Skittles.

Most of my Halloween memories are good ones, but none greater than my encounter with my great uncle. He lived just down the road and was one of our first stops. I walked up to his door one Halloween dressed in my usual Don Cornelius costume, and when he opened the door I said, "Trick or treat!"

He smiled and reached behind the door to grab what I assumed would be a couple of small, "fun-sized" Snickers (Are the normal Snickers considered "serious sized?" Seems there would be more fun to be had with the larger bar, but I digress).

When he reappeared, he did not have candy in hand, rather a football-sized sweet potato. I remember thinking I was too young to have a stroke, but as he smiled and lowered that tumor-looking thing into my plastic bag, I was sure a vacuum tube in my head had busted. I said, "Thank you" and started to walk away, but he started laughing and stopped me.

"I just wanted to see what you'd do," he said as he dumped some real candy into my bag. "Don't eat all of that tater tonight, you hear; save it for your tater gun."

For the next few years, I always laughed to myself whenever I saw a sweet potato. Sadly, around the age of 13, I had to start digging them in the field behind my grandparents' house, and to this day, when I see a sweet potato, I kick it just as hard as I can.

60 Minutes is actually 43 minutes

WAS 60 MINUTES' ANDY ROONEY A CURMUDGEON OR JUST A JERK?
NOVEMBER 3, 2011

I posted an Associated Press story about the passing of Andy Rooney to The Free Press website (Kinston.com) this past Saturday. He'd been mainly absent from "60 Minutes" over the past few months, so his passing at the age of 92 was no great surprise.

According to the AP piece by David Baud-er and Sunday night's "60 Minutes" profile of Rooney, he made his bones as a war correspondent, producer and writer. His biggest claim to fame before "60 Minutes" was being a comedic writer for Arthur Godfrey's radio and TV shows. Although Godfrey's public image was that of folksy gentlemen, Rooney said behind the scenes he could be "quite nasty."

Based on interviews with other Godfrey employees over the years, Rooney's comment on Godfrey's disposition was no shock. What is a bit of a shock — at least to me — was Rooney's attitude towards his fans. When asked by Morley Safer if he responded to fan mail or granted autograph requests, Rooney used the term "idiots" when referring to people who would do such things.

Idiots.

As for myself, I tend to gravitate towards comedy with some teeth, but Rooney was not doing a shtick; he actually referred to people who thought enough of him to write a letter or ask for an autograph as idiots. Now, between my little music stuff and this little column, I've been asked for my autograph approximately 12 times.

Actually, I've been asked for it 13 times, but one of those requests was from a 12-year-old girl in an Atlanta airport who thought I was Jack White of The White Stripes. Not wanting to disappoint her, I duly wrote "For Amy — Love Jack White" on her napkin and made no fuss about it.

I don't know if Rooney ever used the word to describe himself, but most journalists sidled him with the "curmudgeon" tag. According to Merriam-Webster, a curmudgeon is "a crusty, ill-tempered, usually old man." Also according to Merriam-Webster, a jerk is defined as "an unlikable person; especially one who is cruel, rude, or small-minded."

Based on these definitions, which category does Rooney fall into? Would his carwash-sized eyebrows have any effect on the ruling?

Just imagine you've decided to take your elderly parents to New York City. For years, your mom has wanted to see a Broadway show and shop at Macy's, and your dad has wanted to see the Statue of Liberty and maybe scare up a hooker that reminds him of Mamie Van Doren.

After Mom has enjoyed a production of "Guys and Dolls" and Dad has received what could be a life-saving dose of penicillin from the free clinic, you've decided to take them out to dinner at a fancy New York restaurant. I'm not talking about the K&W buffet — I'm talking $8 for a cup of coffee/Tavern on the Green/food-you-can't-pronounce-with-flames-shooting-out-of-it fancy.

After enjoying a $400 meal, you and your parents walk out into the New York night and bump into Andy Rooney on the street. As it turns out, your parents are big-time fans of the Roon, so you very politely tell him your parents are big fans, and ask if he'd mind giving them an autograph. Keep in mind this is a guy who's made millions since 1978 writing about the junk in his desk, his hatred of chocolate chip cookies and the packaging costs of potato chips.

Based on what his colleagues and Rooney himself have said, your parents would have been denied that autograph. A perfect weekend of culture, fine dining and promiscuity ruined by a man made rich by the very people he'd rebuffed.

Does this sound like the actions of a curmudgeon (crusty, ill-tempered, usually old man) or a jerk (unlikable person; especially one who is cruel, rude, or small-minded)? It seems to me the obvious answer is yes.

Let's just hope St. Peter didn't ask Rooney for an autograph.

BILL CLINTON OFFERS HERMAN CAIN SOME ADVICE
NOVEMBER 10, 2011

The following letter was sent by former President Bill Clinton to Republican presidential candidate Herman Cain on Wednesday (The Free Press obtained an exclusive copy):

Dear Mr. Cain,

I know it's been a tough week, but I just want you to know that I feel your pain. My presidential run was marred by accusations of sexual harassment. Shoot, I got so much flack for that cigar thing that I can't even use a toothpick in public anymore.

Can you imagine how hard it is to look cool while using floss at the IHOP?

Since you're a Republican, these allegations of sexual misconduct will not help you … but boy, did they help me. When every woman with a pulse from Arkansas to Alabama accused me of trying to play "hide the dolphin" with them, the press jumped all over them. These women were dragged through the mud and for the most part their claims were discounted.

Shoot, one of 'em even had me on tape and it still didn't stick. I even carried the feminist vote — figure that one out and I'll buy you a steak dinner.

It may seem strange for you to be receiving advice from me, but to be honest, I've had it with the Democratic Party. If they hadn't embraced Barack Obama with kid gloves, Hillary would be in the White House — which means I'd be in the White House. I've got bags of Cheetos and weed hidden all over that place, although judging by the work of my successor, the weed is probably long gone.

Being a black conservative, you won't be able to play the race card. If these accusations were coming out against President Obama, these women would have already been linked to Al Qaeda, Bernie Madoff and Dane Cook by MSNBC. Your best bet is to appear on Fox News wearing a Larry the Cable Guy T-shirt while dueting with Hank Williams, Jr.; challenging Al Sharpton and Jesse Jack-son to a game of lacrosse might help too.

To be honest, I don't know much about your accusers. One of them has had nine jobs in 17 years and filed for bankruptcy twice, but I'm sure that wouldn't have anything to do with her sudden decision to grant more interviews than a crack dealer with a makeup fetish.

Another one has filed complaints more than once at different companies, which means she's either really hot or possibly thinks a little too much of herself; either way I'd like her number if you have it.

I don't know if you're innocent or guilty of the charges levied against you, but I suggest you lawyer up either way. I used a semantic discussion of the meaning of the word "is" to weasel out of my problems, so if you need any help with the legal mumbo jumbo, I'm here to help.

Remember, I'm the guy who left DNA on a woman's dress and my poll numbers still went up; I'm bad and I'm nationwide, Buddie Row.

In closing, remember that the Republican Party is a forgiving party. Dick Cheney shot a man in the face and George W. Bush invaded a country that had nothing to do with the 9/11 attacks, but they weren't lynched in the street.

Shoot, Ted Kennedy let a woman drown and he never received as much as a speeding ticket.

You hang in there, Herman. If this whole presidential thing doesn't pan out for you, come on up to Chappaqua and we'll pull the blinds and watch a DVD of me telling the press that "I did not have sexual relations with that woman" with a straight face.

I'm Rick James, b***h!

Sincerely,

Bill Clinton (dictated but not read)

PATCHES OF IDIOCY FAIL TO RUIN LA GRANGE PARADE
DECEMBER 1, 2011

As some of you out there may know, I participated in the La Grange Christmas Parade last week. To many, I'm sure this appeared to be the equivalent of mixing shrimp into a banana pudding, but I agreed to do it, so I showed up.

When I was a kid, it was common knowledge that if you went to the parade, at some point gobs of candy would be thrown in your general direction. However, in recent years it's become verboten to launch any sugar-based confections from a parade float, tractor, or obscenity-blasting show car.

In case you weren't there, the short version of the story is this: A car club had several vehicles registered in the La Grange parade. One driver decided to blast music with vulgar lyrics from his vehicle during the parade that was viewed by old and young alike.

According to a parade official, the Lenoir County Sheriff 's Office advised the town it couldn't do anything on the day because they didn't actually witness the incident in question. If it had witnessed it, apparently they would have been able to remove the car from the parade and issue the driver a citation.

Monday night, I spoke with the CEO of the car club in question, and he told me the person responsible for the vulgar music was someone who'd been trying to gain membership to their club for a while. According to the club CEO, neither he nor anyone in the club had any idea this person was going to play this music.

The club leader went on to say this person was now banned from their club and, going forward, all drivers would be required to synchronize their music to traditional fare such as "Silent Night."

The only other complaint I've heard is about the motorcycle folks who thought it would be a good idea to periodically rev their engines to the point of hurting people's ears. Honest to God, what is the purpose of making so much noise with a vehicle that it makes little children start to cry? Maybe I'm wrong, but I don't think people should have to invest in earplugs to attend a Christmas parade.

I don't remember anywhere in the Bible where it says the three wise men revved up their camels on their way to the manger.

Now back to the candy thing — why can't we throw candy anymore? Unless you are purdy, you need something to do other than wave when participating in a parade. My guess is some kid chasing down a piece of candy got run over by a Shriner doing 3 mph in a clown car. Instead of allowing nature to skim the weaker strands of DNA from the gene pool, we as a society have decided to make the entire world safe for morons.

Sure, this means within a few decades we'll be overrun with stupid people, but there is no positive side so I'll move on to the next paragraph.

Although I didn't and don't agree with the no-candy policy, since I was representing my employer, I decided to play by the rules. The only other thing I could think to do was film the parade from atop the truck provided by Dan Wise Chevrolet. I was riding in the back of the truck with Official Wonder of Lenoir County Paulette Burroughs, so she handled crowd control while I filmed the parade attendees.

Everyone on the route was nice and it was cool to see the women start to fix their hair as soon as they noticed I was filming. As soon as time permits, we'll try to post the video on Kinston.com.

The marching bands and floats were all mighty impressive, but it's hard to top the jolly dude with the white beard. I thought it was great of Santa Claus to participate in the parade, especially since this is his busy season. Before the parade started, I walked up to him and asked if that "Hot Wheels City Speedway" I asked for back in 1979 was on back order.

He just smiled, reached into his back pocket and produced a copy of a restraining order he took out on me in 1980.

While I myself am not a fan of being in a crowd of more than five people, the people of La Grange were in great spirits. I may be wrong, but this year's La Grange Christmas Parade seemed like the biggest in years — maybe ever. It was good to see a mass of people in a generally festive mood.

With all that's gone wrong this year, it was good to see a massive group of people from diverse backgrounds get along and have a good time. Now if we could only spread some of this over the rest of the year, we'd be in bidness.

By the way — within two minutes of the parade starting, I saw candy flying from three different floats into the crowd. To get around the candy thing next year, I think I'll dump Moon Pies and Nabs on the crowd with a pool skimmer.

LA GRANGE MAN TRAPPED IN CAR WASH
FOR 36 HOURS
JANUARY 12, 2012

A simple trip to the car wash turned into a 36-hour ordeal for a La Grange man last weekend.

Elmore Leonard, 89, of Echo Drive, La Grange, told rescue personnel it all started when he mistakenly inserted a $100 bill into an automated payment machine at the Harlan Car Wash on Wynona Street.

"Apparently, he thought he was putting a five in the machine," said Harlan Car Wash owner Art Mullins. "We've found pennies, bottle caps, Monopoly money and flattened pieces of gum in these machines in the past but never a $100 bill."

Leonard says he realized the mistake instantly and tried to get change from the machine.

"I kicked it, hit it, cussed it and spit on it, but it wouldn't give up nothin'," Leonard said. "Usually, it takes them dang machines 20 minutes to take a brand-new, flat dollar bill with no wrinkles at all. That C-note I put in there looked like Larry King after a hot shower and it nearly ripped my hand off when it sucked it in.

"I could almost swear I heard that machine burp after it took it."

Leonard said he was determined to get his money's worth, so he drove his 1980 Impala into the car wash with the intent of receiving $100 worth of services.

"I hit the button for the $3 option, so that came out to 33 car warshes I was due," Leonard said.

After the fourth wash cycle, Leonard said he dozed off.

"Them jets of water get downright soothin' after a while," Leonard said. "I put a Tanya Tucker tape in the stereo, rared the seat back and took an incredible nap."

While Leonard was napping, the car wash's stop mechanism malfunctioned.

"I woke up between a wash and rinse cycle and everything was dark," Leonard said. "Then the soapy water started up again and scared the oatmeal right out of me."

As it turns out, Leonard had been asleep for five hours.

"I tried to call 911 on my cell phone but forgot the number," Leonard said. "Luckily, I found part of a ham biscuit under the front seat. It looked to be a few months old, but I'd put my weekend teeth in that morning so I was able to gnaw on it a bit. When I got through with the biscuit, I rolled down the window a little bit during a rinse cycle to warsh it down."

Finally at 3 a.m., emergency crews were able to shut the car wash down.

"I've never been so happy to see the five-oh come up behind me," Leonard said. "I tried to ditch my Lipitor and Viagra simply out of habit."

The owners of the car wash apologized to Leonard, although he said he harbors no hard feelings.

"The way I figure it, I won't need a car wash for at least three years," Leonard said.

"It feels good to be ahead of the game."

MACHETE IMPLEMENTED IN MONDAY'S
UNC BASKETBALL PRACTICE
JANUARY 17, 2012

UNC head basketball coach Roy Williams was calm and collected at a press conference that followed the Tar Heels' 90-57 loss to Florida State on Saturday. He took responsibility for his teams' poor performance and praised the Seminoles for playing a good game.

While many were hoping Williams would go on a red-in-the-face, vein-busting scream-a-thon that would make Bobby Knight look like Phil Donahue, the coaching legend apparently decided to channel his energies into correcting the mistakes made by the Heels down in Florida. Based on bits of news creeping out of Chapel Hill since the flogging in Tallahassee, Williams seems to be making progress.

For starters, several pictures of Williams entering the Smith Center with a baseball bat and a machete made their way to the Internet Monday morning. When asked by a passerby what he planned to do with the weapons, Williams smiled gently and said in a soft Bill Anderson-esque tone, "These aren't weapons, these are motivational tools."

With that, Williams playfully mussed the hair of the questioner, pulled the machete out of its sheath and kicked open the door to the Dean Smith Center.

According to Facebook and Twitter posts by UNC students, strange sounds and odors were said to be emanating from the Smith Center on Monday. One student tweeted "lots of shrieks and screams coming from gym area; possibly gunfire." One player tweeted that "having coach bounce a ball on my face for 15 minutes helped me focus." It's not known if this tweet was made under duress.

UNC practices historically start at noon, but due to what was described as a "scheduling conflict," the workout didn't start until 4 a.m.

"There was a scheduling conflict alright," said team manager Rafael Nadal. "The coach wouldn't let them on the bus to come home. As the players stood outside the bus they could see Coach Williams doing all kinds of unspeakable things to their personal belongings; I was completely ignorant to the erotic possibilities of an iPod."

As the players stood outside the team bus, a few of them grumbled about a lack of food.

"A few of the players started complaining about not having any food, so Coach Williams asked if they wanted some doughnuts, to which they replied 'yes,' " Nadal said. "A few minutes later, Coach stepped off the bus with the doughnuts but nobody would take one."

When asked why no one took a doughnut, Nadal said the coach was wearing the doughnuts at the time.

"He kept walking around offering the guys doughnuts but they just kept looking skyward," Nadal said. "Coach was carrying half a dozen of 'em; it was downright impressive."

There were other "motivational" measures for the team when they arrived back in Chapel Hill.

"Students from the UNC engineering department were called in to electrify the free-throw line," said a member of the Dean Smith Center custodial crew. "It's kinda funny to watch the coach sit on the bench with a barbecue sandwich in one hand and a set of jumper cables in the other.

"The downside is every time one of those guys misses a free throw, I'm the one that has to clean up the mess. You'd be surprised how much product a 6-10 basketball player can produce after being juiced. I swear some of the jerseys in the rafters were starting to curl up just to get away from all of it."

Team manager statistics indicate UNC's free-throw percentage went up 457 percent during Monday's practice, as did cases of dyspepsia.

"I haven't seen that much **** on the floor at one time since Rashad McCants was on the team," one player tweeted.

I just saw an NRA sticker on a Prius

FATHER LEAVES DAUGHTER BOX OF GRITS IN WILL
JAN. 19, 2012

I turned 39 on Wednesday. My birthday started off with a 22-month-old tax deduction jumping on my chest at 5 a.m. She gave me a kiss on the cheek as I laid there thinking how sweet she was becoming. Then she sneezed on me seven times with a spray pattern that resembled a busted lawn sprinkler hooked up to a fire engine.

It sounded like someone was slapping the side of a brick wall with a wet mop.

As I got up to take a shower, the moonlight glistened off the beads of toddler spray that were now encrusted in my ample chest hair. The droplets of nose tears shined in the night like diamonds hiding in a briar patch.

I'm probably the only guy on the Eastern seaboard who had to shower with Lava soap, I thought to myself.

The screams from the shower woke up everybody in the house, but they gave me a pass because it was my birthday. Also, they all knew it meant they were one year closer to their inheritance — which, at this point, consists of the third season of "Facts of Life" on VHS, a box of grits autographed by Polly Holliday and 100 shares of Enron stock.

When I got to the office, I flipped the choke on my computer and gave the starter cord a good rip. After 10 or so pulls, it cranked up and my workday began. There were a few "Happy Birthday" emails mixed in with the usual "drop dead" emails, which was nice. Free Press concierge Paulette Burroughs brought me breakfast, and while I don't usually eat cigarette sandwiches before noon, I must admit they hit the spot.

Back at the office, it was hard to concentrate. Coworkers heading to and from the break room rattled their keys so loudly it was as if the ghost of Jacob and Bob Mar-ley were having a jam session out in the hall. I got up and shut the door to my office, but since the heat in this building is set on "Inferno," the door had to be opened to let some of the steam out.

My thoughts then wandered to a debate I've had with myself for years: Since Lorne Greene was on the original Battle-star Galactica AND he used to sell Alpo, how was he able to take his dog outside the spaceship to release a few hostages? If this dog needed to send a fax, as it were, did they let him do his business in an air lock and then shoot it out into space? If so, does that mean there are thousands of pounds of Golden Retriever fertilizer hurtling through space? What if they smashed into each other and formed that new planet they found a year or so back?

Anyway, turning 39 is no big deal. They say your mind starts to go around this time of life, but I don't see any reason why they shouldn't allow the 3-point shot in the NFL. Football takes too long and this new facet to the game will allow the NASCAR drivers to pit with greater frequency.

LIPSTICK LEADS AUTHORITIES TO SUSPECT IN NIGHTCLUB RAMPAGE
JAN. 26, 2012

The scene at the Zirconium Club on King Street was despicable. Busted chairs, glass and bone fragments covered the floor while the string of lights used to illuminate the restroom door dangled like a participle in the wind.

Det. Bolander of the Kinston Sheriff 's Office picked through the rubble looking for clues that could help him arrest whoever was responsible for the carnage that took place the night before.

"According to eyewitnesses, the damage was caused by a woman wearing red lipstick, high heels and not much else," Bo-lander said. "Some say she was wearing a dress; others say she'd wrapped herself in Saran Wrap; a few said she was wearing a dress wrapped in Saran Wrap to keep it from getting dirty.

"Either way, this broad was sealed fresh for trouble."

The boys from the lab were lifting lipstick remnants from straws, glasses, cigarette butts and ankles. The lady had a penchant for the wilder side of life. She wasn't interested in sugar, spice, or anything nice. She was more into alcohol, booze, and sneaking out of Golden Corral with a pocketbook full of macaroni and cheese.

According to the club's manager, celebrated local heathen Paulette Burroughs' rampage was ignited by an argument over which was better, "Battlestar Galactica" or "Walker, Texas Ranger."

Down at the Kinston Sheriff 's Office, four detectives crowded around a TV screen. They were going over Zirconium Club security tapes in hope of identifying the woman who sent 11 men to the hospital the night before.

"THERE SHE IS!" cried out Det. Pembleton as he glared at the screen. "She's standing by the jukebox."

Detectives Bayliss and Munch concurred the woman stealing quarters from the jukebox was an old nemesis.

"On the street she's known as 'The Horror', 'M.C. Krunkloaf ' and 'Grandma Manson'," Pempleton said. "According to the DMV, her name is Paulette Burroughs."

A few minutes later the lab reports came back on the lipstick samples taken from the crime scene.

"The lipstick found at the Zirconium Club match samples taken from crime scenes at the Emerald Club, Club Pearl, and The Tupper-ware Room," Bayliss said. "Many of these brands of lipstick were taken off the market years ago, but apparently Paulette is frugal and buys in bulk."

The brands listed in the report were "Concubine Crimson", "Ben Dover Red", "Fire In The Hole", "Daddy Issue Red", "Moulin Rouge", "Safety Word", "Jersey Shore Orange", "Not A Rash", "Pimp Me Pink", "Scarlet Letter" and "Baboon Butt Red".

Traces of lizard hormones and owl squeezings were also listed in the report.

Although the security tape places Burroughs at the Zirconium Club at 9:42 p.m. on Wednesday, the system seems to have mysteriously shut down before any of the carnage was caught on video. Burroughs' insistence on playing her bootleg "Mama's Family" DVDs may account for the disruption in coverage.

"Apparently, Vicki Lawrence is her 29th cousin or something," said Zirconium Club bartender Isaac Washington. "Back when I worked on cruise ships, she'd show up once in a while. Capt. Slaughter once threw her off the ship in Puerto Rico for trying to smuggle a pool boy onto the ship in her luggage.

"On the other hand, once when our ship was approached by a band of pirates, Paulette fired a few rounds from a .38 over their heads and they decided to go rob one of Kathie Lee's boats instead."

Burroughs was unavailable for comment; the case is still under investigation. According to TMZ.com, Burroughs is believed to be the woman responsible for the bust-up of Kobe Bryant's marriage, the overturned cruise ship in Italy and Dane Cook's career.

Sequins, or how to align penquins in order of age

N.C. STATE PLAYER A DESCENDANT OF HOLLYWOOD ROYALTY
JAN. 31, 2012

Stupid questions — we all get them on a daily basis: "Cold enough for ya?" "Ya think the price of gas is gonna come down? "Why hasn't Clay Aiken gotten married yet?"

If you're a good person, you'll just answer any of the above questions with a shrug, smile and possibly a grunt and go on about your day. I try really, really hard to be a good person — at least during business hours. At other times — say at 8 a.m. on a Saturday when I'm at the dump — not so much.

After a week of working for wages that would make a homeless man hock up a lung with laughter, I loaded up the previous week's trash and headed to the dump. This used to be a fairly simple task: put trash in bag, drive bag to dump, throw bag in dump. Now, trying to get all the bags in the dumpster before the dude comes out of the shack to make sure you haven't mixed in a plastic jug — which would apparently cause the world to spin off its axis and into the sun — requires James Bond-like training and nerves of steel.

"I don't mean to bother you, but if they find any plastic bottles in your trash, they're gonna fine you $1,000," the dude in the shack told me a few months ago.

"That's OK, I appreciate the warning," I said. "But I drop my old landlord's name and address into every bag of trash I bring down here.; if they ever do find that Crisco bucket full of uranium in my trash, they'll know which house to go to."

With a shrug, smile and friendly grunt, he went back into the shed.

As I stood their tossing my bags full of illicit plastic bottles into the dumpster, a guy on the other side of the dumpster started grilling me about a recent story we'd ran that required an amendment the following day.

"Man, y'all really messed that up," he said. "I can't believe...." ...

"Well, the guy had falsified documents, but the error was discovered — and corrected — over a month ago," I said.

"Well what are you all going to do about it?" he said.

Keep in mind I'm knee deep in bags full of baby diapers and illegal Pepsi empties while this is all going on. It's about 94 degrees and mosquitoes the size of golf balls are trying to tote me off.

"Sir, we ran a correction; there's not much more we can do about it," I said.

"Well, I'm still mad about it," he said.

"What else would you like us to do?" I asked. "Do you want us to TP his house or key his car? What exactly do you think needs to be done?"

"You ain't got to git no attitude about it, now," he said.

"Let me ask you something: Did you see my name on the article?" I calmly asked between gritted teeth.

"No," he said.

"Then why are you bothering me with it at 8 o'clock on a Saturday morning?" I asked. "How'd you like it if a stranger started bothering you about the cancellation of 'Gomer Pyle'? I'm pretty sure you didn't write the show, but from where I'm standing, it looks like it could be based on you or your kin. Apparently they made the TV version a little smarter than the real-life version."

At this point, the dude in the shack came out to see what was wrong. As I got in my car to leave, I motioned the dude in the shack over.

"Look, I don't know how to tell you this, but that guy has loads of plastic bottles mixed in with his trash," I whispered. "I tried to stop him but he said nobody told him what to do."

As I drove off enjoying the interrogation that was now going on in my rearview mirror, I remembered possibly the dumbest question I'd ever heard in my life.

After a shooting incident that claimed the life of a law enforcement officer and wounded another, I accompanied the then-Free Press crime reporter to a press conference. The wounded officer entered the room and sat patiently for the onslaught of questions. After a few standard questions, a TV reporter — with a straight face — asked the wounded officer the following question:

"How does it feel to know the community is behind you?"

I'm not sure what happened after that, but when I regained control of my faculties, my colleague and a cameraman were both trying to stop me from stapling that TV reporters' head to the floor.

Because of that incident, my stapling license was permanently revoked and I'm now only allowed to use paper clips.

The greatest and best publicized example of a stewpid question involves N.C. State basketball player Scott Wood and a reporter that was apparently getting his teeth whitened on common sense day at school.

Here's the scene: N.C. State had just been beaten by God's team — the UNC Tar Heels — for the 11th time in a row. After the game, these poor players are required to speak to the media and answer the same questions they answer after every game: What was the key to the victory?

Why do you think you lost? Is Billy Packer still hiding out in the locker rooms asking players to pull his finger?

We've all become conditioned to these types of questions, and, to their credit, the players usually go along with it.

All of that changed when a reporter asked Wood the following: "How frustrating is it to have never beaten UNC?" Woods took a second or two to absorb the question and somehow find the strength not to punch this guy into the following week. Eventually, Woods responded with, "Has your wife ever cheated on you? It's probably that frustrating."

I don't know if this kid is related to Don Rickles or read a lot of those Mad Magazine "Snappy Answers to Stupid Questions" books when he was a kid, but I can tell you it's the first time I've ever stood at attention and saluted a newspaper story.

God bless you, Scott Wood.

And for the record, the reporter who asked the question has been promoted to vice-president of NBC.

ATTENTION: DIAPERS MUST BE BOILED FOR LANDFILL DISPOSAL
FEB. 2, 2012

On Tuesday, I eluded to an unpleasant encounter with a Free Press reader at an area dump site. Little did I know the deluge of responses that column would generate.

According to various emails, texts and phone messages, many area residents have been confused by the rules and procedures of our local trash drop-off sites. Between having to separate plastic from the other trash to no longer being allowed to dispose of corpses, the red tape involved in taking out the trash is getting ridiculous.

I sense some of you city slickers are looking down at us county folk for not having access to a trash pickup service, and in my youth, I was right there with you. My main reason for trash-pickup envy was the dreaded practice of having to beat the top out of a 55-gallon steel drum so it could be turned into a trash barrel.

Unless you had access to a torch — which we did not — the only way to pop the top off those barrels was to take a hammer and chisel to it.

There was nothing like coming home from a day of middle or high school blandness and seeing a new blue barrel waiting for you near the back edge of the yard. There was no sense in pretending not to see it, because it was so blue Ray Charles could have seen it from an airplane.

I firmly believe whoever invented rap music spent many afternoons beating the snot out of a steel drum with a hammer and chisel; you had a dull, repetitive beat mixed in with words and phrases of a lewd nature. The echo of the clanging metal bounced off the woods in a nearly musical way that was easy to dance to, and by the end of it, your pants had probably slid down to the middle of your whoopee cakes.

Once the barrel was topless, trash could be deposited into it and burned. There was a separate barrel for glass and aerosol cans, so even back in the 1980s, we had to separate trash. Was it because we thought in our hearts this practice would stop the earth from devolving into a burnt biscuit by the year 2058?

No, it was done purely for safety.

One afternoon, I had somewhere to go and was in a hurry, so I dumped all the trash in the barrel without separating it. I set the trash on fire and waited for it to burn down enough so I could hit the road without worrying about the neighborhood going up in flames.

As I stood there waiting for the fire to dip below the top of the barrel, one of the aerosol cans I'd neglected to remove from the trash 'sploded. The blast blew a hole in the new barrel the size of Toby Keith's head and caused many within earshot to have involuntary spills of a personal nature.

Fast forward a few years and trash drop-off sites started popping up, which made the backyard trash barrel a thing of the past. Mysteriously, this happened just as I was leaving home.

Come to think of it, my folks didn't get a riding lawn mower until I moved away either. I believe this warrants a call to Oliver Stone.

While the trash barrel nightmare is now a thing of the past, a new refuse-related terror had emerged: trash dump rules.

In the good old days, you could load up any trash — paper, plastic, human — and throw it in the dumpster and be on your way. It was so simple and delightful you almost looked forward to taking the trash off. It wasn't glamorous, but it was cut and dried.

Most things we all have to deal with on a daily basis (jobs, relationships, restraining orders) can get complicated, but taking off the trash was the last bastion of black and white/no questions asked goodness in our lives.

Like anything that is enjoyed by many, it eventually got screwed up. It started with being forced to separate aluminum cans. I'm all for recycling, and if it creates a few thousand jobs then I don't mind doing it. But then we were ordered to separate the plastic from "regular kitchen trash," which in this day and age is like trying to distinguish which part of the air we breath is oxygen and which part is hydrogen.

And by the way, what is "regular kitchen trash?" We've got a baby still in diapers. Historically, we don't diaper the baby on the stove, and the diapers do contain plastic. Does this mean we have to separate the soiled diapers from the used napkins and dead 9-volt batteries?

Maybe if we boiled the soiled diapers with some collards for a few minutes they'd be considered "regular kitchen trash."

The piece de resistance in the world of trash regulation is a sign that was reportedly posted at a local trash dump. The person who emailed this to me swore it was actually taped to a local bin within the last month, so here's what it said: "No spoiled food."

Can you imagine the look on a veterans face after reading that sign? This soldier went halfway around the world to fight for his or her country, only to come home to a world that won't let him dispose of a half-eaten bologna sandwich at the county dump.

Aside from the occasional stick of celery that shows up in my refrigerator from time to time, I've never felt the need to throw away unspoiled food. Maybe by "no spoiled food" they mean food that had a privileged upbringing with heat lamps and private nurseries.

I don't want to perpetuate class warfare between free-range eggs and sweat shop eggs; I think brand-name Oreos should be able to coexist with the cheaper (but still tasty) Almosteos; Mt. Dew should feel privileged to sit in the same landfill with its White Lightening counterpart.

Peace, love and soul.

LOCAL ACTRESS MAKES DEBUT IN SUPER BOWL COMMERCIAL
FEB. 7, 2012

I'm probably the only living mammal that hasn't hooked up with Madonna. I'm also probably the only one who didn't see one second of Super Bowl XXVIIX-IVIXIVI, or whichever one it was.

For the record, I have nothing against the Super Bowl or people who use their public positions to further their own wealth. Consequence-free distractions are a great way to relieve some of the pressure brought on by a stagnant economy, a limp job market and the terrorizing notion of NBC's "Whitney" being renewed for another season.

Personally, I think your time could be better spent reading a selection from a good book; a book such as "Making Gravy in Public" ($2.99 Kindle/Nook, $15 paperback at Amazon.com).

Are words not your friends? How about using that booming surround-sound system of yours to listen to something other than 'splosions from the latest "Transformers" movie? A wise investment would be the new "Life Saver" CD by Third of Never (available on iTunes, Amazon, thirdofnever.com). If you play the song backwards you can clearly hear the vocalist sing "revas efil"; pretty spooky, huh?

While I was busy de-linting my belly button with a claw hammer during most of the game, I did check that infernal Twitter thing a few times. Most of the messages coming across were the same lame wastes of time you'd expect: Demi Moore was "feeling awfully full" after eating half a grape; Jay-Z and Beyonce's baby's first burp debuted at No. 1 on the Billboard Top 200; the Kardashians have signed an exclusive distribution deal with Walmart for their new line of bubble-butt shaped Jello molds — which is expected to increase the sales of Jello in the creepy, lonely men demographic by 7,000 percent.

Usually, those types of updates would make even the sturdiest person look for the car keys and a well-sealed garage, but one piece of good news did filter through. Apparently a local actress/model/motivational speaker/taxidermist made her professional acting debut in a Super Bowl commercial on Sunday.

"One of our scouts was in La Grange visiting relatives, and while at the grocery store she noticed a woman buying ExLax and a plunger at the same time," said Rainn Wilson of Tramp, Trollop and Jezebel Modeling Agency of Tulsa, Okla. "She seemed such a free spirit, and after finding out she worked for a newspaper we figured we'd be able to get her real cheap; I'm talking half-a-bag-of- -Skittles-and-a-loosey cheap."

The woman in question, Paulette Burroughs of The Free Press in Kinston, said she is taking her newfound fame in stride.

"I've been famous before," Burroughs said. "I was the first woman to dance in a bikini on 'Soul Train' back in 1977. After the show, Don Cornelius told me I was so good I was intimidating the other dancers. He gave me enough money for bus fare home and a copy of 'Barry White sings Bing Crosby' on eight-track and that was the end of my career as a professional freakazoid."

If you were watching the game on Sunday, Burroughs' appearance could be seen between Jerry Seinfeld's Acura advert and the Mel Gibson/Louis Farrakhan/ Jeremiah Wright commercial for Klein's Kosher Pickles. In the spot, Burroughs is seen frolicking on the beach with a bottle of the new chewing tobacco-flavored Red Bull energy drink, which is set to debut in test markets in the South beginning March 1.

"Usually, if I need a burst of legal energy, I'll just take a sip of water from the air conditioner run-off," Bur-roughs said. "But this chaw-flavored Red Bull is alright, now."

DUKE PLAYERS CITED FOR CHEATING BEFORE UNC BASKETBALL GAME
FEB. 9, 2012

Another chapter in the soap opera known as the UNC-Duke basketball rivalry was written last night. While reasons for the outcome will be debated amongst sports fans that players on the respective teams would never hang out with in real life, the ugliness that preceded the game was unprecedented.

Social media sites such as Facebook, Twitter and Thirdofnever.com were the first to break the story on Wednesday afternoon. Allegations of rumor mongering and cheese forgery flew back and forth between Durham and Chapel Hill for hours before the following statement was issued by the Atlantic Coast Conference:

"Acting on an anonymous tip, ACC officials searched the belongings of three members of the Duke basketball squad as they entered the Dean Smith Center on Wednesday afternoon. This search resulted in the discovery of several items the Department of Homeland Security has deemed 'potentially problematic'. This investigation is ongoing."

Although no officials at Duke, UNC or the ACC would go into specifics regarding the items in question, a former Duke employee in charge of Mike Krzyzewski's hair dye has decided to speak out.

"They've been doing this for years," said Wynn Duffy. "I don't know how they got away with it for this long."

In the interest of full disclosure, Duffy was fired from the Duke staff at the end of the 2010-11 season.

"It generally takes about 40-50 gallons of industrial grade Bible Black Grecian formula to keep Coach K's hair in tiptop shape," Duffy said. "A couple of times last season, I mixed in ink from some old pens in an attempt to stay within budget. Eventually, some of the ink caramelized, which made it really difficult for the guy who has to come in and file Krzyzewski's horns down every week, so they let me go."

According to Duffy, one of the items seized from the bag of Duke guard Seth Curry was a bag of feathers.

"It's widely known that UNC center Tyler Zeller is extremely ticklish,"

Duffy said. "Coach K has been running feather-tickle drills in practice ever since Zeller came on the scene. A light swipe at his ear used to distract him, but now they have to get him right in the armpit to throw him off. Also, if you say 'TICKLE MONSTER IS GOING TO GET YOUR SUGAR!' while you're doing it he won't be able to hit the backside of a barn."

Duffy says marbles were found in the bag of Duke forward Mason Plumlee.

"I don't know where he finds them, but Krzyzewski imports these weird marbles that are made of a special polymer that causes them to melt as soon as they're stepped on," Duffy says. "UNC Coach Roy Williams actually saw the marbles used in a game last year but he could never scoop one up before they evaporated," Duffy said. "Roy was one 'dadgummit' away from getting a technical foul that night, boy!"

The most controversial item was reportedly attributed to Duke guard and "America's Got Goatee" finalist Austin Rivers.

"The feathers and the marbles are almost comical," Duffy said. "But they've equipped Rivers with something that is downright evil. He sometimes hides it from the media by wearing a little girl-scout brace on his right arm."

An official with the ACC did confirm an item found "on Rivers' person" caused the Obama administration to re-launch the controversial color-coded terrorism warning system and crank it up to "center of the sun red."

"Imagine you're a UNC player and you and Austin Rivers are fighting for the same rebound," Duffy said, as tears welled-up in his eyes. "Just as you're trying to focus on the task at hand, you notice a tattoo on the back of Rivers' right arm; it's not the average 'Mom' or 'Clay Aiken' tattoos that most of the Duke players have.

"Instead, it's a tattoo of a naked Lefty Driesell. I'm too upset to go into what the tattoo does if Rivers' flexes his muscles."

LOCAL COUPLE TO MARRY ON TWITTER FOR VALENTINE'S DAY
FEBRUARY 12, 2012

Like so many couples these days, Ashley Mills and Connie Riblet of Kinston met on the Internet.

"I was on Facebook one day noticed a post titled 'Parallels between 'Star Wars: Episode One' and Da-vid Lee Roth's return to Van Halen,' " Mills said. "When I clicked on the writer's profile picture, I fell in love instantly."

The writer of the post turned out to be local web designer and car crash enthusiast Connie Riblet.

"Anybody who doesn't notice the similarities between Jar Jar Binks and David Lee Roth is insane," Riblet said as she held her hand over a lit candle in her home office. "They're both goofy and you can only stand them in five-minute intervals. Also, the similarity of their voices and style of dress is uncanny. However, I did quite enjoy Dave's choice of leotard back in the 1980s."

The smitten Mills sent Riblet a friend request on Facebook and a follow request on Twitter.

"I'm willing to put in an equal amount of effort, but Facebook and Twitter is all I'm doing," Mills said. "She wanted me to follow her on Critter — which is a social networking site for the animals of Twitter users — but I don't like birds."

A quick check of Critter posts revealed a striking contrast between the different animal species. A random check of posts by dogs reveals much conversation about unconditional love for their owners, dog food vs. table scraps, new fire hydrants and leg fetishes.

In contrast, the few cats that bothered to post seemed to have a rather unpleasant air of entitlement about them. A tabby named Greta opined that "she just wanted to be alone" and "oh, the person that houses and feeds me is home from a tough day at work. To show my gratitude, I'll sit here with a blank stare on my face and emit a general scent of indifference."

Other networking sites Mills refused to join included:

Differ (social networking for the contrary), Dither (social networking for the non-committal), Jitter (social networking for the uneasy), Knitter (social networking for quilters), Litter (social networking for the trashy), Quitter (social networking for those with no follow-through) and Quicker (social networking and support for the premature).

What sets the Mills/Riblet romance apart from others is the fact the two young lovers have yet to meet in the flesh.

"It's much easier to just get together online," Mills said. "By the time you take a woman out to McDonald's, and you factor in gas and tire wear, it can get up into the neighborhood of $10. Typing 'I Love U' online don't cost a daggone thing, yo. I don't see any need to meet Connie in person until it's time to go on the honeymoon."

For her part, Riblet has decided to take the notion of an online relationship even further.

"I've been saving this as a surprise for Ashley, but I've decided we might as well honeymoon online too," Riblet says. "We can hook up online via webcam and watch episodes of 'Rick Steves' Europe' for free on PBS. This option will be even cheaper than Ashley's idea to tour the Chiquita banana factory in Detroit, and we'll save money on bulletproof vests."

When The Free Press told Mill's of his bride-to-be's plans to forego the traditional honeymoon route, he was obviously flustered.

"Maybe I've been taking this idea of frugality a little too far," Mills said as he typed 68 frowny-faces :(symbols on Riblets' Face-book page. "I'm not LOL. I'm thinking OMG, we're not going to ;) on our honeymoon! IMHO I should have a 'dislike' button for this. I thought we were j/k about not having a real honeymoon. What's the point of having a honeymoon without a little ;), you know what I mean?"

He continued, "I am not LMAO about this. I mean, WTH? #whataboutthewhoopee. A honeymoon should be FTF, at least for the first few minutes. IOW, JSYK, my Twaggle is Twaiting about Twaunting me already. The whole experience is making me a little Twittish."

As of this writing, the ceremony is still scheduled to take place at 1 p.m., today. The bride and groom are expecting all 7,041 of their Facebook and Twitter followers to attend the ceremony via Skype. If the marriage indeed takes place, the couple will split their time between residences in 'FarmVille' and 'CityVille'.

In lieu of wedding presents, the couple are requesting donations of SimCash be made in their names to the Virtual Hamster Rescue at www.adoptme.com.

THE DREADED NORVILLE VIRUS CLAIMS LOCAL VICTIM
FEB. 16, 2012

Valentine's Day is just another way businesses scoop in money most of us don't have. Yes, I am a romantic, just not in the way modern culture dictates.

I wasn't in the office on Tuesday, but when I walked in Wednesday, I noticed someone had left a bag of what appeared to be tiny red pieces of cinnamon candy on my desk. Attached to the bag was a note describing the contents as "Cupid Poop."

Anybody can stop off at the drug store and pick up a Whitman's Sampler or a bottle of Kirstie Alley's Chocolate Bubble Bath, but when somebody takes the time to collect, bag and label genuine Cupid Poop — that's a commitment.

The area's No. 1 Tupperware salesman and my boss, Bryan Hanks, cooked homemade lasagna for his sweetie on Valentine's Day. It turned out so well he brought in leftovers to share with the Free Press staff. Since the only form of currency I had on my person was a Canadian Civil War nickel, I was glad to have it.

Turns out not only did I not need that quickie last will and testament from Legal-Zoom.com, but the lasagna was quite tasty. After I took the rest of the lasagna that was set aside for my coworkers and hid it in my car, I headed to Hanks' office to thank him.

When I got to Hanks' office, he had just finished opening a package of "Chocka Ca Ca" chocolate diapers he'd received the day before from archnemesis and Freedom Communications Regional Director of Human Resources, Steven "Ice Pick" Hewitt. Steven got the nickname not from years of nefarious behavior, but rather due to his knack for being able to carve ice sculptures that bear an uncanny resemblance to legendary NFL defensive tackle Rosey Grier.

The Hanks/Hewitt rivalry stems from the fact that Hanks is a staunch Virginia Cavaliers supporter, and Hewitt is a dyed-in-the-wool Virginia Tech supporter. In the interest of full disclosure, I wasn't even aware Virginia or Virginia Tech still had basketball teams, so this intracompany skirmish was news to me.

This week's chocolate diaper incident is the latest in a long line of one-upmanship between these two. Last Valentine's Day, Hewitt had a dozen roses sent to Hanks' better half Tina, but the card was addressed as if the flowers had been sent by Hanks. This all sounds well and good until you find out the card read, "To my Dearest Marcy, we'll be together soon."

I haven't seen a guy walk that crooked for that long since I had a vasectomy a few years back, but you can read all about that in my book, "Making Gravy in Public" — details below.

What did I – a guy who thinks Valentines Day is a colossal schnoinkfest — do for his sweetie on Valentines Day? I protected her from the diabolical Deborah Norville virus that's been wreaking havoc across the entire nation.

See, I was in a recording studio in Chapel Hill all day Saturday. The session went well, and on our way home, we decided to stop at Char-Grill in Raleigh to worship a little flame-cooked cow. While we worshipped at the foot of the hoof, our drummer slowly started to realize something was going wrong down in the engine room.

It was so bad he didn't eat any of his fries, which — by all accounts — were decimated by unknown members of the band in his absence.

Since our buddy was turning six shades of pale at 33 revolutions per minute, we cut the rest of the trip short. I aimed my ancient, 213,000-mile havin' Suburban towards La Grange and applied pressure to the gas pedal with extreme prejudice.

The first 20 miles of the trip home were tense. We were all wondering when the first eruption of Mt. Barfatoa would take place, and my frequent allusions to "driving the porcelain bus," "the Technicolor yawn" and "arguing with the worms" didn't lighten the mood.

Even when I pulled out top-drawer material such as "jazzing up the carpet," "spitting out furry Lifesavers," "reviewing the menu" and "selling a Buick," I was rewarded with rolled eyes and threats of bodily harm.

Suffice to say, between Smithfield and La Grange several stops were made so our friend could "yell at a few ants." Eventually, I made it to my home and my joy at being able to see my family was cut short by the realization that I could possibly pass the dreaded Deborah Norville virus on to my wife and two children. I decided to take a scalding hot shower and spend the rest of the weekend on the couch in my office outside the house.

It was lonely out there on the couch, but in my own way, I was expressing love for my sweetie by not passing on a virus that could potentially cause her and our sweet, beautiful children to throw it in reverse and go all Barffalo Bill for the next few days.

Others may refer to it as "The Call of The Walrus" or "downloading dinner," but it's not pleasant. Even if the dreaded experience is described in a colorful way, such as "the gale force burp" or "making a map," it doesn't help matters one bit.

Happy Valentine's Day, suckers.

RAP SUPERSTAR DONATES MONEY TO HOMELESS
FEB. 23, 2012

Free Press writer Justin Hill's recent story about the good folks at Rhema Word Christian Center's efforts for the less fortunate was a nice reminder that good still exists in our community. It also reminded me of my encoutner with a homeless man in Durham last week, and I'd like to take this opportunity to share it with you all now.

Anyone who has taken exit 270 off Interstate 40 in Durham knows the adjacent median is the Las Vegas for homeless people in the Triangle. I'm not making fun of the homeless, because God knows the way things are going, any of us could be on that stretch of road begging for money, food or Hot Pockets in the blink of an eye.

What gives me comedic domain over this particular group of supposedly homeless people was the fact that nearly all of them were wearing really nice clothes. As I type this, I'm wearing a pair of black Wolverine boots that are two years old. There's a bit of tread left on the bottom, but the Dr. Scholls I stuck in there to replenish the inside have been pulverized into fine blue powder that looks like something Frank Lucas sold on 110th Street in the 1970s.

The shirt I'm currently wearing was purchased from Target for $7 back in 2006, and my pants are actually three pairs of old shorts that have been sewn together. As for underwear, let's just say freedom ain't just for seniors at the Sizzler anymore, okay?

It's painfully obvious to everyone from my family to a cosmonaut stepping outside the International Space Station to take a leak that fashion isn't a major concern for me. If it covers up enough stuff to keep me out of the Gray Bar Hotel, then I'm good to go. That being said, I was a little miffed when one of the "homeless" people off exit 270 was wearing a new pair of Timberland boots that were worth more than my car. My Spidey Sense told me this guy might not actually be homeless.

A few feet down the median stood what at first looked to be a homeless boy. Upon closer inspection, we realized it was actually a homeless midget, which simultaneously brought on feelings of depression, confusion, and — to be honest — a pinch of morbid curiosity.

The homeless midget was holding up a sign, but as we were parked at a gas station across the street we couldn't quite make out what it said. I can't swear to it, but I think the sign read "SHORT ON CASH." As we headed back down the highway, I slowed down to offer the man some food. As I handed him half of my turkey sammich, he waved it off.

"I'm out here for cash, son," the midget said. "Take that crusty sammich back to the house!"

Suffice to say, I was a little ticked off, but I did get a good look at his sign. As it turns out, the midget wasn't homeless at all; rather, he was an employee of www.rentamidget.com. We called the number on his sign and were treated to a prerecorded message by rap superstar 25 Cent. Apparently, 25 Cent was doing a half-price show at a local halfway house. Half of the show proceeds were being donated to a local homeless shelter, and 25 Cent (Quata to his friends) was posing as a homeless man to promote the show.

It just goes to show you can't judge a book or, in this case, a pamphlet by its cover. By all accounts, the show was a success, although the "Home Sweet Home/Mama I'm Coming Home/I'm Your Captain (Closer To Home)/I'm Going Home/Bring It On Home To Me/Green Grass of Home" medley might have been in bad taste.

Keep spittin', Twenny.

ILLEGAL FREON DISCOVERED IN LENOIR COUNTY
FEB. 28, 2012

After a summer that saw grown men dipping their corn-ridden feet in pools of air-conditioner runoff for just a little relief from the heat, I had high hopes for this winter.

I spent approximately 15 summers working in a tobacco field, which meant heat, dust and sweat. The heat and humidity was always tough, but the situation rarely got as stupid as it did last summer. The worst thing that ever happened in the tobacco days was every once in a while a coworker who imbibed a bit too much over the weekend would be forced to make a withdrawal after about an hour in the sun.

It was really funny if this happened as the guy hung his head over the edge of the tailgate of the truck that was hauling us from one field to another. You should have seen the faces of the people driving behind us — especially if they were riding shirtless on a motorcycle.

Let me paint a little word picture for you: You start the day by being gently slapped in the face by row upon row of giant green leaves covered in morning dew. No matter how you position yourself in the seat, the sensation of being pelted in slow motion by thousands of wet fish awaits.

After a few hours, the sun comes up and the dew dissipates. Now the cold slime has been replaced by a sticky film — actually tar — that, at the end of the day, can be scooped off your cropping arm like so much black Parkay.

Eventually, you'll learn to wear a thin, long-sleeved shirt, with the sleeve rolled up on your non-cropping arm. At the end of the summer, you'll say a few words over the former shirt, throw a lit match on it and run for your life.

Confused Canadians will mistake the blaze for the aurora borealis and Gordon Lightfoot, Bryan Adams and Rush will organize a benefit concert. American and Canadian bikers will provide security for the event and they'll clash over who has the best bacon. Anne Murray will be arrested for stabbing a guy during the melee, and the Rolling Stones will finally be off the hook for Altamont.

Last summer, we were pinned down under a blanket of humidity that was as unforgiving and relentless as a Nicolas Cage film festival. By the time the average man or woman walked from their home to their vehicle, any remnants of a shower or personal grooming were mooted. All of that time showering, spraying, rolling on — down the drain. They would, for the rest of the day, be making gravy in public.

It made the sweat on Nixon's lip during his televised debate with Kennedy look like chalk dust.

After the pummeling heat/ humidity eventually started to subside last September, I offered God a deal. I promised him that if we'd be spared another one of these miserably summers that I'd never, ever complain about being cold again. I told him if he wanted to send us blizzards, nor'easters, avalanches or snowicanes, I — nor anyone in my immediate family — would complain. I spend a fair amount of time in New Jersey, so I even offered to bring suitcases full of their snow/ice/ frozen corpses back south.

With temperatures getting up to 70 degrees last week, I knew either God had other plans or the ACLU intercepted my prayers. We in the South have not had a winter. If any of our brothers and sisters in the North or Midwest are reading this and are currently buried under 12 feet of snow, please understand we are jealous of what you have.

This weather is so screwy that my sinuses have gone on strike. As I type this, I have a cough drop under each armpit, in both ears, up both nostrils, in my belly button and in my mouth. Anything beyond that is none of your business.

If we are to suffer another summer of terror, I'm going to be ready for it. I've purchased a second freezer specifically for my clothes. I've already stocked it full of underwear and socks, so if Mother Nature insists on turning my pressure points into miniature squeegee factories, she'll have to fight through subzero clothing to do so. I've been buying most of my sub-zero clothing from FEBE — For Eskimos By Eskimos.

As for the air conditioning, I've been stockpiling some top-notch Antarctic Freon that makes the stuff we get here in America look like Diet Sprite. A test run on Sunday afternoon resulted in a dusting of snow in my living room. My daughters and I made snow angels while the wife looked up "annulment" on Legal-Zoom.com.

I'm not sure what an "annulment" is, but she said it would make the upcoming summer much more bearable.

HIGH GAS PRICES HURTING ILLEGAL DRUG BUSINESS
MARCH 6, 2012

The price for a gallon of gasoline is expected to top off at approximately $5 this summer. Rumors are also afoot that next year, the Daytona 500 will be renamed the Daytona 400 in an attempt to save money.

On the positive side, most car salesmen predict it'll be cheaper for most consumers to trade in their vehicles for a new car than buy a tank of gas by Christmas.

We've been told that gas prices are being pushed up by speculators. I've never met a speculator, and I'd venture to guess none of the people reading this have either. I used to think a speculator was that thing Mr. Peanut wore over his bad eye.

Just the word "speculator" sounds a bit filthy. Can't you just imagine a guy going to the doctor because of an infected speculator? "Doc, I don't know what happened; I woke up in the middle of the night and my speculator had busted. I wrapped it in a towel and got here as fast as I could." According to Investopedia.com, a speculator is "a person who trades derivatives, commodities, bonds, equities or currencies with a higher-than-average risk in return for a higher-than-average profit potential."

First off, I don't think most of those things mentioned in that sentence are real things. Secondly, it sounds like a cleaned-up, Ivy League-sanctioned form of pseudo-gambling that causes people who aren't even at the table to lose money.

Not only are these wormy little speculators causing the cost of everyday goods and services to rise, they're starting to affect the types of businesses that aren't traded on the stock exchange.

"My product is very inexpensive to produce, but it's costing more and more to make deliveries," said local drug dealer Beth Amphetamine. "A little oxy, a pinch of bleach and a teaspoon of windshield wiper fluid is all it takes to make my Wake and Bake Crystal Flakes: Racing Hearts, Dripping Stars, Yellow Tongues, Green Teeth, Blue Bruises and Purple Gums — they're methically delicious!"

Mrs. Amphetamine has added a $5 charge to her normal $25 fee for a quarter gram of crystal meth.

"A lot of my customers got upset when I added the $5, but there was no way I was going to let them pick it up from my house," Amphetamine said. "The way these folks steal stuff to pay for their meth, it's almost like they're addicted to it or something."

Some drug dealers have resulted to car pooling in order to avoid raising their prices.

"I used to enjoy the ride to my corner in the mornings," said local ecstasy salesman Stephen Hawking. "I'd get my baggies packaged the night before. I'd always put a $5 coupon in the bags of my best customers — just as a way to say 'Thank you'. In the morning, I'd have a peaceful drive to my spot, and it was nice to have that bit of calm before a frantic day of selling.

"Now, I have to share the ride with a coke dealer and a weed salesman to save on gas. The coke dealer never shuts up, and the weed guy is always running late. At one time, we had a heroin salesman in the carpool, but I caught him trying to steal my McMuffin one morning, so he had to go."

Hawking would not comment on where the McMuffin thief went or how he got there.

"You just don't mess with a man's muffin," Hawking said. "Don't even lick the cheese off the paper without asking, aight?"

While carpooling seems to have helped these local businesspeople from raising their prices, further measures may have to be taken.

"We've been talking about creating an all-purpose drug that will feature the best of what all our products have to offer," Amphetamine said. "We don't have anything ready to roll out just yet, but we've got a meth/weed/ heroin hybrid in the works called 'Marimethoin'. If this works out, we'll be able to reduce our sales staff and delivery costs.

"Since what everybody wants from an illegal drug could be delivered in one little ball that resembles several partial pieces of soap caked together, our customers will be able to lose their teeth, homes and dignity in a much more timely and inexpensive manner."

FATHER OF BIRTH CONTROL CRUSADER
RESPONDS TO CRITICISM
MARCH 8, 2012

A few days ago, law student Sandra Fluke gave a speech to members of the U.S. House of Representatives detailing her belief that her Je-suit law school should provide free contraception through its health care coverage. Since that time, she's been called a "slut" and a "prostitute" by a conservative talk show host and had to sit on a couch with Joy Behar.

Since national problems such as unemployment, poverty, high gas prices and Ryan Seacrest have apparently been handled, members of the House recently found yet more time to devote to this issue.

On Wednesday, Sandra Fluke's father Randolph spoke to House members about his daughter's ordeal.

The following is a complete transcript:

"My name is Randolph Fluke, and I'm the father of Sandra Fluke. She is a student at George-town Law School. Go Hoyas! (Applause) I'd like to thank the assembled members of the House of Representatives for giving me this forum.

"I, as the father of a law student with a voracious sexual appetite, encourage lawmakers to require health insurance companies to fund all forms of contraception: the pill, condoms, patches, IUD, STP, sponges, Jell-O and glamour shots of Joy Behar.

"My daughter attends a Jesuit law school that does not provide contraceptive coverage in its student health plan. To be honest, I don't have a problem with this. When I was making $8.25 an hour, I had to pay for my own insurance and birth control, but no one offered to put me on television to complain about it. For the record, I also don't agree that Viagra and similar medications should be covered by health insurance either. If Father Time has seen fit to de-starch your shirt, who are we to prop it up?

"All that being said, I'm very tired. I've worked hard all my life, and to be frank with you, I'm not interested in raising more children. The wife and I gave it a shot — and we're proud of our daughter — but we could have done without her telling the nation how bad she needed help paying for birth control. When I turned on the TV that morning, all I wanted to see was Hode Kotb and Kathie Lee; those girls are firecrackers. (Laughter and applause) Anyway, I see a clip of the little girl I taught to ride a bike telling Congress how much she needs birth control. I can't tell you what kind of hell I endured at the lodge that night, but at least it gave Bernard Lewinsky a brief respite.

"If seeing the light of my life plead for birth control on national television wasn't enough, then I had to listen to Rush Limbaugh call her a prostitute and a slut. I used to like Rush, but ever since he got busted for gobbling oxycodone pills as if they were after-dinner mints, he's been a little off. Furthermore, if I ever come face to face/ chin/chin/chin with him, I'm going to plant my foot so far up his backside, his breath will smell like shoe polish in the afterlife.

"While Rush went way over the line, he and his ilk did raise an interesting point last week. Apparently Bill Maher — the liberal version of Limbaugh — recently donated $1 million to a Barack Obama-friendly super-PAC. That's all fine and good, but does anybody remember the salacious things Maher said about Sarah Palin a few years back? The two words he used are too vulgar to repeat here, but they are both one-syllable words used to describe women in a derogatory manner. Maher's comments were just as mean-spirited as Limbaugh's and, in fact, even more vulgar. I'm hoping President Obama will find a way to urge the PAC return Bill Maher's money, as it would be hypocritical to accept it under the circumstances. (Uproarious laughter)

"While Rush wouldn't need to worry about birth control if Brad Pitt was tied around his neck, I can understand why some may be perturbed at having to pay a higher insurance premium so my little ray of sunshine can get her groove on with all the proper roadblocks in place. That being said, the pill only costs about $30 a month - that's $1 per day. I don't mean to sound like Sally Struthers here, but it's only $1 a day. I find it hard to believe anyone in college — be it on scholarship or not — can't find something to cut out that would free up $1 per day. It all comes down to what's more important to you: Birth control or being able to see 'Goodfellas' on cable for the 700th time.

"It's true that contraceptive medications are sometimes prescribed for reasons unrelated to birth control, but the thought that a religious-based organization would be forced to go against their beliefs is troubling to me. My daughter is a smart girl, and she researched Georgetown's policies before she enrolled. She knew birth control was not part of their plan, so I guess you could say this whole thing was about as spontaneous as the formation of the Backstreet Boys. I asked her why she didn't just go to a school that provided what she wanted in their insurance, but I guess that wouldn't have drawn any attention.

"If the government is insistent on everyone being guaranteed contraception, I believe they should mandate we all receive free gasoline. If gas prices keep rising, how are we going to get any use out of all these birth control pills? Contraception without transportation is pointless.

"Thank you for your time."

DRINKING PROBLEM DESTROYS LONG-TERM RELATIONSHIP
MARCH 13, 2012

In 1975, Queen released their classic album, "A Night at the Opera." That album contained many great songs, including "Bohemian Rhapsody" and "You're My Best Friend". Another great song on that album was "I'm In Love with My Car."

I used to think it was unusual for someone to get emotionally attached to a car. I knew a guy in high school who couldn't write his name in cursive without a tutor, but give him a tub of Turtle Wax and an old T-shirt and he could turn Fred Sanford's truck into a Porsche. He used to make fun of my sensible 4-cylinder car.

"That thing ain't got no power," he'd say. "Why don't you quit messin' with that music turnout and get a decent car?"

What you don't know is that ol' Jethro Andretti didn't have to pay for his car. My folks made a deal with me when I was 14; the deal was they would pay for half of my first car. I spent that weekend calculating how many tobacco leaves I'd have to crop to drum up my half of the dough.

Since I'm less mechanically inclined than Woody Allen in a body cast, I knew I'd need something reliable. All things considered, the first car to legally feel the gentle massage of my right foot on its supple accelerator was a 1986 Chevrolet Celebrity. It wasn't flashy, but it was cheap, got me where I wanted to go, and the stereo worked. Anything beyond that was just showing off.

A few years later, I'd graduated from playing music in local dives to playing music in regional dives. This climb to the middle of the East Coast music scene required an upgrade in transportation. I'm a moderately inventive fella, but neither Penn nor Teller could figure out how to cram three guitars, a drum set and amplifiers into a backseat that already contained a minimum of two musicians.

The answer to the problem was a van. Not a mini-van — a long, forest green van that looked like something al-Qaeda would use to haul goat feed in. I bought it from Ed-die Halen's Van and Cigarette Outlet in Smithfield.

Nearly a year to the day after I became a van guy, the van and I were involved in a car accident. I was stopped at a light on U.S. 70, wondering whatever happened to the two guys who temporarily replaced Tom Wopat and John Schneider on "The Dukes of Hazard" during a contract dispute. At first, I thought I could just look them up on Wikipedia when I got home, but then I remembered Wikipedia hadn't been invented yet.

The next thing I know, I hear a loud screeching sound followed by what felt like a bomb blast.

After I stopped seeing stars and checked to see if I'd voided my bowels, I realized a guy driving a moving van had plowed into my vehicle at 45 mph. He left a skid mark 120-feet long and could have killed me, but he didn't get a ticket.

The van was totaled, which meant I had to acquire another vehicle of similar size. This time I ended up with a blue Chevrolet Suburban. It didn't have great gas mileage but at the time, gas was only $1.20 a gallon, and there was no way the price would triple during the vehicle's lifetime, right?

Twelve years and 212,000 miles later, I'm in the market for another car. Ol' Blue has been good to me, but I've reached a level in the music games where we play in bigger dives that furnish their own P.A. system, so there is no need for me to drive an aircraft carrier anymore. Gasoline is now more expensive per gallon than uranium, and I'm in the market for something that has fantastic gas mileage.

I called around but nobody seemed to have anything in a half-cylinder in stock. I thought about putting a roll-cage on a Cub Cadet riding mower, but the DMV wouldn't issue tags for it.

Eventually, a savior appeared to me in the form of a relative who knew the history of a certain 2006 Chevrolet Impala that was in great shape and for sale. It had some miles on it, but it had been serviced properly and still had some good years left in it.

After one test drive, I was smitten with this car, and it looked and drove as if it were brand new. Also, the car was several hundred dollars under what I'd allotted to spend, so it was a win win. Sure, this new car was 6 years old, but it was 13 years newer than my previous car. I guess you just can't hide money.

I didn't know how I was going to break it to Ol' Blue, as we'd been through a lot together. We've gotten each other to Newark, Charlotte, Atlanta and many other bergs over the years. I've slept in that monster more than one time, and on one occasion, used it to smuggle Pat Sajak out of the country. You'd think with all his dough he would have thrown a brother some gas money, but I digress.

Just a month ago, she safely delivered three musicians and a pile of guitars safely to Chapel Hill and back, even at her advanced age of 19. I've never had to do any major work on Ol' Blue, but her drinking problem just became too much for me to bear.

Ol' Blue guzzles gas as if it were free. A tractor, car and moped from my neighborhood held an intervention for her last year, but her "CHECK

ENGINE" light just turned red and her lushful behavior continued.

Eventually, to try and curb her insatiable lust for dinosaur juice, I started leaving 10 minutes earlier than normal for work so I could drive at a slower speed. On the way home, Ol' Blue was restrained by a cruise control that was set on 50. Sure, some people didn't like that, but that's why God created the two-lane highway.

On the bright side, driving home at 50 mph has helped keep the middle finger on my left hand nice and limber over the past year or so. At this point, I can tie it into a frilly bow.

While I'm a little sad at the prospect of selling Ol' Blue, I must say I haven't been this excited to drive since I was 16. While gas is still too expensive, it's nice to be driving what is essentially a new car. It's still painful to fill up the new car with gas, but it's only paper cut painful; filling up Ol' Blue was literally "getting a knot in your drawers" painful.

Instead of telling Ol' Blue what was going on, I decided to park the new car next to her for a few days. At first, I think she believed it was the car of a visiting friend, but at some point I think she remembered I don't really have any friends.

There was noticeably less air in Ol' Blue's tires on Monday morning, but I couldn't let that affect me; I was in love with my car.

HELICOPTERS OVER KINSTON PART OF
'APOCALYPSE NOW' SEQUEL
MARCH 15, 2012

On Monday, a tranquil March night was interrupted by a group of helicopters flying at an alarmingly low altitude.

Social media sites such as Facebook and Twitter were inundated with reports from frightened and confused citizens. Some posters played the activity off to a military exercise, while others believed something more nefarious was afoot.

"I was out walking the dog when this helicopter swooped down out of nowhere," said Walter Kurtz of Cameron Drive, Kinston. "That thing was so low to the ground I could see the Earnhardt sticker on its side."

Outside of Kinston, reports of property damage and animal cruelty clogged emergency communication centers.

"One of those helicopters ducked down so low it pulled up my clothesline, with all of my unmentionables on it," said the viciously buxom Lillie Langtry of Tick Bite. "I thought it was rather uncouth for the pilots to strap one of my bras across the front of their helicopter and use it as a bug shield."

Earlier this week, an official from the Kinston Regional Jetport told Free Press reporter Wes Brown a different story. According to the spokesman, military staff believed to be from Cherry Point MCAS called to inform aviation officials of military exercises that would be taking place near Kinston's air space.

"That was done for authenticity," said Bill Kilgore of Francis Ford Coppola's American Zoetrope production company. "We wanted civilians and government officials to react genuinely to what they perceived to be an alarming situation. That's why Francis cast Marlon Brando in the original 'Apocalypse Now', the role called for a madman, and Bran-do was already out of his mind. We'd just turn on the camera and he'd start rambling about gardenia plantations."

Along with "Apocalypse", Coppola has also directed such classic films as "The Godfather," "The Conversation" and "The Outsiders." Although he was not available for comment, Coppola was spotted by autograph hounds at the Golden Corral breakfast buffet on U.S. 70 last weekend.

According to movie gossip website thirdofnever.net, Martin Sheen will reprise his role as Capt. Willard.

"Willard gets back on the boat and floats up the Neuse River to dethrone a delusional warlord who has converted a troupe of porn stars into a murderous gang," says Hollywood insider Tyrone Miller. "When Willard arrives at the warlord's compound — replete with a tiger blood fountain dispenser — he's stunned to discover the warlord is actually his son (played by Sheen's real-life son Charlie - who ironically does surf)".

Kilgore told The Free Press the low flying helicopters from Monday night were being filmed for a sequence reminiscent of the "Flight of The Valkyries" segment of the original "Apocalypse Now."

"Instead of using Wagner's music to terrify the people they're after, this time the guys in the choppers are blaring Nickelback as they fly over," Kilgore said. "This is a scene in which two war-torn characters are having a discussion about how if they're not in hell they're at least in hell's waiting room."

Kilgore continued, "Ever the stickler for authenticity, Francis believes if hell were to have a waiting room, Nickelback would be piped in over the public address system. We thought about using Kanye West's music, but somehow that seems even too harsh for hell."

LOCAL MAN HAUNTED BY DAMAGED CAR AND SUGAR
MARCH 20, 2012

There's nothing better than waking up at 6 a.m. and realizing you don't have to get up. Sure, 15 minutes later, a diaper-clad tax deduction hopped up on milk full of steroids and penguin hormones will climb on your face as if it were something to conquer, but it's still Saturday.

This past Saturday, I got going pretty early. A few musicians were coming over at noon for a rehearsal, so I needed to run some errands and update my vaccinations before they arrived.

After subduing the diaper ninja with a hit from a jar of "Uncle Rusty's Kiddie Chloroform and Salad Dressing," I eased out of the house with the intention of handling a few small errands before starting work on the things I work on when I'm not at work.

I'd sold some CDs and books during the week, so I headed to the post office to send them on their way. Everything was packaged and marked "fragile" — nothing was left to chance. Many times in the past, I've made the rookie mistake of arriving at the post office near closing time, which usually means you get stuck behind someone trying to mail an aquarium full of macaroni and cheese to the moon or something.

Upon arrival, there were only two other cars in the post office parking lot, so I felt moderately pleased with myself. I walked in to find a guy in the process of shipping a large, bulging box to some exotic locale. I'm not sure where it was going, but from what I observed, it generated more paperwork than that time an astronaut locked himself out of the Space Shuttle.

The postal employee asked the man what was in the box. The customer replied, "DVDs, T-shirts, and shoes." The postal employee then asked the value of the contents. The customer said the contents were worth $60.

(Note: The customer said there were 20 DVDs in the box. Can you even rent a DVD for $2 anymore?)

After much typing, measuring and cipherin', the cheapest postage option — to mail $60 worth of merchandise — was $79.90. Without so much as a raised eyebrow, the customer reached into his pocket and produced four crisp new $20 bills. They were part of the new issue that now features the Walmart logo above the door of the White House.

I tapped the guy on the shoulder and suggested it would be cheaper to just send a money order worth $79.90. Based on the destination of the package, the recipients could use the $79.90 to buy their own T-shirt factory. The guy took one look at me, eased his wallet out of my line of vision, and went on about his business.

I took care of my transaction in about one minute — which is the proper amount of time for any post office transaction — and headed to my next stop: the grocery store.

Since we were rehearsing near dinner time, I felt obliged to feed my band mates something, so — sparing no expense — I loaded up on Tom's pizzas and store brand seltzer. Hey, nothing is too good for my guys. Throw in some apple slices and celery sticks and it's moderately nutritious. Besides, no good rock and roll has ever been made on a diet of tofu.

As I stood in line at the one open register, the cashier was ringing up someone else's groceries. She picked up a bag of sugar and noticed it had a small tear in it. She offered to replace the damaged bag, but the customer was very understanding and said it was fine. The cashier tried a second time to replace it, and the customer said it was going to be dumped into a plastic container anyway, so there was no problem.

With the Senate hearings on Sugargate now over, I moved up to the register. The cashier was in the process of cleaning up the spilled sugar and she apologized for the inconvenience. After a few seconds, she seemed to be finished, but she kept noticing tiny bits of sugar and kept cleaning.

After a few hours, she still wasn't satisfied so she called in the boys from CSI La Grange to remove the sugar particles she couldn't see but suspected were there. I' all for a person taking pride in their work — Lord knows I've seen everything from cracked eggs to afterbirth strewn across supermarket checkout tables — but this was getting a little out of hand.

Before Horatio Cane and the rest of his team cleared the scene, the red-headed policeman eased on his shades, handed the store manager a Who CD and began to speak in a hushed tone: "It looks like this was a sweet assignment."

One quick scream by Roger Daltrey over the P.A., and away he rode in a Hummer that looked like it had been thrown up by Darth Vader.

Next, I drove over to the car wash. My new ride (it's 5-years-old, but it's new to me) is normally as white as I am, but thanks to a bunch of loose plants, was now drenched in pollen. The car looked like it was covered in Big Bird dandruff, so I decided to spend $1.25 on a quick spray wash to rectify the situation.

Here's a little tip for you kids out there: The "pre-soak" option is a joke. Be sure to set that dial on "soak" before you put the money in. Also, unless you want to be plopping in quarters all morning, as soon as that water comes on, start running. Don't worry about being surgical; you're going to want to treat that spray hose as if it were a shotgun of cleanliness.

If you hustle, you can get the entire car soaped up and rinsed before the $1.25 worth of time runs out.

My moves in a car wash are so smooth I was once offered a sneaker endorsement from Nike. Sadly, I felt it was immoral to endorse a shoe that cost more than a school teacher's yearly salary, so I turned them down. If I'm going to cause people to riot over something they can't afford, I want it to at least be made in America; no sweat-shop riots on my watch.

Before I could drive into the car wash stall, I had to wait for a man who was obviously more emotionally invested in his car wash technique than I. This guy had apparently put in a mayonnaise jar full of quarters and was using all sorts of brushes and attachments that I'd always seen hanging in the car was but never seen in action.

While it's perfectly fine for someone to spend more time washing their car than raising a child, this case was special because the vehicle being treated like a senator at a D.C. cathouse was, in fact, wrecked. Both taillights were completely smashed, with nothing but a series of wires hanging from both sides of the vehicle's rear. The entire back of the car was smushed in also.

I know managing editors at certain small-town newspapers that don't clean themselves this thoroughly, much less a vehicle that has been smashed up.

After a small eternity, the guy who was washing the wrecked car drove it away but his plight stuck with me the rest of the day. Was the guy in denial, or was he some sort of trend shaman following his instincts?

When you think about it, a new car with a busted rear-end still doesn't look as insane as those spinning salad-shooter rims. The clean front/damaged back might be the vehicle equivalent of the mullet haircut, which is best described as business in the front, party in the back.

That's my luck, though. Just about the time I obtain a vehicle that's good on gas and looks great, fuel prices are going to rise to $4 a gallon and ratty-looking cars are going to be chic. If you need me, just look for the guy pouring Crisco in his gas tank and customizing the back of his Impala with a hammer.

CHARLES BUCHANAN HAD LIFE FIGURED OUT
MARCH 27, 2012

A few hours ago, The Free Press staff gathered graveside to pay final respects to our much-loved and respected chief photographer, Charles Buchanan.

Many kind words have been spoken about Charles since his passing last week. Speaking well of the recently deceased is almost as involuntary as blinking or breathing — at least while the family and the preacher is within earshot.

Later that night, when everybody is all greased up on fried chicken and pie, a select few will go outside for a cigarette. Within minutes, the once sad throng (now emboldened by an influx of Bojangles' and nicotine) start telling the real story about the person they've been pretending to mourn all day.

"Everybody's boohooing about Bob, but he owed me money," one will say.

"Yeah, Bob and I would say hello to each other, but we were never friends," another might say.

"Bob couldn't return a stapler to save his life," a third will say. "I bet he's been selling them on eBay."

While Bob may have left a string of indifferent acquaintances behind, the same can't be said for Charles Buchanan.

As expected, the people who worked with Charles on a daily basis have been speaking fondly of him. A cynic could argue that saying good things about Charles at this point is just a way for the living to comfort themselves — which may be true. Either way, it doesn't matter, because people routinely told Charles how fond they were of his work.

It always angers me when it takes someone dying for their work to be truly appreciated, but it's a small comfort that Charles knew his work was valued while he was with us.

The most fun I ever had with Charles was at the wedding of his protégé, Free Press photographer Janet Carter. After the ceremony, Charles and his wife Patsy carried on much conversation with our then 4-year-old Tax Deduction. As most people do, Charles commented on how pretty my daughter was and then immediately asked if I was absolutely positive I was her father. I responded that journalism paid so poorly I couldn't afford a DNA test, to which he held up his glass of tea for a toast.

I don't know how we got on the topic, but one morning I mentioned to Charles that I'd recently acquired a vinyl copy of the landmark jazz album "Time Out" by the Dave Brubeck Quartet. As it turns out, Charles was a fan of jazz and big band music. Charles told me he bought the same album roughly 40 years earlier after seeing the band playing on TV. I asked him what show it was, and after he told me, I dialed it up on YouTube. As Charles sat at his computer watching the performance, he spoke of other LPs in his collection. Being a music nerd, I told him I'd love to see his collection sometime, which he welcomed.

Sadly, I never made the time to do it; I assumed it would be something maybe I could do after he retired.

Without a doubt, the thing Charles was most proud of was his marriage. After 15 years together, he and Patsy rejoiced in each other's company as if they were newlyweds. Anyone that denigrates marriage as an institution should have spent five minutes around Charles and Patsy. Sometimes after many years of marriage a couple become no more than roommates with vested interests, but these two obviously hit the matrimonial lottery.

I was not the first, but I tried in vain to convince Charles to compile a book of his photos. For whatever reason, he just closed his eyes and shook his head dismissively. He said there was no need for it, and one of the things I loved about the man was his nearly 0 percent tolerance for anything he deemed unnecessary.

Once after a wave of layoffs had scared the water out of every employee in the building, I stopped by his office. I guess Charles was the closest thing to a Yoda on that side of the building, so I asked him what he thought was going to happen to the rest of us. I've been accused many times of oversimplifying a situation ("If you're going to jump, go ahead already; I've got stuff to do"), but Charles' advice in regards to worrying about layoffs was simple.

"There's absolutely nothing you can do, so there's no reason to worry about it," he said.

In a nutshell, Charles adored his wife and dared to care about his work — everything else was just BS. If you can ever figure out how to drown out the BS and focus on the handful of things that matter, then you've won. Pick up the trophy on Tuesday — make sure they've spelled your name right.

It's puzzling to me that someone who actually had life figured out could be separated from it so prematurely. I guess it's one of those things nobody can do anything about, so I'm going to take Charles' advice and try not to worry about it.

AREA COPPER THIEF CAPTURED IN BEAR TRAP
MARCH 29, 2012

Kinston resident Nick Searcy said he'd just sat down to supper when he started hearing strange noises under the floor of his house.

"I'd taken all the usual precautions to ensure a pleasant meal — the phone was off the hook, the blinds were drawn, and I'd changed out of my good pants into my eatin' pants," Searcy said. "A fork-full of sumptuous barbecue turkey was about 2 inches from my face hole when the noises started."

At first, Searcy believed the noises were being caused by his dog.

"Every once in a while that bag of hair we refer to as a dog will chase something under the house," Searcy said. "One night he got tangled up under there with a cat and I believe he hit his head on every floor joist at least twice; it sounded like somebody was dragging a bag of hammers down a flight of stairs. When he came out there was a knot on his head so big he couldn't close his eyes; we couldn't tell if he was asleep or surprised for eight days."

Searcy said no matter what he did to reinforce the entrance under his residence, the dog would find a way to get under there.

"That dog loves to drag all of his treasures under the house," Searcy said. "If he finds a bone or a toy, he'll eventually drag it under the house and bury it for safekeeping."

While Searcy admits the antics of his psychotic dog sometimes get on his nerves, in this case, the antics of the mangy mutt proved fortuitous.

"The noise under the house Wednesday night wasn't the dog — it was a copper thief," Searcy said. "Apparently, the dog found an old bear trap in the woods and dragged it under the house, and I'm guessing the thief crawled over it just before the screaming started."

Searcy called the Kinston Sheriff 's Office to report the incident. When officers arrived, they weren't sure how to proceed.

"We shined a light under the house and observed several pieces of copper pipe lying next to the alleged thief," said Erica Tazel of the KSO. "The culprit's left leg was caught in the bear trap, while hot water from a cut copper pipe was streaming onto his face. To complicate matters, the dog thought the man was trying to steal the bear trap, which explains why the dog was repeatedly biting him in the groin."

Officers managed to pull the shrieking man — identified as habitual felon Dickey Bennett, 42, of Tick Bite — approximately 3 feet until another problem arose.

"The unseasonably warm weather we've been experiencing has caused the insect population to become abnormally active for March," said Jacob Pitts of the KSO. "The combination of hot running water mixed with blood and other bodily fluids that were emanating from Mr. Bennett at an increasing rate stirred up a nest of fire ants. We couldn't risk any members of our staff being bitten, so we had to exit the area and devise another course of action."

"It took them a long time to pull that guy out," Searcy told The Free Press. "All that beatin' and frammin' under the floor was playing hell with my bric-a-brac."

After nearly four hours, Bennett was pulled from underneath the house after the fire ants were subdued by several rounds of tear gas.

"We had to drag Ben-nett out with a rope, so unfortunately, the bear trap got hung on a few floor joists," Tazel said. "The only way to dislodge the victim was to yank on the rope really hard, which would occasionally cause the trap to open momentarily only to immediately shut again."

Due to budget cutbacks, rescue personnel ran out of bandages and gauze when treating Bennett at the scene.

"Mr. Searcy generously donated a roll of unused roofing insulation at the scene," Pitts said. "Mr. Bennett — apparently feeling guilty about being helped by the very man he was trying to rob — resisted having his wounds wrapped in the insulation, but Mr. Searcy insisted."

LOCAL MAN AUCTIONS SUBURBAN FOR CHARITY
APRIL 5, 2012

A few weeks ago I told you folks about the end of my relationship with Ol' Blue, but as it turns out, you must have thought I was joking.

Just to bring everybody up to speed, thanks to a couple of tax deductions I'm legally bound to clothe and feed from time to time, I was able to upgrade my motobilic situation. While I was delighted to acquire an automobile of the 2006 variety, it meant my longstanding relationship with a 1993 Chevrolet Suburban would have to be terminated.

I'm only going to say this once, and I want you to hear me: I am, in fact, selling my Suburban; it is for sale. Any allegations to the contrary are false. There is no relationship between me and Ms. Lewinski and Oswald acted alone.

I refer to that Chevy as "Ol' Blue" because it's red and I'm naturally contrary. No, it actually is blue; blue as the waters that surround the islands of Jamaica; blue as the eyes of a young Paul Newman; blue as a ham sammich left in the back of a dormitory refrigerator for an entire semester.

Along with its intoxicating coloring, this particular Suburban has a stereo in it that will knock a Nickelback or Drake fan down at 50 paces. You've all been at a stoplight while the moron in the car next to you is doing his or her best to let the world know how awful their taste in music is by cranking it up to Nigel Tufnel levels. But not to worry, the stereo in Ol' Blue has on more than one occasion rendered these squish-headed truants useless with one quick dollop of Roger Daltrey's scream from "Won't Get Fooled Again."

If the allure of the paint job and mammoth stereo isn't enough for you, then think of the space factor. While the rest of the world is moving towards vehicles that look like that thing Capt. Bill Owens drove around in "Fantastic Voyage," you can be the rebel. No matter how small your car, gas prices are going to eventually top off around $27 a gallon. With this in mind, you might as well be comfortable while you're driving to a job that won't generate enough money to cover the gas it took to get there in the first place.

Speaking of "Fantastic Voyage," how hot was Raquel Welch in that movie? As Whitman Mayo used to say, "Goodgoobledygoo; would you like some breakfast, Lamont!?"

Have you thought about safety? This vehicle is the safest thing on the road. About seven months ago, a woman pulled out of a bank parking lot and tagged the left side of Ol' Blue head on. While the brand new, mainly-plastic vehicle that struck Ol' Blue folded up like a $2 lawn chair, Ol' Blue suffered only a minor, small, teeny cosmetic blemish and kept on rolling.

The charity I've decided to donate the proceeds from the sale of Ol' Blue to is a relatively new organization. It's called the Jon Dawson Foundation, and its primary purpose is to feed and clothe Jon Dawson's children. Also, my wife is having a birthday this week, and it would be nice to be able to biggie size her combo when I take her out to celebrate; if I could raise enough for a Happy Meal, that would knock out the meal and present in one shot.

If you would like to purchase Ol' Blue, please contact me at the number below.

CHILD TORTURED WITH HOG ODOR
APRIL 12, 2012

Children should never be allowed to ride in cars. That type of sentiment won't help me land the long coveted role of Danny Tanner in Quentin Tarantino's reboot of the "Full House" franchise, but then again he peaked with "Jackie Brown."

No matter how well behaved or medicated the child, they all have the magical power to turn a car into a living monument to Keith Moon. Even a small child strapped into a car seat that looks like it fell out the backside of NASA has this ability. You can buckle, snap, and zip in a manner that would flummox Houdini, but by the time you make it around to the driver's side of the car, the vehicle has depreciated by at least $2,000.

To prevent my recently acquired, brand new, 5-year-old car from falling victim to the two tax deductions I'm legally required to transport from time to time, I've initiated a 25 cents per ride program. Many people in my family believe this is a little extreme, but I believe it will teach these crumb snatchers the value of money and hopefully prevent them from performing goat sacrifices in the back seat.

It's been tough explaining this program to the 2-year-old tax deduction, as her vocabulary is limited to words/phrases such as "uh-oh," "fish," "Maaauma," "Daaaaady," "me," "duck," "ball" and "patricide."

The 7-year-old deduction understood immediately and was not receptive at all. She tried the smile/hug/"I love you daddy"/second hug routine, but it didn't phase me. She then tried to pacify me with two pennies. I got out the calculator and after a few hours of 'cipherin' determined 2 cents was just about enough to get her from the driveway to the mailbox. She pleaded her case to her mother, who was too busy researching divorce attorneys to give any advice.

Things came to a head on Tuesday night of this week. TD#1 requested a quick ride around the block before she went to bed, so I loaded her up in the space capsule in the back seat and headed out for a pleasant evening drive.

We always take the same route, which is basically a square around the Bucklesberry community. There is a hog farm at about the midway point, and historically, I roll the windows up in order to avoid the full ambience of the Sus domesticus.

About a mile before we hit the bacon stream, I reminded TD#1 that she owed me a quarter for the ride. She protested and offered up some lame excuse about only being 7, the devaluation of the dollar and most of her money being in the Caymans.

Judging from her response she wanted to play hardball, so when we got within noseshot of the pig farm, I rolled down all the windows and eased the car down to about 5 mph. Cries of "WHAT ARE YOU DOING?!" and "MY EYES ARE WATERING!" and "I WANT TO BE AN EMANCIPATED MINOR!" immediately flew from the backseat.

"I can't understand you with your hands covering your nose like that, sweetie," I said. "Are you saying you want to pay me that quarter, now?"

I was promised a quarter, an American Girl Doll and half of her Easter candy if I would "please please please please" roll the windows up — which I did.

The cold, dead stare of an American Girl Doll and the smell of Easter egg omlettes now fill my office with a combination of melancholia and fairground stank. But my car is clean, and that's all that really matters.

LA GRANGE WOMAN TO BE SUBJECT OF REALITY SHOW
APRIL 17, 2012

Reality shows such as "Teen Mom," "Toddlers and Tiaras" and "America's Funniest STDs" have been a financial boon for TV networks and a slow depravation of oxygen to the brains of their viewers. Andy Warhol's flip comment that eventually everyone would be famous for 15 minutes has become oddly prophetic.

While the ability to write a coherent script is becoming about as marketable a skill as VCR repairman or beeper salesman, the reality show craze has positively enhanced the lives of everyday people. The latest person to be ripped from the warm embrace of obscurity is a La Grange grandmother by the name of Paulette Burroughs.

"I've seen a few of those shows over the years," Burroughs told The Free Press. "Most of them are pretty stewpid, but I've caught a few episodes of 'America's Got Candidiasis' and 'Aphasia For Real' that were pretty good."

Burroughs' show — which is set to air on the fledgling NEIO (Nothing Else Is On) Network — will focus on her day-to-day life as a wife, grandmother, newspaper magnate and reprobate. Family members, coworkers and members of local, state and federal law enforcement will round out the cast.

"It'll be interesting to have a TV crew around here," said Jeremy Piven of the La Grange Police Department. "Paulette's got her own cell. To save time, we made a key for her and showed her how to book herself. You'd think one set of prints would do, but she periodically goes to Sweden to have them changed."

"I'm just trying to stay one step ahead of the 5-0," Burroughs said. "If you get me around a display of 'Six Million Dollar Man' DVDs, I tend to get sticky fingers."

While the NEIO Network has made a 12-episode commitment to the series, executive producer Graham Yost says they've yet to settle on a name for the show.

"Paulette has graciously given us several suggestions," Yost said. "There was 'Kiss My ***' and 'Why Don't You All Just Kiss My ***', but my personal favorite was '**** *** *** ***********'s.' The show doesn't air until the 2013-14 season, so I'm sure we'll settle on something all in good time."

On Monday, members of the press and a local methadone clinic were invited to a private screening of the first episode, which was primarily filmed at the La Grange jail.

"The motherly presence she brings to the jail is simply heartwarming," Yost said. "The scene in which Paulette tucks a fellow inmate into bed after touching up his 'Adele' tattoo with a soldering gun sums up the entire show."

"I'll give you $5,000 for a candy bar," said a guy from the methadone clinic.

To coincide with the launch of the show, Burroughs will be issuing official "Paulette" merchandise to beef up her retirement fund.

"We're going to have 'Honk If You Dated Paulette' bumper stickers, 'My Other Girlfriend is Paulette' T-shirts, and 'The Tests Came Back Negative' phone covers for iPhone and Droid," Burroughs said. "We're expecting to have 'God Don't Make No Trash but I Sure Smell Funny' ball caps for sale this summer."

NURSING HOME RESIDENT ACCUSED OF DRUG TRAFFICKING
APRIL 24, 2012

The Wednesday afternoon bingo game at Bayview Retirement Community on N.C. 903 is usually a pretty tame affair.

"Aside from the occasional argument over what is a 6 or a 9, we don't have many problems," said Bayview Executive Director John Inman.

The tranquil game was interrupted when agents from the Bureau of Alcohol, Tobacco and Firearms raided the retirement home to arrest a resident on various drug-related charges. The resident in question — Ernest Grainger, 89, originally of Deep Run, has been a resident at Bayview since 2006.

"Mr. Grainger has always been the model resident," Inman told The Free Press. "He'd get a little cranky now and again when his teeth got mixed up with Mr. Thornton's from across the hall, but generally, he was a delight."

ATF spokesperson Carol Cleveland told The Free Press they received a tip Grainger was selling illegal substances to his fellow residents.

"Apparently, one of Grainger's grandchildren had a bite of his Jell-O during a visit and went on to endure several days of intense hallucinations," Cleveland said. "The spiked dessert concoction is known as Electric Jell-O on the street."

"It was strange to see a 3-year-old reciting Abbie Hoffman's old speeches on the playground," said the child's preschool teacher, Mollie Sudgeon. "That little rascal started ranting about John Sinclair rotting away in prison over a single joint and it just went downhill from there."

Sudgeon continued, "Later on, while the kids were watching Sesame Street, the little fella tried to stab the TV with a red crayon because he thought Big Bird was making eyes at his woman. At that point, we made him stand in the corner, but not before he had the entire class chanting 'Attica! Attica!' "

The ATF believes Grainger was importing "various forms of psychotropic drugs" from Canada and selling them to his fellow residents at Bayview.

"We never understood how Bayview could care for 59 clients with a staff of only three," said Trevor Bannister of the Center for Medicare & Medicaid Services. "It all makes sense now; they were jacked up out of their minds."

While the contents of Grainger's room have now been confiscated by law enforcement officials, it appears a good deal of his product is still in circulation.

"Just last Saturday night, the residents organized a trip to the planetarium to view the Lawrence Welk Laser Show," Inman said. "According to Face-book posts of the planetarium staff, the senior citizens were spotted munching on psychedelic mushrooms in the parking lot before the show. It seems most of them started to peak around the time Pete Fountain took his first solo on 'Bye Bye Bill Bailey.'"

After the light show was over, the stoned seniors relocated to an adjoining pasture owned by local farmer Max Yasgur. By daybreak, the carnage was apparent: sleeping bags, spent roaches and empty tubes of Ben Gay that were reportedly not used for pain relief purposes littered the field. A police helicopter that hovered over the scene photographed what looked like a giant re-creation of the AARP logo fashioned out of trashed adult diapers; apparently, the Age of Anginous was at an end.

From a cell at the La Grange Sheriff 's Office on Monday, Grainger was in good spirits.

"They've been very nice to me here at the jail," Grainger said as he poured a bit of wavy gravy on his potatoes. "I promised I'd behave as long as they didn't Bogart the salt."

Grainger's first court appearance is set for April 20, 2525.

COLUMN: POULTRY COMPANY SCOUTING KINSTON
FOR NEW SITE
MAY 1, 2012

The public relations wing of Valley Mill Poultry has confirmed that Kinston is on the short list for its new processing location.

"Kinston and Lenoir County have been very accommodating to Sanderson Farms," said Valley Mill spokesman Freddie King. "The fact they are able to operate in Kinston without having to use City of Kinston electricity made the area very attractive to us."

While King says everything is still in the planning stages at this point, he believes the plant could bring 400 jobs to the area.

"What we'd be producing at this site wouldn't be your typical chicken or turkey operation," King said. "Based on the data we're receiving from test markets in Afghanistan and Raleigh, this new product could revolutionize the food industry."

The proposed plant would be the first U.S. based processing center for "turkens" — or as they're referred to in some parts of the world, "churkeys."

"This whole business of turkens and churkeys started in a small fishing village in Portugal back in the 1980s," King said. "An elderly blind farmer by the name of Diego Columbus accidentally placed a few turkeys in a chicken pen the same week Luther Vandross was doing an outdoor concert a few blocks away. Apparently, not even chickens or turkeys can resist the power of a seasoned R&B crooner with a velvet delivery and wildly fluctuating weight."

Columbus told the Weekly Publico in 1988, "When Luther hit the chorus in 'The Night I Fell In Love,' there was a caterwaul out in the barnyard you wouldn't believe. A few months later, my omelets started to taste different."

While the process of turkey/chicken crossbreeding has been perfected over the past few decades, the first few generations suffered numerous genetic abnormalities. Many of the animals featured an enlarged wattle that not only covered their head, but their neck, chest and feet. The sight of an apparently turned inside-out bird was not attractive to any potential mate.

"Don't get it twisted, chickens and turkeys are filthy, disgusting animals, but even they don't want to mate with something that looks like an erupting volcano," King said. "Eventually, the boys in the lab got the wandering wattle under control. Aside from a few snoods that looked like that thing on Aaron Neville's head, it's been smooth sailing since '06."

The land at the top of Valley Mill's wish list is located just off N.C. 258 in Kinston on Moreau Road. Several anti-vivisection groups are already planning to protest what they believe to be an abomination on the scale of the Justin Bieber's career or worse.

"Sure, Valley Mill doesn't employ vivisection techniques, but we believe the prospect of a new animal could lead be a slippery slope," said Mary Whitehouse of Citizens against Interspecies Erotica. "The popularity of the McRib sandwich has led to an entire industry of ribless pig farms throughout the Midwest; common decency prevents me from going into detail about the horrors of McNugget harvesting in Central America.

"All I can say is Grimace hasn't been seen since the McNugget was introduced in 1983 ... you do the math."

If the turken/churkey experiment pays off for Valley Mill, the company hopes to bring the cog to the U.S. market in 2015 and the dat to Sri Lanka, Korea and Raleigh by 2016.

TOUCHING IS WELCOME
MAY 3, 2012

Against my better judgment, I've let Free Press Managing Editor and resident "Glee" fanatic Bryan Hanks talk me into mingling with the public.

On Saturday morning at 6 a.m., I'll leave the tranquility of my compound in order to meet Bryan at The Free Press office. We'll load a table and a Free Press banner into Bryan's 1946 Jeep and meet Free Press concierge Paulette Burroughs (as Neil Young would say) down by the river. According to Paulette's autobiography, "I Did It Before Doing It Was Doable," Paulette is no stranger to meeting men down by the river.

I was coerced into sitting at the Free Press booth at the Festival on the Neuse by a couple of people. The first person to blame is Richie Honeycutt at LCC, who after a book signing at the school, broached the idea. At the time she mentioned it, I'd just sold a decent number of books at the signing, and with the assurance that I'd sell a similar amount at the festival, my unrequited lust for money took over.

The other person responsible is Mr. Happy Drawers himself, Bryan. He believes with all of whatever is in the spot where his heart should be I will repeat the success of the LCC signing at the Festival On The Neuse. I'm not so sure, but since newspaper people make less money than a Hawaiian Ice guy in Antarctica, I'm going to be there with bells on and little else.

Additionally, I've been coerced into selling the book for $13 – which is $2 off the normal price. To make up for this disparity, I've come up with a way to further monetize my time at Festival On The Neuse. Any women who'd like a hug can get it for free, but on the odd chance any men would like a hug, that's going to cost you $38.

Some people would call this sexist, and they would be correct.

I'm usually against public drunkenness, but it is my sincere hope that several men with money to burn and a thick set of beer goggles will want a hug from either Paulette or me. Paulette will hug anyone and everything with a pulse, so if you're paying by check, you can just make it out to me.

After the last show I played at Kenny's Castaways in New York, I was asked to sign a CD and a body part. Thankfully, the Sharpie pen malfunctioned so a fair amount of bearing down was needed to make a good impression. This request came from a female, so there was no charge.

For any non-woman wishing to have a body part signed on Saturday, the cost will range from $20 up to $200, depending on the desired location of the signature. If we're talking about a forehead, then $20 will get you squared away. If the area is anywhere below the Mason/Dixon line you're looking at $200, and you will also have to furnish the plastic gloves and isotope holders.

Although it's pompous to think anyone would want it, my autograph is free. The only caveat is the pens I use will only show up on the special paper used to print my book, "Making Gravy in Public." I'm allergic to most ink, and the special pens I use were developed by NASA so astronauts could keep up with their Sudoko in space. I'd love to sign your wet napkin or religious pamphlet that was left on your car, but on the advice of doctors, I can only sign copies of the book.

I love you all, so if you're a female or a dude with money to burn, come see me and Paulette on Saturday.

I am not a prostitute.

ILLNESS DEVASTATES LENOIR COUNTY FAMILY
MAY 10, 2012

There's nothing like a raging intestinal virus to drown out the dull grind of an election.

It all started Sunday night. We'd gotten Tax Deduction No. 1 to bed using the customary 47-step program that involves things such as prayers, nightlights, ocean machines, sips of water, Lou skipping and the arranging of 100 pounds of pillows for a 48-pound girl. By the time she actually gets to bed, it's time for breakfast.

Tax Deduction No. 2 is only 2, so her only requirement is a pacifier which may or may not have been soaking in a vat of Gentleman Jack just to give us a fighting chance. No. 2's latest trick is saying the word "hey", but it's the way she says it that's unique.

Her version is an elongated, Southernized take on Mae West and Paul Lynde. Hearing this diapered lemur cry out "Haaaaaay!" at 2 a.m. as if she were trying to hail a taxi in slow motion is frankly frightening.

The first time she did it, I thought Miley Cyrus had broken into the house.

(Note: I've never actually heard Miley Cyrus speak or sing, but I'm just assuming.)

On Sunday night, we got both of the freeloaders to bed without incident and thought we were in the clear. Then, after about five minutes of blissful silence, our version of Three Mile Island occurred. TD#1 became violently ill and you guessed it — didn't make it to the facilities in time to properly dispose of the involuntary upload of that day's dinner.

The pattern was frantic footsteps, a reverberating splat, followed by more frantic footsteps.

Like a poorly-funded but spirited NASCAR pit crew, the wife and I leapt into action. One of us comforted TD#1 while the other initiated the cleanup. All the commotion caused TD#2 to pop her head up out of the crib and say "haaaaay!" with all the abandon of soused salesman at a convention.

Ten minutes later — with everything and everybody consoled, cleaned and gotten back to sleep — we foolishly tried to go back to bed. A trash can was placed at the edge of TD#1's bed in case she felt the urge to urp again. I took this opportunity to reintroduce my plan to move to Anchorage, home-school the children and avoid all contact with the outside world. I may have actually been winning the argument, but this was all mooted when TD#2 started going off like a car alarm.

"Haaaay!" "Haaaay!" "Haaaay!" alerted us to the fact that TD#1 was again in the throes of a violent refund. As we raced down the hall, the theme from "Chariots of Fire" played in my head. Then I wondered if TD#1 had enough wherewithal to move one foot to the left and direct everything into the trash can.

Sadly, upon entering her room barefoot and without turning on the light, I discovered she had not.

This scenario played out a couple of more times through the night until around 4 a.m., when I put TD#2 (the drooling car alarm) in the bed with the wife and sat next to TD#1 (the little blonde Chernobyl) and rubbed her back until she eased off to sleep. This all worked fine and we all managed to get about two hours of sleep.

Around 6 a.m., Monday I awoke with an odd feeling. Not the kind of odd feeling you get when you put peanut butter on shellfish, but rather the kind of feeling you get just before an actor starts telling you who to vote for.

It was a queasy, borderline-painful feeling in what most surgeons refer to as "the gut." I calmly stood up, realized something horrible was about to happen and excused myself to the proper room for horrible things to happen in.

I spent Monday vacillating between the room where horrible things happen and bed where I lay in a cramped fetal position like the old man at the end of "2001: A Space Odyssey." For a while, I thought there was a mysterious obelisk surrounded by apes at the end of the bed, but I'm 50 percent sure it was just a chest of drawers TD#2 was trying to climb.

I did find it odd the apes were yelling "Haaaaay!" in the voice of a small girl.

All of this nonsense continued till about noon on Tuesday when I started to feel human again. I found out my partner-in-crime Paulette Burroughs — who'd been in a booth with me at the Festival on the Neuse on Saturday — was also stricken with my affliction. Apparently, she came back to work on Tuesday, but after dating Rick James for the better part of the 1980s, her immune system is no doubt tougher than mine.

BREAKING NEWS: City of Kinston customers report several hours of uninterrupted power

LA GRANGE RESIDENTS HAVE TO DIAL 666 STARTING JUNE 1
MAY 15, 2012

For her entire life, Olivia Brown of La Grange has dialed 566 to make a local phone call.

"When I was a girl, we only had to dial the last four digits of the number to make a call," Brown says. "It took me about a year to get used to dialing the 566 and then the number."

While the 566 prefix has been in place for decades, anyone wishing to dial a La Grange number will have to dial a new number starting June 1.

"The new prefix will be 666," says Anton LaVey of the North Carolina Telecommunications Industry Association. "We believe this change will result in fewer dialing mistakes. Besides, the time saved from having to move from the 5 button to the 6 button will add up to several minutes saved per community per year."

As expected, the idea of having to dial 666 to call a La Grange number has created a firestorm of burrito supreme proportions.

"I'm not going to lie to you, when I first heard about this 666 mess, I thought I was going to mess up my good pants," said Michael Talbot of Bug Busters Pest Control of La Grange. "I'm not a prude; I know what it was like when red-headed women were still illegal around here. But this 666 stuff is an abomination.

"There were more phones ripped out of churches this past weekend than the time Oral Roberts was calling for donations to help fund his krunk album."

As of this writing, 3,578 names have been added to a petition demanding the 666 prefix be changed back to 566.

"We understand the connotations that come with the number 666," said Alester Crowley of the American Civil Liberties Union. "In most English translations of the Bible, 666 is linked to the Beast of Revelation. The number is also used by the National Restaurant Association as a distress code to alert buffet owners when Kirstie Alley has been spotted in the area. Either way, the ACLU is committed to sticking our nose into matters that don't concern us, be it religious people who aren't harming anyone or former hotties who've gone the way of the Michelin Man."

Minister Charlie Pettaway of Running Jump Baptist Church in La Grange sees the 666 debacle as the latest in a series of attacks on Christianity.

"Can you imagine how humiliating it is for a minister to have a 666 phone number printed on his business card?" Pettaway asked. "It's like a physical trainer passing out gym passes printed on Krispy Kreme coupons; Lordhammercy."

LaVey says his intent with the change was based solely on practicality, although many claim his ties to a Satanic religious sect may have played a role in his decision.

"It's true, I'm the president of the N.C. Justin Bieber fan club," LaVey said. "He has the charisma of a young Joey Lawrence and the rugged good looks of Rachel Maddow; he's the total package."

To get around the new telephone number, some residents are traveling to 919 and 910 area codes to purchase cell phones.

"This has been the busiest day we've had in a long time," said Bob Weir of Garbled Communications in Duplin County. "We had an entire busload of folks come over on Sunday. Most of the customers were older people who asked me to shut up when I started talking about the various apps the phone had to offer, but a sale is a sale."

LeVay can be reached at 252-527-0175.

LOCAL DESIGNER'S CLOTHES IN STORES THIS SUMMER
MAY 17, 2012

From an early age, Kinston's Sonya Hargrove was interested in clothes.

"When I was 4, I had a subscription to Elle magazine," Hargrove, 29, said from her trendy loft on Kinston's upper west side. "Add to that my obsession with the 'Roseanne' show and my love affair with fashion was born."

Hargrove's mother knew her daughter wasn't going to be an accountant after her first day of kindergarten.

"I was going about my usual day — laundry, dusting, drinking — when I received a call from the principal at Sonya's school," said Ellen Hargrove, 44. "Apparently, the little rascal told the teacher her outfit was all wrong and she'd never get a husband if she insisted on dressing like the night manager at a muffler shop."

It was apparent to everyone that young Sonya possessed the necessary rudeness to make it in the world of fashion, but what about her designing skills?

"The first thing she came up with was a three-legged pair of jeans," said Ivana Bumsen of the Royal Academy of Fashion in Antwerp. "Sonya believed even something as bourgeois as a three-legged-race could be fashionable."

Bumsen went on to say the three-legged jeans were on the way to becoming a hit until the only documented escalator fatality in U.S. history halted production in 2009.

"When that trial was over, I was determined to design something that would catch the world on fire," Har-grove said. "That's when I got the idea for Smoking Pants."

Described as "the first set of pants to literally set the world on fire," Smoking Pants were developed by Sonya for the city dweller who is just bored to tears with simply covering up their naughty bits.

"Sure, there are some cool things on the market — sneakers that light up and underwear that plays the theme from 'A Summer Place' when you tinkle," Bumsen said. "But to have a pair of pants that violates most fire hazard laws is incredibly progressive. These are not your father's pants."

Hargrove won't go into detail about the chemical makeup of her new creation due to a pending patent.

"It's totally safe to take these pants to a dry cleaner," she said. "I wouldn't hang around for long, though."

Along with her line of smoking pants, Hargrove will be introducing a line of designer barf bags for bulimic models called "Toss" and a line of diamond-encrusted gauze pads for Facebook users who inadvertently donate their organs before dying.

"My friend Summer just checks boxes on Facebook without reading anything," Hargrove said. "The next thing she knew, Mark Zuckerberg showed up at her front door with a nurse and an Igloo cooler. Long story short, she now has one less kidney to worry about."

Hargrove has also announced she will be a judge on the 2012-13 edition of "America's Next Top Model."

"I'm taking my role on the show very seriously," Har-grove said. "I'm having a third thumb surgically implanted on my forehead just so I'll be able to give the models three thumbs down."

Hargrove would not respond to rumors she bought the thumb from Zuckerberg.

IS WITN'S HEATHER KING JOINING THE FREE PRESS?
MAY 22, 2012

Local morning show host and "Ink Master" finalist Heather King may be coming to work for The Free Press.

I first met Heather King when I filled in for Free Press Managing Editor Bryan Hanks as a judge for a cooking contest at Vernon Park Mall in 2010. I found Mrs. King to be very pleasant and easy to talk to. We both have children that are roughly the same age so we had plenty to talk about.

That being said, after the fourth time she pointed and yelled "THERE'S OPRAH!" in order to distract me long enough to steal food from my plate, I realized the perky personae masked a tortured soul driven by an insatiable lust for apple fritters and fried chicken.

Since the chicken incident, Heather has been gracious enough to have several members of The Free Press staff on her morning show. I made an appearance last year to promote my book, "Making Gravy in Public", which is currently available at www.jondawson.com and The Free Press office.

At first, she didn't know what to make of me. I distinctly heard her tell WITN Meteorologist Jim Howard to retrieve one of the revolvers from Marvin Daughety's desk in case things got out of hand.

Although I was a bit apprehensive knowing Ol' Jim was packing heat, my appearance (to plug "Making Gravy in Public", which is currently available at www.jondawson.com and The Free Press office) went well. Heather laughed several times, and by the end of the interview dismissed the security guard who stood between us for most of the interview.

When Bryan Hanks has appeared on her show, he was required to wear a burqa, which had something to do with FCC regulations regarding disturbing images.

The latest Free Press personnel to grace the WITN airwaves were publisher/editor Patrick Holmes and advertising director Billy Moore. On Monday, the dynamic duo was promoting the upcoming Relish Cooking Show at LCC and Patrick's new line of spandex trusses. While that may all sound like business as usual, a tweet published by Heather later that morning hinted that Patrick and Billy were up to something.

Mrs. King's Tweet included a link to a "Free Press — Simply Better" notepad she recieved from Patrick and Billy. Many of you are probably thinking, "What's the big deal? It's a notepad."

Let me tell you folks, in the big time world of journalism, a notepad is more than just a notepad. A notepad is a way to send a signal on the QT. A notepad is a way for a business to make an overture without actually making an overture; more like an underture. This is espionage on a level not seen since Bobby Brown was hired as a pharmacist at Walgreen's.

This Free Press/Heather King scenario isn't the first time a company has made a grand gesture to ingratiate themselves to a prospective employee. CBS once sent Jay Leno a job offer attached to a brand new motorcycle. NBC lured Harry Smith from CBS by sending him a salary offer hidden in a schnoinkel bouquet. The Miami Heat sealed the deal with LeBron James when they sent a second car to pick up his ego from the airport.

The much-coveted "Free Press — Simply Better" notepads currently go for $600 to $1,000 on eBay. In one instance, a notepad signed by Free Press Public Relations Director Paulette Burroughs sold for $5,000 at a Sotheby's auction. A notepad signed by myself reportedly sold for a nickel at the SPCA Thrift Shop in Kinston, but only after the page I'd signed had been incinerated.

Over the past few weeks, our parent company Freedom Communications has been shedding newspapers like a copperhead in a blender on a fault line near an active volcano. I don't know if this has anything to do with the covert attempt to lure Heather away from WITN, but as Lee Iacocca wrote in his 1988 book Talking Straight, "It's never a bad idea to hire as many babes as possible."

DIET DRINK MAY CAUSE WEIGHT AND/OR BLOOD LOSS
MAY 24, 2012

After much soul searching and an alarming dream in which Richard Simmons showed up at my house with a forklift, I've decided to go on a diet.

Many people I know are dieting in various forms. Some of them are utilizing portion control; some are walking a few miles a day; others are drinking strange cocktails consisting of Red Bull, air conditioner run-off and Phenphedrine. Me, I'm doing that Slim Fast deal.

There are two ways to do Slim Fast, and neither of them is particularly exciting. The first way is to spend $13 on six bottles of liquid that don't add up to enough to extinguish a lit match. The other option is to buy a can of brown powder for $7 and mix it into 8 ounces of skim milk.

I don't know if you've encountered 8 ounces of liquid lately, but by the time it hits your throat you've already forgotten you drank anything in the first place. The sensation of standing in the kitchen holding an empty glass and not knowing why has sent me running to the Alzheimer's hot line on more than one occasion this past week.

All kidding aside, I've gotta say this Slim Fast stuff really does work fast. As I dumped a glob of the allegedly chocolate powder into a thimble of milk Tuesday morning, one of the tax deductions that inhabit my residence awoke screaming from a nightmare. In my hurry to calm the little piranha down, I sat the drink down on the counter without mixing it.

After a few minutes, the TD calmed down and told us she dreamed we forced her to watch "American Idol." To console the child, I explained that making her watch "American Idol," "Dancing with the Stars," "Survivor" or any of the non-scripted pus being transmitted to North American homes would be in violation of the Fourth Geneva Convention. Legally, the worst thing I could expose her to would be NBC's "Whitney."

With the childronic unit taken care of, I went back to the kitchen to drink my breakfast. I picked up the cup and took a fairly healthy swig. As I soon discovered, in my haste to neutralize the shrieking child so as to avoid the fire detectors going off — again — I'd forgotten to actually mix the powder into the milk. The sensation can best be described as drinking sod and chasing it with mud.

The ball of chocolate dust that was now obstructing my windpipe caused me to cough in a full-body heave type of motion; the type of motion that can cause extremities such as feet to flail uncontrollably. Sometimes when feet flail uncontrollably, they will accidentally come into contact with inanimate objects. In this case, the inanimate object my foot came into contact with was the leg of a kitchen table.

Technically, it wasn't my foot that came into contact with the table, but rather the webbing between the little piggy that ate roast beef and the one that went "weeweewee" all the way home. I don't know why he went "weeweewee" all the way home; maybe he had a small bladder. In any event, I knocked the bark off of my person something awful.

With two young tax deductions in the house, I was not able to relieve any stress by yelling anything close to an expletive. All I could muster was a "SONOFABISCUIT" and a "JAMIE FARR THAT HURT" — neither of which eased the pain as much as the words Mr. Rogers' used to berate his staff whenever the train to Make Believe would accidentally run off the rails and boing him in the groin.

Due to the collision of fleshy-white underfoot and oak, there was a bit of blood loss. Factor in the ensuing tears and I lost approximately a pound of bodily fluids within two minutes.

Thanks, Slim Fast! If you need a news spokesperson, my digits are below, yo.

KINSTON ANNEXES ENTIRE COUNTY WHILE RESIDENTS AT BEACH
MAY 29, 2012

Lenoir County residents were in for a shock when they returned home from their Memorial Day vacation.

Shortley after midnight on Monday, members of the Kinston City Council dispatched several G.I.M. (Gimmie It's Mine) Teams to infiltrate all quadrants of Lenoir County in an attempt to annex all of it. As it turns out, the low flying helicopters that had the entire county in an uproar back in March were rented by the Kinston City Council so as to devise the best routes for their G.I.M. Teams to follow.

"For the past few years we've been trying to grab ... uh ... acquire the areas around Crestview," said one council member who wished to remain anonymous. "Those areas are just a bridge to the big moolah, which would be the area around Falling Creek Country Club and Castle Oaks. Since no one on the planet other than us seems to want this to happen, we've decided it would be easier to swoop in while everybody was at the beach and just take the whole thing."

As the dozens of G.I.M. Teams crept around Lenoir County during the early morning hours Monday, they placed tiny orange stickers on the mailboxes of unsuspecting county dwellers to let them know they were now part of Kinston.

"If you see one of those orange stickers on your mailbox, we gotcha!" said another council member, wishing to remain anonymous. "Next year we're going to launch a campaign to replace DVD players with VCRs, but one unpopular project at a time."

While the 30,000-plus county residents living outside any town limits are against the annexation, upwards of six or possibly seven politicians think it's a good idea.

"We've got to grow real bad," said one prominent political figure. "When I was a young person, a whole generation went to war to stop Hitler from taking over areas that didn't belong to him. Many of that generation now live in the areas we want to annex, and, well, I seem to have talked myself into a corner."

According to information provided by head G.I.M. Team Captain Julius Schreck, the Kinston City Council acquired nearly 68 percent of Lenoir County during the night raid.

"We knew we couldn't get it all in one night, but one more sweep around the Fourth of July and there should be an orange sticker on ever mailbox in the county," Schreck said. "I haven't had this much fun since I drove the Führer to that cat house in Munich."

While most Lenoir County residents were out of town during the raid, the few that were not didn't seem pleased with the Kinston City Council's unorthodox methods.

"One G.I.M. worker did have to return to home base to have 1,456 orange stickers removed from his bathing suit area," said EMS technician Ash-ley Mills. "Apparently a 90-year-old World War II veteran in the Bucklesberry area of La Grange subdued one of our workers, removed all 50 pages of orange stickers from the worker's briefcase and proceeded to apply each of them in areas that the good Lord never intended for sticker activity."

Mills went on to say after the stickers were removed, the worker in question would probably only be able to find work at Seaworld as a dolphin.

When asked who or what entity gave them the authority to just claim Lenoir County for Kinston, the anonymous council member stopped in the middle of lighting a cigar with a borrowed $10 bill to respond.

"We went to Staples and bought clipboards for all of our G.I.M. Team members," the council member said. "I'm no expert on parliamentary procedure or the basic concept or right vs. wrong, but I think if you have a clipboard you can pretty much do whatever you want."

In an attempt to smooth over a potentially contentious situation, the Kinston City Council issued this press release late Monday afternoon:

We on the council would like to welcome you into the Kinston Family.

As with all families, there will be hard times and hurt feelings. Many of you are probably a little persnickety over the fact that we pulled you into the city limits while you were out of town. While it's not your fault that decisions made in the distant and not so distant past have turned our fair city into what some commentators are referring to as "Detroit Jr." or "Little Hanoi," we just want you to know that you'll be getting something for that money you'll be handing over in a few months.

Just think of the wear and tear you'll save on your car now that you won't be able to afford to go out to eat or take in a movie. You'll probably save a gallon of gas per week from just driving to and from work and nowhere else. Can't afford to give your grandchildren a dollar when you see them? It'll teach them that if they work hard, save their money and build a house out in the county, that the city council can come in and take over whenever they want.

Oh, and we'll try to get somebody out there to pick up your trash for

you, although with less money to buy things with, those pesky garbage cans probably won't get filled nearly as quickly as they
used to.

Sorry for any inconvenience.

Love,

The Kinston City Council (dictated but not read)

LOCAL COUPLE CELEBRATES 22 YEARS OF
WEDDED BLISS
MAY 31, 2012

The world was different in 1990. A gallon of gas cost $1.34; Johnny Carson was the host of the Tonight Show, and Ste-vie B's "Because I Love You (The Postman Song)" was at the top of the Billboard charts.

Fast forward to 2012 and the cost of a gallon of gas has tripled, Dudley Do-Right's nephew is hosting the Tonight Show, and Ste-vie B recently was arrested after a concert for owing $420,000 in child support.

While the Tonight Show and Stevie B have devolved into a quagmire of chin envy and baby-daddy nonsense over the last 22 years, this time period has been good to me. Let it be written and let it be done that 1990 was the year that I met the future mother of my tax deductions; my buddy; my shrink; my consigliere; my shawty; my wife.

Things didn't start out uproariously for us. We met via telephone that summer as she was looking for a ride to school. I was the proud owner of a 1988 Chevrolet Celebrity with about 80,000 miles on it and a clean driving record. The car featured working air conditioner and a Delco tape deck.

If all of that wasn't enough, when the route didn't involve a dirt road the CD Walkman with cassette adaptor would emerge from under the seat.

The trouble was I was already transporting three people to school, so I didn't have room for anyone else. After a few days I called back to see if she'd found a ride, which she had. After about two minutes of talking to her, I was resolved to ask her out.

At this point I had no idea what she looked like, but I didn't care. A tentative date was set up over the phone a few weeks before school started back.

After an entire summer of communicating only via the phone (even though she lived about five miles away), we finally met face to face when school started back up. I was in the band room trying to fix the tuning peg on a guitar when this cute girl walked up to the door and asked for Jon. The guy with me tried to claim he was Jon, but after a solid but justified elbow to the stomach he got out of the way.

As I type this I can't remember what I had for supper last night or if I have enough money in my pocket to rent a used toothbrush, but I remember what she was wearing that day. I remember what movie we watched on our first date, and I remember my mom making us a snack that included iced Pepsi served in glasses with little cows on them.

By the way, the movie I'd rented was 'The War of the Roses,' which was a dark comedy about a once loving couple that ended up literally killing each other in the middle of a nasty divorce. I realize the average guy would have picked something romantic like "When Harry Met Sally" or "Pet Cemetery," but I figured I might as well go ahead and let her know from the jump that I was a little off.

After seven years of courtship that included a tour of duty commuting to East Carolina University together, we got married in 1997. During the years that ensued, we served a stint in the Jonestown Acres trailer park in La Grange.

This place was so exciting the producers of the show 'Cops' eventually set up a live video feed from our roof so as to save money sending out a production truck every week. I used to sit with my neighbor William Tyndall on his deck on Saturday nights, and we'd bet quarters on which house the cops would show up at first — but I digress.

We got out of Jonestown Acres about three hours before they started passing out the cups of Electric Kool-Aid, and eventually scraped enough dough and mentally unstable bankers together to build a house in the country. That house is now inhabited by two Tax Deductions that keep trying to rent the "Melendez Brothers Story," myself, and their mother who doesn't look a day over 25.

Today is our anniversary, so we're going out for a nice dinner. My parents have agreed to keep TD#1 and TD#2 so we can have a little time to ourselves. They did this for us last year also, but that's the night my throat locked into a spasm which lasted for four hours and the evening was, to quote my late grandmother, "ruint."

To play it safe, I'm probably just going to order a bowl of miniature marshmallows.

For all you weird looking dudes out there don't give up hope. Women are less shallow than men, and more often than not you'll see a gorgeous woman on the arm of a guy who fell out of the goofy tree and hit every limb on the way down. Luckily, I found one who didn't start wearing glasses until it was much too late.

At this point it would be too much of a hassle to change the names on her driver's license and various legal forms, so I guess she's mine.

BREAKING NEWS: No City of Kinston customers reporting power outtages....unless the phone lines are down too.

JOHN EDWARDS' HAIR TO SPEAK AT KINSTON ROTARY CLUB
JUNE 5, 2012

Late last week, the case against former U.S. presidential candidate John Edwards ended in a mistrial. As of this writing, it's uncertain as to whether or not the government will retry Edwards at a later date.

Edwards is currently not granting interviews — but his hair will be speaking at the weekly Kinston Rotary Club luncheon on Thursday.

Edwards' hair first gained national attention when a video of the well-coiffed politician prettying himself up for an interview made its way to the Internet during the 2008 presidential campaign (see link below to view video). Shortly thereafter, a small uproar ensued after David Letterman reached over and messed up the candidate's hair at the conclusion of an interview. Paramedics were called in; lawsuits were filed — it was a big mess.

After the Letterman incident, things got worse for Edwards' hair. Reportedly drunk on Grecian Formula, it stumbled into a bar in Manhattan and ended up in a fight with Donald Trump's hair.

"Trump's hair used to come in here all the time," said Hoyt Maxton, bartender at the Koala Room Bar in New York City. "Trump's hair has been exposed to so much hair-spray and raccoon hormones over the years it developed a drinking problem. Usually Trump's hair was a happy drunk, but seeing Ed-wards' naturally youthful hair saunter in the room with a comb on each arm just drove him over the edge."

According to an incident report obtained from the New York City Police Department, Trump's hair knocked Edwards' hair to the ground, poured several sample packets of Aveda Men Pure-formance shampoo all over it and verbally taunted the heavenly, caramel-colored locks until police arrived.

"Trump's hair said some really hateful things to Edwards' hair," Maxton said. "Stuff like, 'I haven't seen ends that split since Chris Christie wore spanks' and 'I didn't realize the Village People were back on the road' and 'When the squirrels are in heat, do you have to wear a helmet?' "

Trump was unavailable for comment, but through a representative did question whether or not Edwards' hair was in fact born in the United States.

For years, Edwards has denied artificially coloring his hair. According to his 2005 autobiography, "How to Chase Ambulances and Women at the Same Time," Edwards gives his personal stylist, Dr. Diane DiMassa, all the credit for turning him into "the prettiest man on the scene since Peabo Bryson."

"Each of the hairs on Mr. Ed-wards' head has its own serial number and is cataloged just like a library book," DiMassa said. "Each hair on Mr. Ed-wards' head — approximately 100,000 to be exact — has its own personal caregiver. If hair No. 47,897 shows signs of distress during one of our bi-weekly CAT scans of his head, then the person in charge of hair No. 47,897 is flown in from Switzerland to rectify the situation."

In response to the artificial coloring controversy, DiMassa flatly denied the accusation.

"The only substance to touch John's head other than the cheap glue-on nails of Reille Hunter over the last decade has been the all-natural shampoo we import from Europe," Di-Massa said. "It's derived from jojoba, aloe vera and butterfly tears."

Asked if he thinks employing 100,000 people to deal with one head of hair isn't a tad excessive, Edwards' hair frizzed at the notion.

"Listen, I'm from the street, OK?" Edwards' hair exclaimed. "I'm a survivor. I've been feathered, French-braided, Jhericurled, permed, pompadoured and duck-butted. When John Edwards was a poor kid in the South, all he could afford to wash me with was Pepsi mixed with government peanut butter.

"No, I don't think there's anything wrong with each of my beautiful hairs having its own personal attendant. If Joy Be-har can pay a blind man $800 a week to tell her she's gorgeous, then my situation seems frugal by comparison."

The Kinston Rotary Club will meet at King's Restaurant on Thursday at 1 p.m. Edwards' hair is scheduled to speak for 30 minutes after a meal of angel hair pasta. Afterwards, Edwards' hair will sign autographs and pose for photographs on the heads of any bald attendees for a $50 tax-refundable fee.

BUCKLESBERRY FATHER HAS 2-YEAR-OLD ARRESTED
JUNE 7, 2012

Four hours may be long enough to properly digest a Hot Pocket or perform an amateur liver transplant, but it's not long enough to get a good night's rest.

As I type this on what must be the oldest Compaq computer in captivity, I'm going on four hours of sleep. I know this is the point where many of you stop reading and turn the page to see who died, who got married or who got accepted to mime college. Normally, this would bother me, but I'm just going to clickity-clack on this prehistoric piece of technology until there are enough little black squiggly things on the screen to fill up my allotted space.

By the way — the marriage announcements are all fakes. No one has gotten married in this county since 2007, so go run tell that.

I only slept for four hours because of a small, blonde-headed orangutan that, according to her birth certificate, is my second born child lovingly designated as Tax Deduction No. 2. She's as cute as a sack full of kittens but every man has his limit, and last night she took it to the limit, looked over it and dived in head-first.

Around 12:15 a.m., I went to bed. At this time, she'd been in her crib for nearly four hours with not so much as a whimper. With my wife in her 'kerchief and I in my cap, I flopped on the mattress for a long summer's nap.

At 12:35 a.m., I heard a sound that no parent wants to hear in the middle of the night. Was it a prowler crawling through a window? No. Was it a busted pipe in a wall? No. Was it a door-to-door door salesman from Alaska who forgot to reset his watch? No.

It was TD#2 calling out for "Daaaadeeeee."

In all my agony, I got up, put my Teddy Bear back in his special chair, and eased down the hallway to her room. After a quick rub on the back she eased off to sleep. I went back to my room, grabbed Teddy and once again tried to grab some shuteye.

A few minutes later, I was in the middle of a dream. For some reason, Eliza-beth Hurley was trying to sell me flood insurance, but just as I was about to sign the policy, Mrs. Hathaway from the Beverly Hillbillies barged into the room and I woke up.

"Daaaadeeeee" was being paged yet again.

My wife had been up with TD#2 three or four times the night before. Since I was (allegedly) 50 percent responsible for bringing TD#2 into this world from apparently the psych ward of another, I was determined to handle this situation so she could get some well-deserved sleep.

I went through the whole production again: Teddy in the chair, ease down the hall, rub the back for a minute and go back to bed.

At 1 a.m., I'm dreaming again. I'm walking around the insurance office trying to return Elizabeth Hurley's pen, but every time I open a door, Frances Bavier is standing there with a jar of kerosene pickles.

I wake up again.

"Daaaadeeeee" was paged for the third time.

This time, I took drastic measures. After walking down the hallway, (which after midnight becomes the Bridge of Sighs), I removed TD#2 from her crib, grabbed a quilt and headed to the living room. On the way to the living room in the dark of night, I stepped on what felt like a Swiss Army Barbie as whatever it was nearly sliced my foot in two.

The urge to curse was nearly overpowering, but since TD#2 has turned into a bit of a walking tape recorder as of late, I held the profanity in, although it did cause my ears to pop.

With the quilt spread out and a little fan running close by, I just knew this would soothe TD#2 into a deep slumber. For the first two minutes everything was heavenly, but for the remaining hour and 58 minutes of the ordeal, she flipped and flopped like a fish on methamphetamine.

After a while, the flipping and flopping stopped and those tiny little hands started smacking me in the face. There is nothing like the sensation of a soft little hand popping you in the eye, nose, mouth and other eye for the better part of an hour. I tried to go back to bed but she grabbed onto my leg, refusing to let me go.

With a bloody foot, bruised face and the realization that I was being held against my will, I realized there was only one thing left to do. I called the La Grange Police Department and had the kid arrested for assault and kidnapping.

They tried to take her in without using handcuffs, but after she dismantled the backseat of the police car before it got out of the driveway, they changed their minds. She's being held on $500 bond, and her first appearance is scheduled for Friday, but I'm going to ask the judge for a continuance.

FREE PRESS STAFF GRATEFUL FOR NEW OWNERSHIP
JUNE 14, 2012

As many of you know, The Free Press has been purchased by Halifax Media. To give you a little background, here's a section of the press release provided by Freedom News Service on June 2:

Founded in 2010, Halifax Media is headquartered in Daytona Beach, Fla. The company's investment group includes Stephens Capital Partners, JAARSSS Media, and Redding Investments. The group consists of 16 publications in six states, primarily situated in the Southeast. Halifax Media's strategy is to invest long-term capital in quality companies positioned in strong markets that are closely connected to the community.

We at The Free Press are incredibly grateful this purchase happened. Between you and me, I was one step away from playing "Love Is a Battlefield" in a low-rent cruise ship band for the rest of my days.

While I have nothing but love and respect for the work of Patricia Mae Andrzejewski, with a set of legs like mine, I'll only ever be allowed to do Tina Turner songs.

Just the name "Halifax" kinda puts you in a sunny, Burt Bacharach kind of mood, doesn't it? I'll give a five-spot to anyone who can say "Halifax" without cracking a smile. There's something about the way the sounds of the letters bounce between syllables that forces the Zygomaticus major and minor muscles to contract, which, in turn, pulls up the each side of the lower face.

Halifax Media is also a very patient company. For example, I sent each member of their board of director's pictures of my two young children every day for three months. On the back of each photo, I would write something like, "Please help our daddy keep his job" or "If you don't buy the Free Press, our daddy said we could get a few good hams off of the dog if we run out of food money."

To its credit, Halifax Media waited an entire month before I was hit with a cease and desist request; and even then, it wasn't an order — simply a request.

Did I mention we at The Free Press are incredibly grateful to Halifax Media? Our new owner's reputation is so spectacular it's hard to look at without one of those sheets of paper with a hole in it usually used for eclipse gazing or Joy Behar sightings.

I'm not sure there are enough letters in the alphabet to construct the proper adjectives needed to fully describe how fantastically awesome Halifax Media is — but I will try. For starters, did you know Halifax Media was partially responsible for curing polio?

In 1950, Monroe Koprowski — then an administrative assistant with Halifax Media — accidentally spilled some chocolate from a company gift basket into a coworker's jar of peanut butter. Not wanting to waste anything, young Monroe took the peanut-butter stained chocolate home to his mother, noted virologist Hilary Koprowski.

After placing the chocolate/peanut butter hybrid under a telescope, Hilary Koprowski realized this combination could supercharge the trypsin and invertase enzymes. This discovery led to the first polio vaccine, and — more importantly — one heck of an impulse buy in the checkout lane.

We've also found out recently that Halifax Media is extremely generous when it comes to their employees. Although we haven't received new employee handbooks yet, based on conversations with other Halifax Media properties, we can all expect to not only have our pre-meltdown pay rates reinstated, but also pay raises, a daily food per diem, an on-site masseuse and a Jacuzzi in the break room.

Hopefully, the presence of a masseuse will do away with the mandatory deep-tissue massage our Managing Editor Bryan Hanks requires from all employees on a rotating basis. Most people think reporters have been leaving due to the low pay and uncertainty of the business, but it's been mainly because of the backrubs.

SIX OUTAGES IN 10 DAYS FOR CITY OF KINSTON CUSTOMERS
JUNE 19, 2012

As of this past Sunday morning, residents in the Bucklesberry and Little Baltimore communities had suffered five power outages in 10 days. For the record, I am one of those residents.

Before any of you start lighting torches, I've assembled a loose collection of facts linked together by logic and bailing wire — the same bailing wire apparently used to deliver electricity and phone service to anyone living between Kennedy Home Road and U.S. 70 in La Grange. I'm not saying our power grid is out of date, but allegedly the wire on the poles in this part of the county are from the same spool Alexander Graham Bell used to call Watson.

In case anyone thinks I'm exaggerating, keep this in mind: Anyone in the aforementioned area who tries to gain Internet access via the telephone lines are only able to achieve a 26.4kps connection — HALF the speed of the slowest Internet option, dial-up. This is the equivalent of only being able to drive 22.5 mph in a 55 mph zone.

Oh, Sprint keeps sending out acres of junk mail detailing the delights of their wonderful high-speed Internet options. Occasionally, I'll call and ask them to sign me up, but when I give them my phone number, they take on the quivering, concerned voice Ms. Garrett used to have when about to lay some worldly advice on Tootie and Blair.

"Oh, I'm so sorry, but our high-speed Internet service isn't available in your area," the crestfallen operator will say.

"Well why do you send me a steamer trunk full of these flyers every week which are begging me to sign up for it?" I retort. "Does your company get off on taunting folks that live out in the country? Were the families of your board of directors killed by a band of homicidal trees and they're seeking revenge by decimating the pulp wood population one glossy flyer at a time?"

I don't believe in throwing the messenger under the bus. The people who answer the phones down at the City of Kinston have no control over power outages. Anyone who yells and curses at them because the power is out is A) wasting their time and B) in the words of my grandma, "Being mighty ugly."

Also, it's no good yelling at a guy in a bucket truck trying to fix the problem. He's on your side, and he's not trying to do shoddy work. If he does shoddy work, the chances of him being called in at 2:48 a.m. increase.

As far as my own business goes, I've never understood why people try to corner me at the gas station or bail bond office with complaints about their paper delivery. I politely tell them that while I do, in fact, write for the paper, I don't actually deliver them — yet. I give them our customer service number and if the people are actually polite, I'll take down their name and number and pass it along.

Additionally, if you're upset by something written by someone at The Free Press, their contact information is listed at the bottom of every article or column. I know I'm goofy-looking and easy to spot, but if you have a problem with Managing Editor Bryan Hanks' eight-part series on Wang Chung, don't come crying to me about it.

In all seriousness, as I was typing this very column, the power went out for the sixth time in 10 days. Since I was alone in my private home office/ studio/bat cave, the ball of socks I usually have to cram in my mouth to keep any nearby children from hearing all sorts of profanity wasn't necessary.

I'm not advocating the use of salty language, I'm just saying for once it was cathartic to be able to let a couple of dozen of them bad boys rattle off the walls and curl up the wallpaper a bit.

A very nice woman from the City of Kinston called me later in the day and said the problem lay with a piece of equipment called a "recloser." Apparently — when working properly — this piece of equipment actually lowers the risk of a fallen tree limb or a curious squirrel interfering with electrical service.

I was told the re-closer in our area was faulty and would be bypassed until a replacement could be installed. In the meantime, she said to monitor any limbs hanging close to power lines and to shoot as many squirrels as possible.

As I see it, the administrators and technicians in the area are doing the best they can with the resources they've been given. The only way electrical service out here in the territories is going to improve is if the powers-that-be in Kinston channel some of this insane amount of money we're being charged for electrical service into improving the grid.

I know we're in trouble because of the ElectriCities debt and decisions from decades ago and blah blah blah … I'm tired of hearing it. We all realize we're 20 years away from paying off the debt, but in the meantime, you people in charge of the money need to stop pulling money from electrical proceeds to pay for the other stuff you can't afford and put it towards at least bringing the grid up to 1970s standards.

If you can't do that, can we get the same deal Sanderson Farms gets on its electricity — you know, the ability to buy our electricity from someone else?

If you all will excuse me now, I have to buy four miles of extension cord and run it down to my buddy's house; he's on Tri-County Electric. If you see a tree limb hanging close to a power line or a squirrel trying to bury his nuts in a transformer, alert the authorities.

I've changed some bad diapers in my day, but this thing has a pulse.

FORMER PETA MEMBER BRINGS BACON RESTAURANT TO KINSTON
JUNE 21, 2012

A former tofu eating entrepreneur is making a huge investment in what he calls "the crack cocaine" of food: bacon.

The entrepreneur in question — Miles Silverstein — recently terminated his 17-year membership in People For The Ethical Treatment of Animals, which was originally known as PFTETOA until a marketing consultant initiated the change to PETA in 1981.

"My association with PETA started when I was in college," Silverstein said. "I became infatuated with this girl named Sandoz in my political studies of mythological Greece class. She had curly brown hair, a smile that could melt snow and enough hair under her arms to sop up a gallon of Grandma's molasses."

Silverstein added that once while tripping on a combination of psychedelic mushrooms and Pledge, he and Sandoz realized that if you divide the word "molasses" between its third and fourth letters the results are incredibly funny.

"Sandoz was really into PETA big time," Silverstein said. "So in turn, I decided the plight of the tree lobster was going to be my focus — along with Sandoz."

For the rest of their college careers, Miles and Sandoz attended every PETA event and Phish concert within a 200-mile radius. As their romance grew, Miles' dedication to PETA became stronger.

"We took part in the 'To Animals, All People are Nazis' protest, along with the movement to get Ben & Jerry's to use human breast milk in their ice cream instead of cow's milk," Silverstein said. "Sandoz and I even spearheaded the 'Flyswatters Genocide' campaign."

Eventually, Silverstein's mellow was harshed when his romance with Sandoz ended.

"I made a harmless remark about Dave Mat-thews' voice sounding like a British police siren, and Sandoz took offense," Silverstein said sadly. "She packed up her clothes and her homemade jewelry display table and left me for a Patchouli rep."

Devastated by the departure of Sandoz, Silverstein decided to hang out with some old friends to take his mind off his troubles.

"Me and some buddies went out on a Friday night and grabbed some dinner," Silverstein said. "Sticking by my PETA pledge, I ordered a broccoli salad. As the night wore on, I noticed my voice got a little deeper, I started to grow facial hair for the first time and my scurvy cleared up."

After speaking to the manager of the restaurant, Miles Silverstein realized someone had dosed his broccoli salad with bacon.

"I'd gone so long without meat I forgot how good it was," Silverstein said. "The following Monday, I went down to the bank and applied for a business loan."

Six months after receiving loan approval, Silverstein is in Kinston scouting locations for his new restaurant, "Squealers."

"We're going to have fried bacon, baked bacon, boiled bacon, char-grilled bacon," Silverstein said. "On the weekends, the menu will feature chicken stuffed with bacon, veal wrapped in bacon, and the ever popular pork-stuffed bacon topped with bacon bits."

While Silverstein hopes to eventually buy bacon from local farmers, for the time being he's sticking with the brand that turned his life around.

"Farmland bacon was in that broccoli salad that straightened out my spine and finally helped me pass through puberty," Silverstein said. "Suffice to say, this is a farmland-friendly establishment."

While Silverstein is now up to three double cheeseburgers per week, he says he doesn't regret much about his time spent supporting PETA.

"I'm still against animals being used for the testing of perfumes and iPhone apps," he said. "I think the only time we went too far was when we picketed Rob Reiner's house because he once played 'Meathead' on 'All in the Family.'"

FLOODING SENDS CSS NEUSE BACK TO RIVER
JUNE 28, 2012

Although its recent move was billed as its final journey, the CSS Neuse is now once again at the mercy of river currents and artifact poachers.

According to a recent article written by David Anderson of The Free Press, the CSS Neuse was transported to its final resting place last Saturday. That resting place — the $2.8 million CSS Neuse Civil War Interpretive Center located at 100 N. Queen St. — was expected to be the centerpiece of Kinston tourism for years to come.

By all accounts, the move of the ironclad ship was virtually flawless. Aside from the moving crew trying to access a Bojangles' drive-thru window with the boat in tow, no major damages were reported. Once the boat was firmly in place at its new home, officials in charge of the move branded it a success.

Everything was fine until it started raining early Tuesday morning.

"The Kinston area received about 2 inches of rain in the space of 45 minutes around 1 a.m. on Tuesday," WITN Meteorologist Marvin Daugherty said. "I was driving back from a Phish concert in Virginia and, to be frank, was a little confused, but 2 inches sounds about right."

The deluge of rain caused the Civil War Interpretive Center's septic system to malfunction, which resulted in several busted pipes near the area housing the remains of the CSS Neuse.

"Apparently, somebody forgot to lock the large bay doors in the main room and the influx of water just shoved the boat out the back door," said center director Michael Brown.

According to a list of 911 calls obtained from the Lenoir County Emergency Center, 27 people called in with reports of a large boat floating down Queen Street in the middle of the night.

"Apparently, a man under the influence of alcohol got a case of instant religion and started trying to round up two of each animal," said Det. Meldrick Lewis of the Kinston Sheriff's Office. "He did okay until he tried to match up a squirrel with a muffler. He swore the puppies would be pretty, but we had to shut it down."

With the sewers backed up and several inches of rain pouring through the streets, the CSS Neuse eventually made its way over to Pearson Park and back into the Neuse River. Crews found the remains of the ship intact 20 feet from its original place of discovery back in the early 1960s.

No concrete plans have been made in regards to a re-retrieval of the CSS Neuse. Anyone missing a muffler is asked to contact Det. Meldrick Lewis at 252-939-6460.

SEVEN-FINGERED MAN STILL LOVES FIREWORKS
JULY 3, 2012

When Curtis Payne was a young boy, he always looked forward to July 4th.

"Unless the rain had messed us up, we'd didn't have to work on the 4th," Payne, 67, said. "There were so many charcoal grills lit on the 4th of July, the cows in the neighborhood would just walk up in the yard and surrender."

A native of Atlanta who moved to Kinston last year after retiring, Payne was — and still is — a big fan of another 4th of July stalwart: fireworks. While he's looking forward to his first Fourth of July in Kinston, he thinks half of the people at the event won't even see it.

"These kids today can't make water without having some phone turnout to play with," Payne said as he carved a bust of Lola Falana out of a bar of Lava soap on his front porch. "The fireworks we saw on the 4th were special because they only happened once a year.

"I'll bet you a Johnnycake most of the knucklehead teenagers at the fireworks display on Wednesday will have their heads buried in a Bill Berry or an Eye Phone during the whole thing."

While Payne believes most teenagers should have to barn tobacco for at least one summer and wear a chastity belt until passing a basic skills test, he is concerned about their safety. Payne says his concern stems from the fact that between 1955 and 1960, he lost three fingers on his right hand due to fireworks-related accidents.

"You know that three-fingered 'hang loose' hand signal surfers used to greet each other? They got that from me," Payne said. "Don Ho was visiting some old Ho he knew from my neighborhood in 1961. He was sitting outside the general store with his ukulele singing 'Tiny Bubbles' when I walked up. He waved at me and I waved back with my hand that was missing three fingers.

"Next thing I know, Annette Fullajello and Frankie Telethon are using it in a beach movie."

Payne says he lost his first finger after a failed experiment with a new type of recreational explosive in 1955.

"Back in '55, one of the older boys came up with a bag of Nub Maker

Roman Candles," he recalled. "At first, I didn't understand why they were called 'Nub Makers,' but after we lit the thing and my finger landed on top of a pack-house, it became clear to me."

The following text is from Payne's unpublished autobiography, "Call Me 7-Up":

"For my birthday in 1960, my folks got me a real pretty pit/boxer bulldog named Katie. For months, I trained that dog do tricks — sit up, roll over, give yourself a bath — but she had trouble getting the hang of playing fetch. If I threw a stick or a bone, she'd pick it up and just run away with it.

"When the 4th of July rolled around, me and my buddies put all our fireworks in a pile and proceeded to arrange them in order of importance. The sparklers and firecrackers were at the front of the line, while the M80s, Cherry Bombs and Hoyt Axtons were saved for the grand finale.

"After about 30 minutes of shooting these things off, I found something called 'The Helicopter' that was supposed to spin in a circle while shooting sparks in two different directions. I lit the thing, threw it and ran for my life.

"Oddly enough, the more I ran, the louder The Helicopter seemed to get. For some reason, Katie had now decided to play catch properly. Before I could reach down to remove The Helicopter from her mouth, sparks flew from both sides of her mouth, causing her considerable jowls to flap up over her eyes. At this point, the temporarily-blinded bulldog was putting a lot of effort into trying to give the thing to me, but every time she'd open her mouth to drop it the thing would spin back up into her mouth.

"One of the boys in our little group arrived late and had snuck out a bottle of his daddy's Jack Daniels whiskey. He'd had a snort or two on his way to meet us, and when he got there, he was greeted by a blind pit/boxer bull dog running down a dirt road in the middle of the night with flames shooting out both sides of its mouth. He turned to run but after only a few steps ran smack into an oak tree. The collision caused him to drop the bottle of Jack Daniels, which Katie in turned lapped up.

"Thankfully, the alcohol sterilized her singed jowls and she made a full recovery; although, from that night forward, the sight of matches caused her to run under the nearest porch."

Never one to complain, Payne says losing a few fingers was actually a blessing.

"I lost a few fingers, but fireworks helped me in my career as a firefighter," Payne said. "Since my right hand was missing those three middle fingers, I could feed hose quicker than anybody else on the squad."

Upon hearing this, Payne's wife Ella let out an emphatic, "You've got that right!" from the living room.

"To all the young people out there, I just want to say: The world is your oyster," Payne said. "Unless you're allergic to seafood; then you're just in a mess."

LA GRANGE MAN APPEALS SENTENCE TO PLAY 'TEA POT'
JULY 10, 2012

If you've ever had to sit in traffic listening to a nearby vehicle blast music at a volume capable of diverting the flight pattern of migrating fowl, you're not alone. Chances are the La Grange man who was recently issued a bizarre penalty for noise pollution was the source of your involuntary ear wax removal.

Larry Storch, 89, of 667 Calamity Lane, La Grange, was recently cited for misdemeanor noise pollution; it was his 17th citation since 2005.

"They've been giving me noise tickets for years," Storch said. "I guess they thought their tickets would deter me, but every time I paid off a ticket I'd stop by the speaker place on the way home and add a little more boom to my zoom."

When Storch was brought before Lenoir County District Judge Robert T. Iron-side for his latest infraction, the judge alluded to what he described as "wanton disregard for the public."

"You've come before this court many times over the years Mr. Storch," Judge Ironside said. "In the past I've fined you, sentenced you to community service, and at one point even forced you to watch the fourth hour of the 'Today Show.' Since none of those punishments have done anything to curb your jackassory behavior, I've decided to get medieval on where your butt — if you had one — would be."

Storch - who drives a 1976 Aston Martin Lagonda — has been sentenced to blare the Teapot song ("I'm A Little Teapot") out of his stereo for 45 days. A bailiff gave Storch a homemade CD featuring 37 different versions of the beloved children's poem as he left the Lenoir County courthouse on Friday.

"I think it's kinda sweet, really," said Storch's girlfriend of 27 minutes, Paulette Burroughs of La Grange. "I've dated many a rapper in my day, and they all cite 'I'm A Little Teapot' as the joint that got them started in hip hop. 50 Cent was weaving 'Tea Pot' into his rhymes when he was still 16 Cent."

Storch — who usually blares the likes of Kenny Chesney and Eddie

Rabbit from his system — has appealed the decision. When interviewed by The Free Press regarding the unusual sentence, Judge Ironside stood by his decision.

"I enjoy a good sound system in the car — nothing like a little Bobby Womack on a Saturday night — sookie sookie, now," Ironside said. "But anyone who insists their stereo rattle every mailbox open it passes is in dire need of a daily flogging with a baseball bat wrapped in barbed wire until they get better."

Clinical psychologist Ken Strayhorn of Miller-Monty University says there are several types of psychosis that could cause a person to parade around town with a stereo system that would run Iron Maiden up a tree.

"Massive, bone-rattling stereo systems are usually the by-product of low self-esteem," Strayhorn said. "This type of scenario most often occurs in males who are feeling inadequate in some way. These feelings of inadequacy usually result from the subject's inability to count to 10 or properly satisfy a woman. In the case of Mr. Storch, since he is 89, he may just have it loud because a stereo upgrade is cheaper than being fitted for a hearing aid."

As Storch drove down Vernon Avenue blasting out "I'm A Little Teapot" on Monday morning, he was met with stunned faces. As usual, Storch's stereo set off many car alarms burglary systems as he cruised along.

"There was one bright spot," Storch said. "I had every 3-year-old within a five-mile radius jamming along to the teapot song; they were waving their little hands in the air like they just didn't care."

HOW MUCH DO THINGS COST AT THE DOLLAR STORE? JULY 12, 2012

I'd had too many good days in a row, and I couldn't even enjoy those. As soon as I noticed how great things were going last week, I also realized I'd be paying for it soon.

Things took a turn when I visited my spa — the Dollar Store. I consider it a spa for many reasons, not least of which is the backrub the guy who hangs around in front of the store offers every time I go. Alas, I don't think there's enough stress in this universe or any other to change my mind.

Typically at spas, people like to sit in a steam room and sweat. Since I have no desire to sit in a room full of toweled men while natural juices ooze from their body, I simply stand in the little room that houses the carts between the Dollar Store and the parking lot.

According to my educated guess, last Thursday at 3:15 p.m., it was about 300 degrees Fahrenheit in that little room. Maybe it's kept hot to keep all the wheels and bearings loosey-goosey on the carts. Either way, I was schvitzing like a carnal worker in a house of worship.

Upon entering the store, a wave of cool air collides with your still glistening pores, causing a chill to run up your back as you pick through the latest batch of Keebler batteries. In most stores, the only products you'll find by Keebler items are cookies, but somehow the Dollar Store has an exclusive contract with their battery division.

There is also a row of batteries manufactured by Sunbeam, but the Keebler batteries go better with milk.

With your delicious batteries in hand, you walk around the store with the realization that $10 will pretty much allow you to purchase one of everything in the store. How far will $10 get you at Wal-Mart? Back in the day I'd have to tip the Wal-Mart greeters $10 just to speak to me when I came in the front door; $5 would only get you an insincere smirk; $15 would get you a pat-down.

Starting near the middle of the Dollar Store at the two o'clock position, there are two rows dedicated to candles. Being a bit of a scamp, I always light a few dozen candles while I'm in there just to make sure the sprinkler system works – better safe than sorry!

Luckily, there is a wide selection of ponchos available on Aisle 5. The ponchos can be found next to the six-pack of Toby Keith cigarette lighters I used to light the "Scents of The DMV Waiting Room" candles. Man oh man, that smells like America!

You can't have the full spa experience without some music, so I picked up a "Lee Greenwood's Greatest Hits" CD, although it only had one song on it. I got a little excited when I saw a DJ Jazzy Jeff and The Fresh Prince cassette in the bin, but sadly it was their poorly-received collaboration with Wayne Newton named "He's The DJ, I'm The Rapper, and This Is The Old Dude The Grandhonies Throw Their Teeth At."

The final step of any good day at the spa is to let someone pack some type of guacamole-looking mud all over your face. While there are no guacas or moles to be found in The Dollar Store, there is plenty of candy. I grabbed a bag of Hershey's kisses and a bag of Lifesavers and headed back to the little cart holding area at the front of the store. Within minutes the contents of both bags had melted into spreadable goo which I then applied to my face with the help of an ice scraper obtained from Aisle 9.

With my visit nearing the end, I added up all the items I'd picked up while shopping. The total number of items came to nine, and since this was The Dollar Store, I figured I owed them between $9 and $38 — plus tax. Being aware that I'm not the only human on the planet, I make it a point to have my wallet out and debit card in the ready position at least 20 seconds before it's my turn at the register.

Sadly, the knuckle-dragger in front of me didn't incorporate the same policy. He waited until the cashier had rung up all 19 of his items before making a move on his wallet. Of course, it wasn't a smooth maneuver; he reached into the wrong pocket a time or two.

At one point, he looked at me as if I had it, so I took him by the wrist and guided his hand toward the upper-right quadrant of his right buttock. After a few minutes, he dislodged the wallet from his pants and we all cheered as if trapped miners had emerged from the center of the earth.

Next, in a one-by-one fashion, he removed one dollar bills from his wallet — licking his thumb between each retrieval. About five minutes into this, I offered to pay for his stuff if it would get me out of the store before Halloween, but he soldiered on.

As the sun set in the west, the dollars continued to creep from the man's wallet. The couple in line behind me had purchased a $1 pregnancy test a few hours before, but as it turns out, it was a wasted dollar because the woman gave birth while waiting in line. I think the baby was born between the removal of the 13th and 14th dollar bill.

Finally, the man got all of the money out of his wallet and the cashier — who went through menopause during the exchange — sent him on his way. I plopped my items down and slid the ol' debit card through the machine in 1.7 seconds flat. I was home free until the previous customer turned around and asked the cashier for directions to the nearest adult novelty store.

I'm not sure what happened after that because I blacked out. I woke up with a newborn gnawing on my thumb while a cashier waved an open bag of Chernobyl Strength Chicharones under my nose.

We deflated a silver balloon and used it as a makeshift diaper; not sure what they used for the baby.

FORMER FREE PRESS REPORTER ARRESTED
JULY 17, 2012

Every Thursday, Free Press Managing Editor Bryan Hanks and I record a podcast (see the PODCAST link at the top of Kinston.com). For the uninitiated, a podcast is a nerd term for a radio show you can listen to over the Internet. It can also be downloaded to the phone, iPod, tablet or electric panties of your choice.

Last week, former Free Press reporter and Miss Thunder Bay 2005 Vanessa Clarke Shortley was scheduled to be a guest on our show via telephone. Suffice to say, when she showed up in person for the interview, Hanks and I were both pleasantly surprised.

Nessa was much loved during her tenure with The Free Press, and while we interviewed her in my office, Free Press Publisher Patrick Homes had her car towed in an attempt to make her stay a permanent one.

During the show, a few local issues were discussed, Bryan gave me a minute or two to schill my non-Free Press work, and issues local to Orange County (Nessa's new home) were also discussed. Once finished, I took a picture of Ness and Hanks to post on the website.

Horror of horrors, they both decided to make happy faces for the photo — this will come into play later.

After the podcast was recorded, Vanessa hung out while I edited the program into something Tesla himself would have been proud of. There were a few things to edit out — principally Nessa's incessant burping and the 38 seconds of shocked silence around minute 3 when Paulette Burroughs decided to moonwalk past our door sans pants.

Afterwards, we grabbed a sammich at the Queen Street Deli where, after chugging a can of Sierra Mist, Nessa wowed the joint with a belched, gangsta-style rendition of Gordon Lightfoot's "Sundown."

Once Vanessa retrieved her car from the impound yard, she headed back to Orange County. The following day, the podcast was posted on Kinston.com with the aforementioned photo of two people (Hanks and Nessa) making happy faces. It had been a rough week, and having an old buddy surprise us with a visit sort of evened things out.

I was actually motoring along quite well on Friday morning until I found out somebody posted something rather tasteless under the photo of Hanks and Vanessa. Apparently, the person who typed the negative comment (no doubt one key at a time over a 45-minute period) saw the photo of two happy people and it irked him to no end.

The guy who typed this also took an opportunity to take a shot at The Free Press and myself — something this guy does as if it were a bodily function. Judging by his attitude, it's one of the few functions his body can perform properly anymore.

It's human nature to complain about the local newspaper; archaeologists have even found nasty letters to the editor scratched into rocks that were rolled to the entrance of prehistoric newspaper the Mesolithic Daily. Apparently somebody's daughter's won first place in a regional coprolite tossing contest and they were upset it didn't make the sports section. A response to the letter was found to have read the following:

"We apologize for not getting the coprolite winner's in the latest edition of the Mesolithic Daily. In our defense, our edition goes to chisel everyday at 6 p.m., while the coprolite tournament wasn't over until 7:30 p.m. Due to recent cutbacks (three sports editors have been eaten by a Corposaurus over the last three weeks) we are unable to have a person at every event. In the future, feel free to drop off any stats/cave drawings from the event to our office and we'll do our best to work them in. Thanks for reading the Mesolithic Daily."

Now this adult male has taken many potshots at me on the Internet over the last year, and I've yet to stoop to his level in retaliation. He's retired and I have to work to keep pumping money into a bankrupt Social Security system to make sure he has enough dough to pay for Internet access.

I've received emails and phone calls from people who used to work with him, and although I'm within my rights to publish them, I haven't. I feel so sorry for those who had to work with him all those years I figure they've suffered enough already.

In his most recent award-winning post, he referred to me as "stupid." When he's not busy calling me stupid, he's busy making racist comments on our message boards. I wanted to write back and ask him how he was even able to read our paper with that white hood obstructing his view, but they won't let me do that, so I won't.

Perhaps I have this guy all wrong; maybe he's trying to follow Al Sharpton's road to success. Sharpton has made a career out of race-baiting and distortions of the truth, and he's now a millionaire with a cable news show. Perhaps racism does pay off, and this guy on our message board is just trying to become Al's sidekick. Hopefully one day. they'll be sharing a mint julep at a Duke lacrosse game.

This guy's posts angered me for about 30 seconds, and then I realized it comes with the territory. He's probably a great family man who loves his children and grandchildren, but for some reason has a problem with me and anyone who resembles Slappy White.

None of that matters, as it is with heavy heart that I have to report that Vanessa Clarke Shortley was arrested Thursday afternoon for stealing office supplies from The Free Press supply closet. She was found making a daisy chain out of stolen paper clips at a rest stop in Garner.

The guy who hates me and makes racist remarks online was reportedly only concerned about the White Out.

Thursday: The third base of weekdays.

THE FREE PRESS WILL NO LONGER COVER POLITICS
JULY 19, 2012

Since we as a society have yet to come up with a better idea, I'm sad to report another election season is upon us.

Some people argue about politics in lieu of arguing over sports. Being a dullard in regards to both subjects, the best I can do is raise an eyebrow and nod knowingly when somebody appears to have made a point.

If I'm feeling generous, I'll throw out a "Harrumph!"

Free Press Managing Editor and Eastern Regional Rhythmic Gymnastics First Runner-Up 1943 Bryan Hanks refers to me as a music elitist because I happen to know what I'm talking about.

Conversely, Hanks is — without a doubt — a sports elitist. If you call him at 3 a.m. and ask him the score of a North Lenoir/ South Lenoir mahjong solitaire game from 1976, he can tell you the players, the weather on the day of the match, the brand of hot dog sold at the concession stand and if either player tested positive for performance enhancing substances.

Political elitists also have the type of mind that allows them to recall small details from years ago, but usually only when it shines a positive light on their political party of choice. A Republican remembers Bill Clinton nearly being impeached for lying about playing "Chutes and Ladders" with an intern, but he'll forget the part about spending tens of millions of dollars on the investigation that yielded nothing in the form of a legal ramification.

Democrats remember JFK's "Ask not what your country can do for you" speech, but they seem to forget the bit about his father buying votes in some of his early political campaigns.

Trying to report on this group of knuckleheads isn't a pic-a-nic either. During the good ol' days of the Stephen LaRoque/Van Braxton wars, we were accused of choosing sides more than the publicist for Kim Kardashian's buttocks. No matter how straight down the middle a story on either of those two guys was reported, we were immediately accused of showing bias for and against both of them.

One nut job actually counted the number of words in all stories pertaining to Braxton and La-Roque, and apparently one week we'd "let our true bias show" by printing 17 more words about one man than the other.

I like to get out ahead of potential problems and not get caught with my pants down, because, to be frank, that would intimidate a lot of people. With that in mind, we've decided not to cover any political stories from here on out.

There will be no stories about Barack Obama, Mitt Romney, Walter Dalton, Pat McCrory, Barbara Howe or Pat Paulsen published in The Free Press from here on out. If you want hard-hitting political news, you'll have to watch Comedy Central like everyone else.

In the space that would usually be filled with political stories, we'll be running cute pictures of babies with spaghetti on their head and monkeys flinging their waste at each other.

Like any man-made solution, there's bound to be a downside. Eventually, there will be those who say we're favoring one species of monkey over another and that broad who lived with the monkeys will call for a boycott.

Some pasta enthusiast will notice we're favoring spaghetti over vermicelli, and then the powerful ziti lobby will cry foul, and, before you know it, Chef Boyardee is being burned in effigy in our parking lot.

For now, we're trading in politics for dirty babies and monkey steamers; you probably won't even notice the difference.

CUSTOMER SERVICE ISN'T DEAD; IT JUST SMELLS FUNNY
JULY 24, 2012

Frank Zappa once told a reporter that jazz wasn't dead, it just smelled funny. This wasn't a swipe at jazz, but a sad commentary on its standing in the culture. I believe this can also be said for customer service.

I've worked in the service industry a bit and I've encountered customers so boorish no court in the country would convict me if I jammed mashed potatoes into all of their orifices with the back side of a claw hammer.

The guy that habitually showed up 30 seconds before closing with his entire family in tow really needed a couple of weeks at Gitmo. I once saw him pull into the parking lot and managed to get the front door locked before he got in. He kept knocking and waving and I kept looking in every direction but his.

After 10 minutes of this, I called the cops and told them some crazy man was trying to break in. When the police showed up, they had a brisk conversation with Mr. Timex and he went on his way.

Having worked in a restaurant, I'm an extremely good customer. Unless the waitress is doing a line of cocaine off of her shoulder while pouring my water, I'm not usually one to complain. That being said, when I took Tax Deduction No. 1 our for Daddy/TD time on Saturday, I nearly ended up in the police blotter.

The day before our excursion took place, I stopped by the object of TD's desire to see what time it opened. According to the hours posted on the door, they opened at 9 a.m. on Saturday. To be sure this was the case, I went in and asked someone if the hours posted on the door were current, which — after a few blank stares — resulted in a "yeah."

To recap — the door states 9 a.m. and the staff states 9 a.m. This will be important later.

On Saturday morning, we headed out for breakfast and then to our destination. We reached Mecca at 9:15 a.m. only to find the doors locked. I peered inside and knocked on the door a few times; an employee arrived after me and went around to the front and a few minutes later someone unlocked the door and let us in — at 9:17 a.m.

Instead of asking the staff person if they were on some sort of new quasi-daylight savings time that caused them to be 17 minutes behind the rest of the universe, I stood mute. Not wanting TD No. 1's last memory of me to be berating a slack attendant before stroking out, I just took a deep breath and soldiered on.

Unbeknownst to me, the seemingly straightforward activity we were going to partake in relied on a computer system of the Cape Canaveral variety — a computer that no one had even turned on at 9:17 a.m. At this point, I'm looking around the facility for something to steal.

At 9:27 a.m., the computer finally juices up and we're ready to go. TD No. 1 had a good time and never realized how close her father was to either a massive cerebrovascular incident or a misdemeanor charge of larceny. My belief that no real good can come from leaving the house is reinforced and we go on about our day.

On Sunday when I try to get online to see if any of you folks have made naughty comments on Kinston.com that have to be deleted, my wireless Internet card isn't working. My first call to Sprint customer service was less successful than Kanye West's Oak Ridge Boys audition. I kept trying to tell the customer service rep that I was calling about Internet service, but she kept trying to upgrade my cell phone.

"Would you like to upgrade your phone service to include Canada and Saturn?" she asked.

Wishing I had an old-school phone that could be slammed down, I ended the call and tried again. This time, a man named Ernest answered the phone — and changed my life.

Ernest spent the subsequent hour trying to help me resuscitate the blinking-but-not-functioning wireless card. While we waited for the computer to shutdown and restart several times, we got to know each other pretty well.

In a voice that was a cross between actor Yaphet Kotto and jazz critic Stanley Crouch, Er-nest told me he was from Greensboro. After a stint in the military, he took a job with Sprint in Texas. I told him I was headed to Greensboro for a concert in November. Our meeting was a clear-cut case of kismet, which ironically is also the name of a network detector for ... wireless internet cards.

Eventually, Ernest's shift ended, but he suggested I download the previous version of the card's software.

"My shift was over a few minutes ago," Er-nest said. "But I'm back on tonight at 8 p.m., so I'll call back and see if it worked."

I was a bit shocked to encounter this level of commitment from a technician working at a far away call center, but it was nice. THEN, Ernest called back to make sure I knew 8 p.m. for him meant 9 p.m. for me.

"I just didn't want you to think I'd forgotten to call back," Ernest said.

Usually, I find men repulsive, but I'll admit — at this point — I was a little bit in love with Ernest.

I drive to my folks' house, download the previous software to a flash drive, bring it home, install it and the card comes back to life. A few #*$& &$**'s and $*# $&@*'s are removed from the website and life is good — until I realize that it's 9:12 p.m. and my phone is in the car.

I retrieve the phone and sure enough, I missed Ernest's call at 9:07 p.m. For the next half hour, I call every Sprint number on this and any other earth trying to track down Er-nest in the Texas call center.

Finally, I reach a Brooklyn transplant in the Texas call center. I tell him I'm looking for Ernest to thank him for his amazing service. Mr. Brooklyn then makes everybody within earshot of him stop talking and tells them who I'm looking for and why, and a few of them start clapping. A few minutes later, Ernest and I are reunited on the phone while "Chariots of Fire" plays in the background.

I told Ernest I was going to write about him and asked for an email address so I could forward it along. If you're Ernest's boss or the person in charge of the purse strings, please give this man a raise and actively recruit any of his offspring.

Thanks Ernest!

KINSTON THE NEXT CITY TO HOST 2018 OLYMPICS?
JULY 31, 2012

While literally hundreds of people around the world are glued to their TV sets to see who wins the gold medal for nostril grooming, Kinston and Lenoir County leaders are looking ahead to 2018.

"It's no coincidence Mitt Romney ordered barbecue from Kinston's King's Restaurant last week," said ABC News Psychic Brian Ross. "Romney was in charge of the 2002 Winter Olympics, and he's trying to ingratiate himself to the locals. Since he ordered pork, this is his way of distancing himself from the orthodox Jewish community. I have no real evidence to back up my claim, but I have a fantastic speaking voice and impeccably parted hair."

Conspiracy theorists point to new road construction and the new Woodmen Center as proof that something big may be in the cards for Kinston.

But then, there was the strange series of tweets sent out by @MittRomney on July 25:

10:25 a.m.: "Great to be in K-Vegas again."

11:06 a.m.: "Having a hard time finding any fried food around here."

11:42 a.m.: "This climate isn't conducive to wearing many layers of clothing."

12:08 p.m.: "Cup of sweet tea hit the spot; maybe I'll actually drink the next one."

12:59 p.m.: "Enjoying throwing the rock around at the Woodmen Center... FOUL ON RICHARD CLARK!...gotta go."

While no one at the Woodmen Center would go on record with The Free Press, several employees speaking on the condition of anonymity reported Romney and several of his staffers engaged in a slam dunk contest.

"They warmed up by playing a few rounds of something like Horse," said one Woodmen employee. "And they weren't spelling 'horse;' instead, they were spelling Mark Pryor's favorite 12-letter word — Machiavellian. Later on, they calmed down and used words like 'Solyndra,' although when someone suggested they use 'Bain,' the staffer in question was immediately replaced with an answering service based out of India."

Although no one was permitted to use their phones during his visit, all reports indicate Romney did well on the court.

"The Mittster can ball," said one impressed Woodmen employee. "I thought he'd be laying more bricks than a masonry dominatrix, but he was good. Only thing is, after every dunk he would stop the game to wipe his hands with an antibacterial towelette — which is the same problem that ended Bill Laimbeer's career."

After Romney finished playing hoops, he toured the Woodmen Center to see if it could handle an Olympic sized event — specifically, the new waterslide luge. In years past, this would be unthinkable, but even the Olympic games aren't immune to the failing economy.

"Even at the current Olympics in London, they're having to cut corners," said Kinston Free Press Sports Editor Ryan Herman. "For instance, the U.S. Olympic swim team only has four pairs of Speedo swim trunks. That's why Phelps isn't doing well this year; his boys are in an unfamiliar neighborhood and they're frightened. If they hold the 2018 games in Kinston, they'll save enough money to buy at least six Speedos."

Romney also had personal business to attend to while in Kinston.

"Mittney and I had a bad break-up back in the fall of '93," said Free Press Concierge Paulette Burroughs. "The CDs never got divided up and he's been bugging me about it for years. With his money, he could have purchased the Bangles; but no, Mr. Millionaire has to hound me over a scratched 'Walk Like An Egyptian' CD single.

"When Obama broke up with me, he was a real gentleman; he didn't even ask for his Alabama box set back."

LA GRANGE MAN SEEKS LAROQUE HOUSE SEAT
AUGUST, 2, 2012

There is an empty desk in Raleigh — and I want it.

No matter what side of the Stephen LaRoque controversy you come down on, I think we can all agree we need someone from our area in his recently-vacated slot. Although I have no prior political experience and only recently graduated to big boy pants, I'd like to give this public servant thing a try.

As some of you may know, I've historically shunned the Democrats and Republicans. The way I see it, they've been in charge for several decades and their tenure coincides with our national decline. I will go to my grave a card-carrying member of the After Party.

When I say "card-carrying," we don't have After Party cards per se, I just feel more comfortable walking around with cards in my pocket. Playing cards, greeting cards, baseball cards — for whatever reason, having them near keeps my chi in alignment with my chakras. We were going to print up After Party cards a while back, but we decided to spend the money on stock in a beeper company.

As I understand it, I must register as a Republican to take the vacant seat, so I will do so under the proviso that as soon as I'm in I'll be switching parties. When this happens, I will be the first After Party candidate to ever hold elected office. The years my former running mate Patrick Holmes spent as President of NASL (National Association of Spandex Lovers) are only officially recognized by Somalia and at participating Denny's in Nicaragua.

While the annexation horror seems to be handled for the moment, the latest thing we have to deal with locally is the closing of two Queen Street bridges. On one side of the issue, business owners believe it will be a detriment, while local political leaders believe the new bridges will be a tourist attraction. One city official said the lights on the bridge will be so beautiful people will drive in just to walk out on the bridge.

As far as I know, the only time anyone walks out on a bridge is to jump off of it, but I'm just a country boy so I'll leave the tourist trade to the experts.

Now I will demonstrate my skills at straddling an issue. James Brown referred to this as "talking loud and saying nothing."

The business owners have a point. Anytime the flow of traffic is disrupted, habits are changed and this may cause drivers to switch to businesses that are easier to access. On the other hand, if a bus full of nuns on their way to a fundraiser for an orphanage plummets into the Neuse due to a faulty bridge, it's going to be a public relations nightmare. The press from an event like this will be mostly negative.

With the bridge problem solved, here is the rest of my platform:

• Anyone who allows horrible music to blast out of a $45 car stereo while they walk into a gas station will be fined $1,000 and charged with misdemeanor crimes against intelligence

• All female government employees will be permitted to wear bikinis to work. I don't have a fiscal reason for this; it probably plays into that whole "pursuit of happiness" deal

• Replace all grass and shrubbery at government buildings with Astroturf and plastic plants. This will save thousands of dollars per year in maintenance fees and the guy walking in the middle of the street during rush hour with a leaf blower won't look at you like you're a Judas for daring to drive your car on a public road

• The only staff member I'll be taking with me to Raleigh will be Free Press Concierge Paulette Hussein Burroughs. Paulette has lived a timely life and has amassed several boxes of love letters, photos and VHS cassettes documenting her time with 78 percent of the representatives in Raleigh

"I've made tapes with N.C. politicians that make Paris Hilton's tape look like a Bugs Bunny cartoon; you wouldn't believe what one of them likes to do with slaw," Burroughs said. "Some of the stuff on there wasn't even legal until recently; some of it's still illegal in Mississippi."

If the Republicans won't have me, I'm sure a Democrat will get in trouble soon enough; those scamps.

EATEN ANY GAY CHICKEN LATELY?
AUGUST 7, 2012

Once upon a time, it was no big deal to push down the pangs of anxiety in our stomach with a delicious fried chicken sammich.

Immediately after typing that opening sentence, someone from my bank called to ask if I wanted to purchase identity theft protection for $13/month. I politely turned down her offer, but now I'm worried she'll post my account information online just to teach me a lesson.

Man, some fried chicken sure would be good right now.

As a people, we've been blessed with an overabundance of chicken sandwich delivery services. It all started in 1930 with Kentucky Fried Chicken, which is now blasphemously referred to as KFC. The first time I noticed "KFC" on a billboard, I thought it was an advertisement for the Kung Fu Channel. Later, Chick-fil-A and Bojangles' came along and carved out their share of the fowl-mouthed business.

For decades, all three companies were slinging birds and making a ton of money — and good for them. Kentucky Fried Chicken did come under attack for the way one of their suppliers was treating their birds. After disassociating themselves from the offending company, the Kentucky crew still had PETA to contend with. To make everybody happy, Kentucky Fried Chicken agreed to hire suppliers who only killed chickens by hitting them over the head with a copy of James Herriot's "All Creatures Great and Small."

The latest chicken chain to suffer the bad end of a protest is, of course, Chick-fil-A. To be honest, when I'm deciding which chicken joint to patronize, I'm usually apolitical. For a while, I tried to carry around a copy of "Zagat's Guide to the Religious Beliefs of Chicken Joint CEOs," but we all know how those New York critics can be, so I let it go.

I don't think I'm alone in my lazy attitude towards the associations of people I'll never meet if I live to be 200-years-old. Apparently, most of the country feels the same way: our current president and his family sat and listened to a racist, anti-Semitic preacher for years.

Shoot, this racist, anti-Semitic preacher even officiated the wedding of our president and first lady. Apparently, this type of behavior is OK, but if you buy a chicken sandwich you're branded a hate monger.

Hopefully, Harriet Tubman is too busy playing checkers with Jesus to see how things have devolved down here.

While some people on both sides of this issue have shifted into uberberserk mode, there is one question that hasn't been asked: What is the sexual orientation of the chickens used in these sandwiches? If you're against gay marriage, how would you feel about chewing on chicken that might be gay? How long before don't ask/don't tell is outlawed in the poultry community and we finally learn what a Mc-Nugget is really made of?

You may scoff, but homosexuality in the poultry community is a hot button issue, forcing many gay and lesbian chickens to stay in the coup. For years, beloved Looney Tunes character Foghorn J. Leghorn has disputed rumors that he once spent a lurid weekend in El Segundo with the San Diego Chicken.

"I say, that was, I say all blown out of proportion," Leghorn said from the set of "Pullet Surprise II" in Malibu. "During the 1960s, I was smashed out of my mind most of the time. I'm sure that on occasion some experimenting went on while I was high as a kite, but everybody had long hair then and it was hard to focus most of the time.

"I never dated the San Diego Chicken. I was at a ball game and happened to lunge for a fowl, I say, foul ball and accidentally knocked him down, end of story."

Foghorn currently resides in Kentucky with his wife Miss Prissy and their 478 children.

Recently, Mike Huckabee encouraged people on his side of the gay marriage issue to visit Chick-fil-A with extreme prejudice. The result? People were lined up around the building to buy them some Chick-fil-A. The success of this promotion has led one of Chick-fil-A's competitors to rethink their marketing strategy.

"We're considering coming out as anti-kitten," said a spokesperson for Advent International, the current owners of Bojangles'.

Steve Forbert, 47, is the manager of a Chick-fil-A in Ohio.

"I'm gay and I work for Chick-fil-A," said the Gulf War vet on Monday. "I fought for my country and now I'm just trying to sell it some chicken to make a mortgage payment. I honestly appreciate those who support my struggle, but please don't do anything that could shut this place down; I need the gig right now."

Personally, I wouldn't mind getting fooled again. The last time it happened I thought my uncle had my nose, which was pretty cool.

NBC SHIFTS FROM BROADCASTING TO PROCTOLOGY
AUGUST 14, 2012

The Olympics are over — forgive me if I don't go through a box of Kleenex at that realization.

Loads of people love the Olympics, and if you're one of those people, then good for you. Anything that stimulates or entertains millions of people that doesn't involve a Kardashian or Simon Cow-ell is OK by me.

If nothing else, the Olympics were enough of a spectacle to distract us from the upcoming godforsaken presidential election. I'm already so sick of both candidates that one of those soap opera comas that drags out for a few months but does zero permanent damage is looking mighty appetizing to me.

While my stance on the actual Olympic games is a firm "to each his own," I was interested in the closing ceremony due to the musical acts scheduled to appear. Several favorites of mine were on the bill (Ray Davies, Muse, Queen), but my favorite band — The Who — were headlining the show.

This meant The Who would be appearing last. This meant I'd have to sit through an hour or so of pop tarts and rappers to see roughly 10 minutes of music that interested me, so I took the biggest patience pill I could find and buckled down for a bumpy ride.

The on-air team of Bob Costas and Al Michaels may know how to make a guy running in a circle seem interesting, but they have no bidness giving play-by-play on a musical event. When the band Madness kicked things off with a performance of their hit "Our House," Michaels interjected a story about the "madness" he and John Madden encountered once in a Chicago bath house. Ever the professional, Costas pretended to have trouble with his headphones and told a heartwarming story about the lead singer's battle to overcome a crippling case of Botanophobia.

Later on, the Pet Shop Boys ran through "West End Girls," dressed in something that was part Harry Potter and part Klan member. Eric Idle of Monty Python fame led a contingent through a humorous reading of "Always Look on the Bright Side of Life" complete with a bleep for the one naughty word.

Sadly, the fact Russell Brand was even allowed in the stadium — much less to perform the Beatles' "I Am The Walrus" — caused John Lennon to spin in his grave at a rate that set a new Olympic record.

I forgot to mention earlier that NBC was showing this ceremony on a tape delay since we're six hours behind the U.K. This will be important later.

As the show progressed, Bob Costas would preface each commercial break with "coming up, The Who." I'm just a naive country boy with a penchant for Jim Varney memorabilia, but I took that to mean The Who were coming up.

A few minutes later, Jessie J walked out in some sort of S&M pajamas and warbled through some hideous song, then she teamed up with Tenie Tem-pah for another auditory felony. If that wasn't bad enough, One Direction and Take That showered the crowd with enough sugary nothingness to send anyone who'd ever looked at a candy bar to go into diabetic shock.

After this group of performances, Bob Costas said, "Coming up, The Who." After the commercial, Costas and Michaels were onscreen and, apparently, blindingly drunk. For five minutes, Costas talked about a great piece of fish he had at a Denny's, while Al Michaels got on his cell phone to confirm his reservations at Golden Corral.

Then they showed pictures of what doctors found during their latest colonoscopies: for Costas, it was a set of keys to a 1978 Hon-da Civic; for Michaels, it was Oakland Raiders' general manager Al Davis.

Now while all this witty banter is flying around, I know the ceremonies are over and these two stooges are killing time. I threw a few pieces of furniture at my TV in anger, but my TV is so old you couldn't dent it with a pall-been hammer.

At this point, I've read online that NBC is cutting Ray Davies and Muse out of their broadcast. Upon reading this, my left arm went numb. The guy that wrote "You Really Got Me" and "Waterloo Sunset" was bumped to make room for the Spice Girls, who, frankly, looked like they were on their way to a truck stop pole dancing competition.

At least at the truck stop you'd be able to get some grits and eggs while these lobotomized Barbies screeched through their songs.

Again, after all of this nonsense, Costas says, "Coming up, The Who." After another commercial, Costas invited everyone to come back in one hour to see The Who on the Olympic Encore Show — but first, enjoy a commercial-free sneak-peek of the new NBC comedy, "Animal Practice."

I was so enraged while this idiotic drivel was on I can't really remember it. To me, it looked like a lame attempt at setting the great show "Scrubs" in a vet's office. To quote a Jonathan Clarke piece from Forbes.com, "NBC's 'Animal Practice' hasn't even premiered, and yet it could already be the most hated show on television."

I stayed up for another hour to see The Who because, to be honest, there are few things in this decaying culture of ours I still care about. Whenever something meaningful comes along, I put in the effort to observe and engage. I became a fan of The Who during their Live Aid performance in 1985 and, as of a few years ago, began collaborating with John Bundrick, their keyboard player from 1979 through 2010. I guess you could say I'm more than a casual fan, so take all the potshots you want.

Although it was a TV show that had to be choreographed and controlled, it was great to (finally) see The Who. Ryan Seacrest introduced them as the grand finale of the show, so why did we have to wait an hour to see them? Because NBC knew the legions of Who fans who tuned in would keep watching until their set was shown. Basically, they used The Who to promote a sitcom that won't last six weeks.

I called NBC (212-664-4444) while on the road Monday morning. I asked about the one-hour gap and the stupid sitcom, and a woman at NBC Sports told me the network wanted to use their captive audience to promote "Animal Practice."

I then asked for the one-celled organism in charge of programming but was only allowed to make a complaint that I was assured would be forwarded to the proper person.

Here's the message I left:

"To whomever bumped Ray Davies and Muse and used The Who to promote the worst sitcom in the history of electronic media, I hope whichever brain-attling venereal disease you're currently suffering from advances at a rapid pace. I'm not sure who you married or serviced to get your job, but they could have done better by giving a chimpanzee a Nielson card and a thermos of coffee. Hopefully, the next time I get off the New Jersey turnpike to visit the powder room, you'll be scrubbing the floor of the bathroom with a toothpick you had to retrieve from a backed-up toilet."

See y'all in Rio.

I just saw four seconds of Justin Bieber "All Around the World" and immediately projectile vomited "All Over The Floor".

NEW RESTAURANT OPENING COULD BE DELAYED
AUGUST 16, 2012

A restaurant scheduled to open in the vacant Piggly Wiggly building on Washington Street in La Grange will feature a menu that may turn some heads — and a few stomachs.

According to flyers left on the windshields of vehicles parked at area tractor pulls and poetry slams, the Cyst & Schnoinkel aims to provide "exquisite dining for the diminutive budget." The owner, manager, chef and waitress of the Cyst & Schnoinkel realizes most restaurants fail, but she believes her new enterprise will make it.

"We've got plenty of burger, barbecue and buffet joints around here," said Paulette Bur-roughs of the Cyst & Schnoinkel. "It's about to get advanced up in here."

Although reporters from WNCT, WCTI and WITN have been camped out in front of the Cyst & Schnoinkel for the past few weeks, Burroughs has provided The Free Press with an exclusive advance copy of the new restaurant's menu.

"When a customer sits down, we're going to bring them a variety basket of Nabs," Burroughs said. "Toastchee, Nekot Cookies, Malt — we're trying to get Nip Chee in there, but the health department said we needed a different license for those; I like 'em cold myself."

Instead of traditional Southern fare such as fried chicken and barbecue, Bur-roughs will be offering dishes she's sampled during her formative years working as the cigarette girl at dozens of racetrack infields and illegal dice games.

"We're going to have gourmet tater tots marinated in Kool-Aid sauce, Moon Pie & Spam sandwiches and Twinkies stuffed with tarter sauce," Burroughs said. "The kids will be able to bob for peanuts in a tub of Pepsi on Saturdays."

Burroughs said the dinery's marquee item is a play on the traditional "pig in a blanket."

"Our croissants come wrapped in chitlins," Bur-roughs said. "We call it 'blanket in a pig'."

Although the staff of the Cyst & Schnoinkel — Burroughs and her grandsons Kevin and Josh — is optimistic about their chances, the 2012-13 issue of Zagat's Restaurant Guide didn't include a Cyst & Schnoinkel rating.

"We couldn't find words in English or any other language to describe how we felt about the 'queasine' at the Cyst & Schnoinkel," said Larry Zagat.

If anyone from the Lenoir County Health Department can be convinced to enter the premises, the Cyst & Schnoinkel is expected to open on Nov. 1.

"We do catering also," Burroughs said. "If you'd like to place an order for food or a tetanus shot, I can be reached at 252-527-3131."

TODDLER CHARGED WITH SHOPLIFTING
AUGUST 21, 2012

After a lifetime free of any criminal activity, a young mother of two unwittingly got involved in a bra heist last Wednesday. The woman in question is — as of this writing — my wife. The children — to the best of my knowledge — are hers and mine.

While the Wife's taste in men is questionable at best, she is a genius when it comes to finding nice clothes for little money. Sometimes, she'll just get lucky and find a $50 dress marked down to $6; other times, she'll buy something off the damaged rack, run it through her sewing machine and have it looking good as new in a matter of minutes.

Occasionally, she'll just make a dress or skirt from scratch with little more invested than time and a bit of fabric.

One of the few things the Wife has yet to sew on her own are bras — which reminds me of one of my favorite jokes: A dyslexic man walks into a bra.

Last week while Tax Deduction No. 1 was enjoying an end-of-summer day out with her aunt, the Wife and Tax Deduction No. 2 set out to run some errands. After a little grocery shopping and checking in with my parole officer for me (thanks, Frank!), the Wife and TD No. 2 headed into a local clothing store with coupons and prayer aplenty.

Bypassing flashy displays with a single bound, the wife headed straight to the back of the store to the reduced/damaged section. As usual, she found five high-quality pieces of clothing for a grand total of $7. After a few more minutes of searching, she stumbled upon what is evidently considered the Holy Grail of bargain clothes shopping: Bras that were on sale.

From what I understand, it's easy to find cheap bras, but it's difficult to find high-quality cheap bras. Apparently the disposable bras that can be purchased by the pound from the guy who sells steaks out of his car aren't the most comfortable in the world.

A woman I used to work with bought a bag of bras for $3 at a flea market, and while they weren't comfortable they contained enough wire to pick up Radio Israel. All she had to do was bump into something chest-level and we'd get a few minutes of "All-Star Bris with Michael Ian Black" in crystal clear FM stereo.

After picking out a few bras to try on, the wife and TD No. 2 headed to a dressing room. This doesn't sound like a big deal, but as some of you may know, the calm, easy-to-deal-with genes possessed by TD No. 1 were not passed on to TD No. 2. Apparently, the recessive "insane badger" gene that has been lurking in our families for years has decided to make a comeback via our second-born.

I'm a little ashamed to admit it, but after TD No. 2 woke us up at 4 a.m. on a recent Sun-day morning, I put her up for sale on eBay — no reserve. The bidding is going pretty good, so if you'd like this one-of-a-kind Jon Dawson keepsake, just visit jondawson.com.

One of TD No. 2's most recent fascinations is disrobing at the drop of a hat. When we need her to disrobe for, say a bath or weapons check, she runs in the other direction. When we're trying to get her to give Grandma a kiss, she decides to rip off her clothes and run around with a trajectory not unlike a busted sprinkler.

This was mildly cute until she started ripping off the diaper along with her clothes — nothing like a shiny hiney motoring away from you in the middle of the day.

One of the older members of the family who walked in on one of these freak streaks said, "Those hams are going to be too small to boil."

So the wife and TD No. 2 are in the dressing room, and for a while, everything is going fine. Three of the bras are deemed suitable and none of them are picking up radio signals from the Middle East.

Just as the wife is trying on the last bra, she looks down and realizes TD No. 2 has disrobed and is trying to wear one of the bras. Since TD No. 2 is only 34 inches tall, the bra is actually wearing her.

Oh, did I mention TD No. 2 also has a penchant for opening doors?

Within a split second, TD No. 2 — minus clothing, plus bra — darts from the dressing room with the speed of Usain Bolt and the precision of Chris Farley. In her rush to apprehend TD No. 2 before the fire department was called in, the wife accidentally puts her shirt on backwards and runs after the child. A security guard noticed the attractive but frazzled woman running through the store with her shirt on backwards and immediately hit the panic button under the nearest cash register.

While the guard was chasing the wife, the wife was chasing the nearly-nekked-exceptfor-a-bra TD No. 2. The electronic security tabs on the bra has now set off every alarm in the store, while TD No. 2 is now wearing the bra as a giant set of goggles. She yanked a scarf off a mannequin to use as a cape and — if I do say so myself — the ensemble looked fabulous.

Just as the wife caught up to TD No. 2, law enforcement arrived and secured the scene. Instead of relaying the entire string of events to the officers, my wife simply told them who her husband was. The officers — who were now weeping openly — gave the Wife their card and said if she needed help obtaining a gun permit to just give them a call.

Oddly, none of the officers took the time to point out to the Wife that the shirt she had on backwards was backless.

The officers then questioned TD No. 2:

Officer: Did you steal this bra, young lady?

TD No. 2: COW!

Officer: Do you have a criminal record?

TD No. 2: ELMO!

Officer: Do you have an attorney?

TD No. 2: COW!

Before the officer could ask a fourth question, TD No. 2 had swiped his gun and thinking it was a water pistol from the tub fired a few rounds into the men's shoe department. She took out a few pairs of Air Jordans and turned a pair of penny loafers into wing tips, but no injuries occurred.

Her first appearance is scheduled for Thursday.

Although TD No. 2's bail was set at only $5, her parents have decided not to post it at this time.

I've been accused of being cynical, but even I think stapling a McDonalds application to all college diplomas is a tad defeatest.

FATHER AND SON REUNITED DURING BURGLARY
AUGUST 23, 2012

A double-burglary took an unusual turn on Wednesday when a father and his estranged son reunited for the first time in 13 years.

"A residence on Desdemona Road, Kinston, was burglarized twice on the evening of Aug. 18," said Lenoir County Police Department spokesman Warren Trucks. "One suspect came in through a window at approximately 3:47 p.m., while the second suspect kicked in a door at approximately 3:58 p.m."

Officials with the LCPD do not believe the double-burglary was premeditated.

"I've had my eye on that house for a few weeks," said Luther Mahoney, 58, of Little Baltimore. "The garage was empty and the grass looked like it hadn't been cut in a while, so it seemed like easy pickings. I was busy putting some jewelry in my bag when all of a sudden I heard a loud noise coming from front of the house."

The crash Mahoney heard was the sound of Junior Mahoney, 28, of Goldsboro kicking in the front door of the residence.

"I busted in through the front door and saw a wrinkled up, crusty, threehot-dog-eatin' version of me standing in the living room," the younger Ma-honey said. "My mom told me my father died in a crochet accident; I couldn't believe he was alive!"

According to both suspects, they hugged for several minutes before sitting down on the living room couch to catch up on old times.

"We turned on the Wii and played video games just like we used to when I was a kid," Junior Ma-honey said. "Dad even took the stuff he'd just stole out of his bag and gave it to me to make up for all the birthdays he missed."

The first responders to the scene could not believe what they were seeing.

"They were sitting on the couch watching reruns of 'The Andy Griffith Show'," said Det. Clark Johnson. "They were watching the episode where Opie kills the bird and then feels guilty about leaving the baby birds without a mama. Mahoney Sr. and Jr. were already crying, which, in turn, caused me and my men to start crying as well. After we secured a box of Kleenex Splash 'N Go Moist Wipes from the bathroom of the crime scene, we composed ourselves and made the arrests."

Before the two Mahoneys could be processed, representatives of ABC and NBC fought over which one of them could post bail.

"This is the type of feel-good story the boys in Bur-bank have been looking for," said Craig Bauer of NBC Prime Time Programming and Animal Husbandry. "We can already tell our new show 'Animal Practice' is DOA, so we're looking for something to fill its timeslot."

Bauer went on to say that if the father/son burglary sitcom was given the green light, NBC had a unique marketing strategy for the new show.

"We'll insert an entire episode of 'Breaking Into My Heart' into the Macy's Thanksgiving Day Parade — just before Santa's float appears," Bauer said. "We'll then make every kid in the United States stay up till midnight to see the rest of the parade, because at NBC, we're all about some jackassory programming."

STUDIES SHOW CAFETERIA MILK HELPS
CURB ALCOHOLISM
AUGUST 28, 2012

On Monday many people awoke to the smell of No. 2 pencils and sweatshop backpacks. Usually when this happens, it means they've pulled a drunk and broken into a Staples to take a nap on a pallet of copier paper.

In this instance, for most, it meant someone within their abode was getting ready for the next phase of their education.

The thrill of new school stuff is a short-lived venture. I vividly remember being excited about getting a Trapper Keeper binder for my third grade year. From an early age, I'd always loved James Bond-ish gadgets, and that Trapper Keeper had so many functions and secret compartments I just knew Q had invented it.

Sadly, the luster of the Trapper Keeper wore off after a few weeks. For starters, I had to use it to do a lot of math homework, which, for the third grade and current me, is the equivalent of checking yourself for ticks with a Brillo pad dipped in roofing insulation.

By January, the Trapper Keeper was showing signs of wear. Eventually, my folks hooked me up with an old school three-ring binder that was apparently made from scrapped WWII tanks. It wasn't stylish, but it was highly functional.

With a blue, tweed-like outer material, a clipboard on the inside-left and a binder-snap that popped like a car backfire, that binder taught me an early lesson in practicality. Also, if things got out of line on the school bus, it doubled as a scutum.

The first day of school is bittersweet on many different levels. The parents, teachers and children each deal with many layers of emotions and — in some cases — psychotropic medications on this momentous day. Most of you have either had children or have at one time in your life been a child, so this is as good a time as any stop being fake and break it down like Ricki Lake.

Parents realize with each new school year their little piranhas are growing older. In the blink of an eye, they'll be posing for prom photos and then heading off to college. Within a year of graduation, they'll be heading home because the only way to use their degree is to move to India. The monsoon season was particularly moist this year, so they've got good brownie weather over there.

Those poor teachers; why they're not all alcoholics, I'll never know. The ball of anxiety churning in their stomachs as the summer winds down can only be silenced by a carton of cafeteria milk and a delicious peanut butter cookie that could double as a coaster.

I'm not sure how things are now, but when I was in school, the teacher's lounge was smokier than that bear who mauls people who don't put their campfires out. If they ran out of cigarettes, they'd send whichever student had given them the most trouble that week up into the ceiling with an empty Tab can to harvest some asbestos.

Since they were poorly paid, one of the teachers supplemented his income by selling loosey's to the other teachers. The height of my entrepreneurial prowess was to take the stick from a Nestlé's Crunch ice cream bar and stick it up the end of a similarly-shaped fish patty. I would then slide the Nestlé's Crunch ice cream wrapper over the fish-sickle and sell it to an unsuspecting colleague for 25 cents.

That dude hated my guts for it at the time, but now he's a fish-stick vending machine mogul in Anchorage.

Then there's the children — or as Whitney Houston and most politicians would tell you, the future. I don't like to refer to children as our future, because if that's true, then my peer group can be thanked for the world we're currently inheriting. Yep, these politically correct, Snooki-watching, Hot Pocket-eating bags of protoplasm can upload a photo to Twitter while giving birth but can't properly operate a vehicle are my people.

On second thought, they are not my people. As much grief as I suffered in school for being chubby, having curly hair and a charisma the ladies just couldn't resist, I can't really say I was ever a part of that group of people. While the in-crowd was laying the foundation for the rise of azithromycin-resistant syphilis and Dane Cook, I was working on important things like placing shopping carts on the roof of libraries (see the 1990 North Lenoir High School yearbook).

If I could pass along any wisdom to the children of the world, it would be to learn from the mistakes of your parents instead of using them as an excuse to act like a lobotomized Kardashian. The only difference between a regular Kardashian and a lobotomized one is that the lobotomized one has an excuse and in most cases better manners.

NEWS ANCHOR GOES INTO LABOR ON AIR
AUGUST 30, 2012

On Wednesday, news — and a bit of water — broke during the televised coverage of the 2012 Republican National Convention.

Although no reports of her pregnancy had previously surfaced in the press, MSN-BC's Rachel Maddow went into labor at approximately 10:42 p.m. while commenting on the GOP convention with her MSNBC colleague, the Rev. Al Sharpton.

Earlier in the evening, Maddow spent several minutes chastising the gathered Republicans for being racist while repeatedly referring to their race. Maddow's disgust grew to such a fever pitch after Gov. Chris Christie's speech that one of her producers wrote "DON'T HAVE A COW!" on a cue card to calm Maddow down.

"If Maddow keeps foaming at the mouth like that, Christie is going to think it's whipped cream and storm the booth," Sharp-ton warned the crew during a commercial.

While Sarasota Springs Mayor Mia Love addressed the convention, Maddow reportedly had to be restrained.

"Mayor Love is an African-American woman who is also a Republican and a Mormon," said Dan Rather as he reported on the convention for Arby's Closed Circuit News Channel. "The high-pitched noise you heard during her speech was Rachel Maddow screaming at a frequency only dolphins and Sean Hannity can hear."

Fox News Channel analyst Bill O'Reilly noticed his nemesis was in distress and quickly leapt into action.

"I keep a surgical mask and gloves on my person at all times," O'Reilly said. "I'm liable to bump into Karl Rove at any given moment, so I have to be careful."

Many of the stunned onlookers were shocked that Maddow's co-host didn't come to her aid.

"I have the utmost respect for Rachel," Sharpton said. "But we've got too many white people around here as it is; I don't want to make things worse."

Sharpton kept his comments short as he was on his way to a lacrosse game in Durham.

Known for his take-charge attitude, O'Reilly could be heard shouting instructions to the baby during the labor.

"Okay, what we're going to do here is guide you through the birth canal," he yelled into a megaphone pointed towards Maddow's cervix. "This is the no-spin zone, so I don't want to see any of that breach garbage and if you come on 'The Factor' with an umbilical chord wrapped around your neck, your microphone will be cut off."

Ever the jokester, at one point, O'Reilly leapt up from the birthing area and held a Newt Gingrich bobblehead doll wrapped in swaddling clothes over his head.

"IT'S A BOY!" O'Reilly shouted as Al Franken fainted into Ann Coulter's freakishly skinny arms.

When the actual birth occurred, veteran journalist Tom Brokaw summed it up succinctly.

"She had a cow," Brokaw said in a dialect reminiscent of an inebriated Stephen Hawking. "Rachel Maddow just gave birth to an actual cow."

As the newborn calf struggled to its feet and Bill Clinton tried in vain to pass out cigars, a satisfied looking Bill O'Reilly removed his mask and gloves and placed them in his coat pocket.

"That was a miracle," O'Reilly said as he handed fellow Fox News analyst Brit Hume $20 and sent him to the grocery store for charcoal. "Who's up for some veal?"

BISCUITS TO BAGELS = BUCKLESBERRY TO NEW YORK
SEPTEMBER 11, 2012

Growing up in Eastern North Carolina, New York City might as well have been Mars.

When I was in the eighth grade at E.B. Frink Middle School, our eighth-grade class took a trip to Washing-ton, D.C.

The gridlock and mass of humanity I witnessed in the nation's capital scared me off of big cities for years. For a country boy used to wide open spaces and indoor urination, the mean streets of D.C. seemed like war zone during a cease fire.

I (literally) bumped into Ted Kennedy and his rosy-red nose on the capital steps. When N.C. Senator Jesse Helms — complete with a trickle of snuff creeping out of his mouth — realized our group was from N.C., he gestured us beyond the red rope and took us down on the Senate floor.

Feeling pretty chuffed as the other school groups had to stand around the edge of the room with the other losers, I took the liberty of sitting in Bob Dole's desk. Before both buttocks had fully landed in the chair, a guy in a suit with a little white earpiece walked over and asked me to not sit in the senator's chair.

After the D.C. trip, I assumed I'd never have to deal with a city any larger than Raleigh. The first time some buddies and I drove to Raleigh to invade some record stores, I realized we'd been driving 20 minutes without being able to make a left turn.

Thinking I'd never see my family again, we set up camp on Hillsborough Street and set about establishing a new town. Eventually, somebody pointed us towards a left turn and we all made it home, swearing to never drive past Goldsboro again.

Fast forward a few years and I'm playing in a band. Since all of the members except me lived in New Jersey, we based our operations out of New Jersey.

I know it sounds crazy, but being able to play original material to crowds that want it, instead of dudes flipping you the bird because you won't play the song that was on the radio when they got their first chest hair, is worth the eight-hour trip. I'd played a few shows in New Your City in 1999, but my next foray occurred after 9/11.

My friend Paul allowed us to crash on the floor of his Greenwich Village apartment. I'll never forget waking up to the sound of pipes clanging to life during the first days of winter. Whenever I saw pipes making that racket on a TV show, I assumed it was an exaggerated gag, but when I woke up, I thought a gang war had broken out.

And this wasn't just happening in our building; it was as if the inhabitants of every building on the block were building their own submarines.

Also, I'd never been in a place where biscuits weren't readily available; the closest thing they had was a bagel. With a little cream cheese, a bagel is pretty good, just be prepared to bite the thing with your back teeth. I've gnawed on tractor tires that were easier to chew.

One day after working in the House of Vibes recording studio for around 10 hours, Paul picked us up and took us down to Ground Zero. By this time, the debris had been removed and all that was left was a large gaping hole in the ground.

Across the street from the site, a small church that served as a makeshift hospital/cafeteria for emergency workers in the aftermath of the attack had been turned into a living memorial. Somewhere in a drawer I have pictures of the memorial, but to be honest, they're so sad I haven't looked at them since I took them.

Next to the fenced-off area around the crater, a woman was handing out leaflets begging people to be more tolerant of other religions. This same woman then went on a tirade when she noticed some of the workers at Ground Zero had taken two steel beams from the Trade Center wreckage and welded them into a cross for all to see.

I asked the woman who was ranting about the cross if this was her idea of tolerance, while one of my friends pulled me away. To be honest, in that moment I wanted to take a stack of those fliers and feed them to the person who was handing them out.

Aside from a fellow band member who was trapped in a building with Rudy Giuliani on the day of the attacks, I didn't personally know anyone who was directly affected by the events of that day. I'm so cynical now that whenever I hear people talk about that day, I'm wondering if they're being genuine or turning on the jingoism to build themselves up.

Whenever a relative or friend of a 9/11 victim speaks, I catch myself feeling guilty by even watching it. Am I helping a major news network sell another cell phone plan because I watched this woman fall to pieces when remembering the last phone call she got from her husband?

Like any tragedy, it's important to never forget 9/11, but I've lost the patience to listen to people who try to make sense of it. There is no sense to be made from what happened. For today, I believe the best thing I can do is spend a moment or two thinking about the families who are reminded of their losses whenever birthdays, anniversaries, September or Christmas come around.

The first time the band went to New York, the guy that was supposed to meet us at Grand Central Station got held up in traffic. A couple of policemen could tell we weren't in our natural habitat and asked if they could help. We told them where we had to go and asked for some help deciphering the subway routes. Instead of giving directions, these two guys who didn't know us from Adam put us in their police car and drove us to our destination.

I was too wrapped up in being in NYC to get their badge numbers so I could write a letter of thanks, but I've often wondered if either one of those guys ran into the World Trade Center just as it was about to collapse, and if I would have had the stones to do it.

I think I know the answer to the last question, and I try not to think about the first one for too long.

POLITICAL BIAS SURFACES AGAIN IN THE FREE PRESS
SEPTEMBER 13, 2012

For most of my life, I've never given a fig about zombies. To me, a zombie is a mythical creature like a unicorn or a discreet intern. All of that changed when I started writing for a newspaper, though.

While it's true most people who work for newspapers look like zombies, this is a purely monetary issue. Years of licking Apple-bee's coupons in the hopes the picture might actually taste like a steak is the type of steady carcinogenic intake that won't kill you — but over time it will cause you to morph into Steve Buscemi.

The real zombies I speak of are the political ones — the Democrats and the Republicans.

To be fair to the members of both parties who simply cast their vote and get on with their lives — I have no problem with you people. Everybody thinks the exchange of ideas and interacting with their fellow man is such a noble pursuit, but I'm here to tell you that — in most cases — your fellow man is a flaming idiot.

If every citizen would just cast their votes and be cordial to their neighbor, this whole election thing might be a little bit easier to stomach. It's similar to when a doctor decides he wants to be Steven Spiel-berg and rams a camera up your derriere. This uncomfortable procedure has to be done, but there is no need to bring it up at every meal or write about it on Facebook or tweet pictures of it to your Proctogram account.

Once that thing is up around your Adam's apple, the doctor yells "ACTION!" while the nurses prepare some popcorn. While the camera is moving through you like a truck stop burrito, the health care professionals marvel at the footage being beamed back from your innards: a set of car keys, an undigested Hot Pocket from 1987 and a Redd Foxx Fan Club membership card — but I digress.

Recently, a man called the office and accused The Free Press of "never putting pictures of Republicans" on the front page of the paper. According to the caller (and all of his friends), we "only put Democrats on the front of the paper."

When we offered to send him a copy of the previous day's edition with a giant photo of Paul Ryan on the front, he stammered, duh-ruh'd and back-peddled in a manner similar to Lance Armstrong without his meds.

Similarly, when the story of Rep. Stephen LaRoque's troubles first surfaced — approximately 15 minutes before we went to press — a woman (who swore she never read our paper) typed herself into a coma on Facebook accusing us of burying the story because we were in the bag for the Republicans.

Like a moron, I tried to explain to her the rumor broke early in the day but that it had to be confirmed as fact before we printed it — but according to her, we were working for the Republican Party.

Someone once called and complained that a story on a Republican candidate contained 17 more words than the story on his Democratic contender, which PROVED we were biased. The all-time winner is when people got angry with us for putting a picture of Barack Obama on the front page the day after he won the presidential election.

I've typed it before and I'll probably type it until they find the weapons cache in my office and fire me: If both political parties are mad with us, we must be doing something right.

To my Libertarian friends, don't feel left out — your time will come. Also, I'm going to mention Ron Paul here so a bunch of guys in khakis don't camp out in our parking lot tonight. There, I think I've offended everyone now.

I understand why people are touchy about media bias — particularly when you start talking about MS-NBC or Fox, and for that matter ABC, NBC and CBS. The cold, hard truth is opinions garner higher ratings than facts, and higher ratings mean TV executives can afford to send their children to private schools and house their mistresses in the swankiest apartment buildings in town.

I'm not saying this is the way things out to be, rather simply stating a fact.

(By the way, I realize Rush Limbaugh once wrote a book called "The Way Things Ought to Be" but my previous statement was in no way intended as an endorsement. Also my previous use of the term "moron" was not a swipe at Joe Biden.)

For every liberal who accuses you of being a racist for merely disagreeing with President Obama, there is a conservative who thinks you're a communist if you don't agree with him. I ask you, how on earth are we supposed to report on politics in this type of climate? We could print what the candidates said, but how much of that is fact and how much is fertilizer?

For all I care, we could run an extra page of recipes and cover no politics at all. At least with the recipes we could be sure of what we were being fed.

CONTROVERSIAL RIDES, FOODS HIGHLIGHT
LENOIR CO. FAIR SEASON
SEPTEMBER 18, 2012

Candy apples, bearded ladies and plenty of farm animals all in one place? This can mean one of two things: Either the fair is in town or Bill Maher is throwing his ego its weekly birthday party.

Fairs were once a place for young and old alike to enjoy some comfort food, pet a yak and ride on a big twirly swing. Depending on the order of events, sometimes the comfort food ended up being barfed on the yak during the big twirly swing ride. Conversely, anyone who was barfed on by the yak felt ironically lucky.

While some communities are sticking to traditional fair fare, a growing number have decided to modernize their attractions and menus.

"Kids and people today are overstimulated," said Chris Blizzard of LCFB Amusements. "If they're not glued to Twitter, Facebook or YouTube, they're busy huffing Lava soap or getting stoned on Freon. It's tough to impress these little vipers or their medicated parents with a Ferris wheel alone."

Some of the new rides and food items LCFB will be renting out this year include:

TWEETY BIRD — The Tweety Bird is powered by the tweets of its riders. Mean, catty tweets will power the Tweety Bird for about 30 seconds, while forwarded Tweets from famous people who could care less if the rest of the world lived or died will keep the Tweety Bird in the air for up to a minute. Tweets filled with vulgar, profane language may prevent the rider from ever obtaining a decent job, but it will keep the Tweety Bird airborne for nearly five minutes.

OCCUPY PETTING ZOO — Liberal fair-goers will be encouraged to jump in the pen with the pigs and goats, get good and stanky, refuse to leave and expect some sort of positive change to result from their actions. When the fair leaves town, the smelly protesters will be left to ponder why nothing changed, while the first one to realize the pigs and goats actually have jobs will win a medium-sized "Where's The Beef?" T-shirt.

ICE-T PARTY RAP HOUSE — Conservative fair-goers will be able to participate in epic rap battles regarding the U.S. Constitution, illegal immigration and taxes. All are welcome to spit, but anyone caught rhyming "Obama" with "yo mama" will be escorted to their vehicle by fairground security personnel. Additionally, anyone caught trying to recreate Dave Chapelle's rapping goat sketch will be fined $50.

BOILED STUFF SCRAPED FROM UNDER YOUR CAR — It doesn't get any more free range than a possum peeled off the undercarriage of a 1972 Ford Zephyr. Free of any injected hormones or steroids, the only flavor stronger than the charcoal it's cooked over will be the fumes it inhaled just before everything went dark.

FOOT-LONG DACHSUND — Tired of being sold a hot dog with no dog in it? Look no further.

FRIED DETACHED LIMBS OF MAIMED FAIR WORKERS — Just because Skeeter and Rufus both lost fingers while trying to clean the gearbox on the Tilt-a-Whirl while it was in motion is no need for those pardoned digits to go to waste. After a little time in some boiling grease and a healthy dollop of mayonnaise, you've got some good eatin' — and Skeeter and Rufus both have an extra dollar in their envelope that week.

Other new food items to be on the lookout for include Fried Whiskey, Okracicles, Pocket Lint Dumplings, Polyester Candy and Prozac Pops.

A spokesperson for People for the Ethical Treatment of Animals, or PFTETOA (shortened to PETA in 2003) said most of the staff had left early for the day to catch a Ted Nugent concert.

JESUS SPOTTED IN THE DOLLAR STORE
SEPTEMBER 25, 2012

Everybody with kids loves to talk about them, and I'm no exception. What differentiates me from the herd is my desire to only open my yapper about the little Tax Deductions if they've done something worthy of a conversation.

I haven't spent more than 10 minutes at a party since ever, but even in that short space of time, you can find at least seven conversations peppered with some of the most mind numbing kiddie talk this side of a pilled-up Kathie Lee Gifford:

"Well, Chrysanthemum is four months old and she's already figured out how to fill up her diaper. We were skeptical about hiring a tutor, but it paid off in the end."

"Here's a picture of Manzano staring blankly into the distance."

"Florian is so advanced for his age; he's drooling on his own now."

There is some notable news in the Tax Deduction Department at Dawson Manor. Tax Deduction No. 1 is now in the second grade. When her teachers found out who her father was, they offered to skip her on up to the third grade.

We weren't sure about letting her skip a grade, especially when her prospective third-grade teacher read the first 700 pages of the school's file on her father and immediately signed up for a teaching exchange program in Afghanistan.

TD No. 1 also is taking piano lessons, has started her first job as a floor/furniture maintenance specialist (vacuuming and dusting), and now has her own Netflix account.

The impetus for giving TD No. 1 a Netflix account was twofold: Firstly, she'd have to use the $2/week she earns from doing housework to pay the $8/month Netflix fee, thus teaching her the value of money; secondly, it means I won't have to wait another week to get season three of "Justified" through my account because TD No. 1 wants to rent "Barbie: The Mermaid and Sardine Salesman."

Tax Deduction No. 2 is growing like the wildebeest-camouflaging weeds on either side of U.S. 70. She's now in pre-school three days per week from 9 a.m. to noon. We believe being in a daycare nine hours per week will help TD No. 2 learn to interact with other children.

Also, nine hours is plenty of time for The Wife to get estimates on the damage TD No. 2 inflicted on the house during the previous week. Even the painters that come over every month have noticed how quickly TD No. 2 is growing.

"Just a few weeks ago we were having to bend down to our knees to paint over the gang signs TD NO. 2 was spray-painting in the hallway," said Keith Emerson of ELP Painters. "She's gotten so tall we can just hold the roller at about waist level and start running laps."

Last week while The Wife took TD No. 1 to her piano lesson, I took TD No. 2 to the Dollar Store to get some early Christmas shopping done. As we perused the coloring book section, TD No. 2 called out what she saw — "FISH!" "DOG!" "ELMO!"

As we made our way to the battery aisle, we crossed paths with a tall man with long brown hair and a beard. He was wearing a white linen shirt and sandals. Without missing a beat, TD No. 2 pointed at the man and yelled, "JESUS!"

I don't know if you've ever experienced a 2 year old in full rapture mode, but it's a site to behold. If she pointed and yelled "JE-SUS!" once, she yelled it 20 times. While yelling it, she was jumping up and down in the shopping cart like a lone piece of popcorn in a well oiled and heated pot. After I peeled TD No. 2 off the ceiling, I walked over to the long-haired gentleman to make sure everything was OK.

As it turns out, the long-haired/bearded/sandal-wearing man is the lead singer of a Christian-themed Def Leppard cover band called Def Leper.

"I love Jesus and I like rock music, so touring with Def Leper seemed like a good way to spread the word," said Christian rocker Pete Willis. "Our songs include 'Pour Salvation on Me,' 'Billy's Got a Bible,' 'Samaria,' 'Capernaum It' and, of course, 'Rock of Ages'."

Later that night, TD No. 2 was having trouble getting to sleep, so I camped out on the floor next to her crib and held her hand. For a few minutes this worked, then she took my hand and placed it under her right cheek and dosed off.

Not wanting to wake her up, I stayed on the floor with my hand cradling her right cheek. Whenever I'd try to ease my hand out of the crib, TD No. 2 would start muttering about pancakes and ammunition in her sleep, so I'd lay back down on the floor in defeat.

After about 10 minutes of this, my left arm went to sleep; after 30 minutes, the rigor mortis had worked its way up to my elbow. Even- tually I escaped and, after wrapping my arm in some Saran Wrap and putting it in the freezer, TD No. 1 decided to have a coughing fit — which in turn woke up TD No. 2.

I go back to TD No. 2's room and lay on the floor next to the crib.

Now she's decided to jettison everything from her crib: Dolls, toys, books and lighters. After everything seemed to be out of the crib, TD No. 2 lay down and appeared to be going to sleep.

Eventually, I dosed off and woke up about a hundredth of a second before a large, hardback edition of "Where the Wild Things Are" flew out of the crib and struck me in an area described by Charles H. Baker as the Gentleman's Companion. I could see it happening, but the fear of what was about to happen caused my entire body to freeze up.

To my credit, I made it to the front porch before the crying/cursing/more crying started. I eventually recovered, and it's now much easier to sing along to the Bee Gees' "New York Mining Disaster 1941."

WHICH IS EASIER — BUYING GUM OR VOTING?
OCTOBER 12, 2012

"Sign! Sign! Everywhere a sign!" Did you ignore Jack Donaghy's advice and go to a second location with a hippie? No, you're just a human walking around a giant blue ball while it spins around the sun. You don't want any hassle, yet you're constantly swimming in it.

Regulations, forms and proper procedure are your friends if you're about to undergo exploratory surgery or go on a date with Joy Behar. On the other hand, having to fill out a stack of forms thicker than Cam Newton's sense of self to pay for a honey bun and an R.C. Cola is a bit much.

When debit cards burst onto the scene a few decades ago, they were advertised as a way to make things easier. I clearly remember a commercial depicting a guy tossing his groceries in the air, swiping his debit card through the little machine and being finished with his transaction before the groceries landed on the counter.

I may be a little hazy on the details, but you get the gist of what the banks were trying to convey.

For my money, swipe-card technology reached its zenith in the early days of pay-at-the-pump gas stations. The ability to pump and pay without having to go into a gas station was revolutionary.

I have nothing against the inside of gas stations in theory, but the chances of getting stuck behind some yabo who wants to pay for a pack of jerky, a can of Red Bull and a copy of Paul Ryan's "Kegal's For Men" DVD with a combination of Canadian, Confederate and Monopoly money have increased over the years.

In this great new world that my generation is going to have to start taking some of the blame for, it is easier to vote in a presidential election than it is to buy a pack of gum. Whenever I've voted, usually, a very nice lady will ask for my address and nothing more. The last time I voted I wasn't even asked for my address.

Conversely, I recently witnessed a man attempt to pay for a pack of gum with a debit card. Instead of letting the man swipe his card and get his chew on, the checkout clerk asked to see the man's identification before letting the sale go through.

Apparently, the meth cookers have figured out a way to extract pseudoephedrine from Juicy Fruit.

I've also recently witnessed a woman trying to pay for some food with a $5 bill, only to have the manager of the establishment jump over several tables and a few employees to intercept the bill. The manager pulled a monocle from what was hopefully his back pocket and began inspecting the $5 bill.

He commented on the cotton vs. linen ratio of the paper, the consistency of the ink and after receiving an "ALL CLEAR" text message from the boys in Quantico, he allowed the purchase to proceed.

For years, the drive-thru window was a ray of light for the anti-social restaurant-goer. In the old days, you'd have to stand in line behind a group of sociopaths who would debate the nuances of the short-lived McRabbit sandwich while your major organs slowly began to shut down due to lack of nourishment.

When the drive-thru was first introduced, there were only three items on the menu — the way it should be. Customers would order a burger, fries and a drink, and in turn, the attendant would repeat the order through a cheap speaker that turned English into some sort of garbled language that only twins and dolphins could understand.

Your order may not have been rendered perfectly all the time, but you knew you were now in possession of something that used to moo that was now resting between two pieces of bread. So what if they forgot the cheese or you found a band-aid on it? A hamburger was not a major decision, so you got on with your life.

Nowadays, the fast-food places are hung up on this "cook-to-order" nonsense. Unless you're ordering water with a side of napkin, chances are you'll have to pull up after paying and burn half a tank of gas before they bring your food out. If you'd like to get your kid a small milkshake, you will be interrogated in a Guantanamo-like fashion.

The following exchange took place just a few days ago:

Carby's attendant: May I take your order?

Me: I'd like a small vanilla shake and that's it.

Carby's attendant: That was one small vanilla shake?

Me: Right on.

Carby's attendant: You don't want a sandwich or some fries with that shake?

Me: (Sound of car driving off in disgust)

Carby's attendant: Sir!?

I'd chosen to do business with that restaurant because they had the lowest prices. Since the policy of said establishment was to coerce people into buying things they didn't want, I drove across the street and purchased a small milkshake from another restaurant. It cost about $1 more, but I don't believe in rewarding hooliganism with commerce.

I'm sure motoring away in a controlled snit will have zero effect on anything, but for one shining moment I'd defeated the Man's efforts to grab my money.

By the way, please notice the book I have for sale below.

You know what all of these little annoyances and unnecessary procedures do? They take up valuable brain power. Do you think Albert Einstein would've been able to come up with the Theory of Relativity in today's world? I think all of the so-called aforementioned minor inconveniences would cloud his brain to the point he wouldn't even be able to solve one side of a Rubik's cube.

About a thousand levels down from Einstein, I admit the brain power I've used up on these hindrances has crippled me as well. Somehow, this column started off as a tirade on debit cards, only to end rather uneventfully with a Rubik's cube allegory.

Is that good-lookin' big girl from "Cheers" on "Dancing with the Stars" this year?

WOULD GAYLE DO THIS FOR OPRAH?
OCTOBER 16, 2012

Nature is a beautiful and terrifying thing. For every rainbow, there's a hurricane; for every pile of autumn leave,s there's an earthquake; for every sunset, there's a Behar.

Last week while parked outside a government building, I witnessed two squirrels frolicking in an oak tree. The frolicking led to wrestling, and before it was over, the two squirrels were involved in a bout of family expansion. A small crowd of government employees, tourists, truants and ne'er-do-wells gathered at the base of the tree to witness these two squirrels fill out their tax returns in public.

When it was over, there was a smattering of clapping which shifted into shrieking when the male squirrel jumped out of the tree and yanked a lit cigarette from a spectator's mouth. When he finished the cigarette, he scampered down the backside of a spectator whose pants only rose to the bottom of his buttocks. Apparently the little guy was looking for something to stow away for the winter.

Judging by the gyrations and screams coming from the guy with the squirrel performing exploratory surgery around his undercarriage, I'd say that little fella found enough provisions to get his new family through the winter.

That night I took advantage of a rare window of calm to take stock of my life. Depending on your personal beliefs regarding open-air erotica, the unpleasantness/bolt of clarity I witnessed in that oak tree made me realize two things: Squirrels are freaks and never, ever wear loose fitting clothes in the presence of freaks.

Most of us pretend we care about the welfare of others, but how many of us are truly better than that chain-smoking, giblet-maiming Lothario of a squirrel? Do you think Gay-le would drop what she was doing to help Oprah dispose of a body?

Over the past two years, I've bought a couple of DVD players from a friend of mine for $15 each. Truth be told, I didn't really need them, but due to a second-grade level of finance management skills, he was in a financial bind.

Figuring I'd eventually use the DVD players, I bought them and stuck them on a shelf. Fast forward a few months and this same friend (who will henceforth be referred to as "Lummox") is having phone trouble. I'd switched over to cell-only phone service a while back and had a nice phone/answering machine w/two cordless phone package just sitting in a box.

My first inclination was to just give Lummox the phones, but then I remembered he charged me for the two DVD players. Just so I could sleep at night, I told him if the phones fixed his problems to just give me $10 for them.

Sure enough, the phones fixed the problem but the funds were not forthcoming. At first I didn't say anything. After a few weeks, I started to joke about it. Once when Lummox called to ask a favor of me, I responded by asking if he was using the phone system he hadn't paid me for to call and ask for a favor.

He put the phone down and looked up "irony" in the dictionary.

Lummox then told me about the roughly $1,200 he'd received over the past 10 days for doing absolutely nothing. He'd used some of the money to buy a couple of movies on Blu-Ray and a third guitar — even though, after supposedly practicing for the better part of a year, he only knew two chords.

I pointed out it seemed strange for the number of guitars in his collection to be greater than the number of guitar chords in his arsenal. Lummox admitted that was a funny observation but again the matter of the 10 big ones was skirted.

A few weeks later, I had a day off so I decided to stop by his job and take him to lunch. My plan was to guilt-trip him into paying me for the phones and use the money to pay for his food. I'm not sure if that's how Gandhi did it but the man wore a diaper. I've been in big boy pants for over a decade, so take that, Mohandas.

I told Lummox I was there to take him out to lunch. Before we left, he showed me a new CD he'd purchased with his recent financial windfall. After seeing that, I'd had enough. I told him to quit being a tightwad and come up with the money.

Lummox produced his wallet to show that it was empty, but I know my Lummox. He keeps his money — honest to God — in a clear, see-through plastic bucket in his car. I suggested he visit the Lummoxmobile and get the money.

After a few minutes he returned and handed me a piece of folded currency. I opened it and discovered it was only $5. I reminded him that he owed me $10, and his entire head, neck and face turned ketchup red. He couldn't believe I wanted $10 for something that would've cost him around $65.

As he turned to go get the other money, I told him what he could do with the phones and the other $5. As the song "Redneck Riviera" states, "friends will fade/it's the way that they're made."

This little tiff isn't just about the $10 — it's about the dozens of times I've stuck my neck out for Lummox over the years. I've gotten Lummox dates to the prom; I've kept bullies from beating Lummox up; a few months ago, I even had to give Lummox a refresher course on shoe-tying.

I never did those things so Lummox would owe me, I did the because in my naiveté thought that's what friends did for one another.

That evening, I lay on the floor while Tax Deductions No. 1 and No. 2 pounced on me as if I were a trampoline that owed them money. As bedtime grew near, I got them calmed down. While TD No. 1 began her four-hour going-to-bed ritual, TD No. 2 sat in my lap and looked me right in the eye.

All of a sudden, every joy and hardship we'd experienced since her arrival came flooding back: her first steps, her first word, her first misdemeanor. I kept looking into her eyes and had visions of her future: her first day of school, her first boyfriend, her first felony.

For several minutes, I just sat there staring at this beautiful little creature and realized what was really important in life. She started cooing and touching my face just as she had done when she was a baby. The ugliness of the Lummox drifted from my memory and at that moment I thanked God for blessing me with a great wife and two great children.

Then — as if on cue from above — TD No. 2 grinned and broke wind with the force of an Evinrude boat motor.

The force was so powerful it tore two buttons off my shirt, but in an odd way, the whole episode was reassuring. If you got a Lummox in your life, just cut it loose. If you've got a couple of TDs, make friends with a good seamstress.

ADULT-THEMED HAUNTED HOUSE
SPARKS CONTROVERSY
OCTOBER 18, 2012

From now until Halloween, children of all ages will be paying money to visit a haunted house and have someone scare them senseless. Most of the haunted houses will feature fog machines, zombies and chain saw-wielding lunatics, but a local man has decided to create a haunted house with adult themes that wouldn't be appropriate for children.

"Anybody lookin' for mummies or werewolves need not come to my haunted house," said Dennis Weaver of Seven Springs. "It's going to get adult all up in here."

Weaver says he's spent the last month acquiring the necessary permits to open a for-profit haunted house on his property located just off of N.C. 55 in Seven Springs. Opponents of the adult-themed haunted house say even though Weaver has done everything legally required to open such an enterprise, that doesn't mean it's a good idea.

"How's it going to look if some folks come in from outta town to scout a location for a new business," said Ken Curtis, one of many concerned Seven Springs residents. "We're never gonna to get them Walmart people to build here if they think their young'uns are going to have to walk around a hoochie show just to go trick or treatin'; Target might put up with that mess but Walmart won't." Weaver believes people who have such a problem with his new enterprise should check it out before they condemn it. "These folks are worse than people who'll protest a movie before they've even seen it," Weaver said. "Sure, my haunted house is adult-themed; it's full of stuff that will scare the breakfast out of anyone over the age of 18."

The following is a partial list of attractions at Weaver's "Adult House of Horrors":

The Hall of Mortgages
The Tunnel of Taxes
The Visiting In-Laws
The Prenup Cleanup
The Husband Who Thinks Bodily Noises Are Funny

The Wife Who Doesn't Recognize "Yes" or "No" As Acceptable Answers

The Political Zombie Who Thinks Their Candidate Is Somehow Less A Dirt Bag Than The Other Guy

The Intern Who Can't Keep A Secret

The Blood For Gasoline ATM

The "Dancing With The Stars" Discussion Group

"The View"

The Student Loan Mice Wheel

The 90-Year-Old Who Claims To Have No Appetite While Looking For The Chocolate Cake

The New Parent Who Believes They Were The First Human To Ever Procreate

The Brand New $75 Geometry Text Book That Contains The Same Information As Every Other Geometry Book Ever Printed — That Will Also Be Out Of Date By The End Of The Semester

The College Graduate Who Can't Find a Job

The Parents of the College Graduate Who Can't Find A Job

The Second Grader With Homework Too Advanced For The Parent

Dennis Weaver's Adult House of Horrors is located at 666 N.C. 55, Seven Springs, across from The Garnished Wage restaurant. Adult diapers will be available at all exits.

DON'T MIND THE BAG OF KITTENS
OCTOBER 23, 2012

I've written about dumps before. Some of them were clubs I've played music in, while others were the type that occur when a computer has decided to make years of work disappear in an instant. Even the "William Tell Overture" — better known as the Lone Ranger theme — extols the virtues of the dump, da-da-dump, da-da-dump, da-da-dump-dump-dump.

Last Friday afternoon, I had an intense encounter with a lovely woman at a dump of the trashy variety. No, this wasn't a house of ill-repute or a Denny's, it was an actual trash dump … a place where seemingly good people routinely deposit the most disgusting byproducts of their existence: used tissues, food scraps, spent deodorant canisters and, if you're like me and live with a 2 year old who routinely mistakes gun powder for pepper, once-clean diapers that have been transformed into glowing orbs of inconclusive hazard.

For the past several months, my trips to the dump have been blissfully non-eventful. I play along to the point of separating cans and plastic bottles, but I will neither confirm nor deny my adherence to local policies such as keeping used Tic-Tac containers separate from "regular" trash. Is there a concern that the worms chowing down on this stuff might end up with fresh breath?

There's also some rule about mixing in yard waste with the rest of your trash. I guess it would be toxic if something like part of a tree that was meant to biodegrade in a safe manner was thrown into the mix. A friend of mine in Boston said he could be fined if old clothes were found in his garbage. I guess it's feasible that a pair of worn-out socks could accidentally mix with lasagna remnants and the resulting Socksagna mutant could terrorize the eastern seaboard. This would explain how we ended up with that yenta Joy Behar.

So I pull up to the dump and pop the trunk on my car. Before I get the first bag completely out of the trunk, a woman — who was a civilian, not an employee of the dump — got in my face in a Joe Pescilike manner and asked what was in the bag.

"Do you work here?" I asked.

"No, but that doesn't matter," she said. "I want to know if you've got cans or bottles in that bag."

I didn't know if this person was for real or if she had her buddy filming this for a potential lawsuit, so I turned away and went on about my bidness. After tossing the first bag of trash into the giant bin with the power and grace of a young Johnny Unitas, I headed back to the car and picked up the second and final bag.

"You're going to tell me what's in that bag!" the self-appointed Sheriff of the Landfill demanded.

I saw this as a chance to be an adult and diffuse a potential volatile situation with a cool head and a kind word. In actuality, THE BAG WAS FULL OF OLD PAPERS AND NOTHING MORE. Instead of simply telling the boring truth, I looked this twit straight in the eye and said the following:

"Okay, you got me — it's full of kittens."

Just as I finished the sentence, I shook the bag a little and made a little "reower" cat noise under my breath.

"I thought it would be cool to have some kittens, but they whine all night and it turns out I'm allergic to them ..."

With that comment the lady screamed as if someone had pinched her bottom with a rusty pair of salad tongs.

"WHAT IS WRONG WITH YOU!?" she shrieked as I twirled the bag in a Roger Daltrey-esque fashion, while still making the corresponding "reower" cat noises, before flinging it a good 20 feet into the back of the big metal bin.

"Can I help you with anything else?" I asked as the woman ran over to the little office to bother the attendant on duty.

As I drove off and watched as that crazy person dug through my trash with the attendant watching from a safe distance, I realized any chance I'd ever had at becoming a well-balanced adult was now gone forever. My slide into inevitable dementia will be as flawless as the great Shelly Long/Kirstie Alley transformation of 1987.

Here kitty-kitty-kitty.

MEMORIES OF LICE, HERPES ABOUND
ON SENIOR NIGHT
OCTOBER 25, 2012

As the 2012 high school football season comes to an end, many area teams have their annual senior nights coming up on Friday. Around these parts, Senior Night is a chance for local sports teams to give former stars a few more minutes in the spotlight against their younger counterparts.

One of those former players is Wheat Swamp/North Lenoir graduate Justin Hayward of Snow Hill.

"The game has changed so much since my playing days," the 86-year-old said. "There was so little money in the athletic budgets that we had to share footballs, helmets and jock straps with South Lenoir. This practice led to the Great Head Lice and Herpes Panic of '44."

Hayward — who was a running back for the Wheat Swamp Tigers as they were then known — credits the tumultuous weeks of soaking, rinsing and repeating with his decision to become a penicillin salesman later in life.

"Gosh, the sound of the scratching was unbelievable," Hayward said. "It sounded as if all of humanity were trying to start a fire by rubbing two sticks together; it really confused the crickets."

When reminded that Wheat Swamp didn't actually have a football team, Hayward played it off as "media bias."

"I'm looking forward to getting back on the field," said former Greene Central star John Lodge, 78. "These guys today have it easy with their shoulder pads and safety helmets. All we had for protection was a thick leather swim cap and a mouth guard made out of old brick shavings.

"It'll be great to show some of these 250-pound 18-year-old players how to kick it old school."

Dr. Mike Pinder is an osteopathologist at La Grange Memorial Hospital.

"I applaud Mr. Lodge's tenacity, but if he plays football against a bunch of high school kids, his hip is going to splinter like gas station peanut brittle," Dr. Pinder said. "No matter how much Ensure is sold at the concession stand, this game will make 'Sophie's Choice' look like an Adam Sandler movie. The impact of an 18-year-old running back colliding with an

86-year-old man at full speed would be the equivalent of hitting one of those trick golf balls that explodes into dust.

"Much like Joey Lawrence, the poor guy would just cease to exist."

Ray Thomas of the Lenoir County Recreation Association hopes Senior Night 2012 will be the first step towards erasing the black eye that was Senior Night 2011.

"Last year, players from the Greene Central class of '51, Wheat Swamp '45 and South Lenoir '39 tested positive for hard candy," Thomas said. "They all claimed to have prescriptions for Cialis, but our tests show it was combination of peppermint and Werther's Originals. The non-stop crinkling of the candy wrappers could be heard over the marching band for goodness sake."

Grahame Edge was the star quarterback for South Lenoir in 1943.

"Old age and treachery will always overcome youth and skill," Edge said. "There will be lots of what I like to call 'sympathy jabs' during the game. What I love to do is grab my chest like something is wrong, and when the young guys come over to see if I'm OK, I throw my teeth at 'em."

"If that don't cause a fumble, I'll just punch 'em in the dolphin."

Sure the world is your oyster, but what if you're allergic to seafood?

A TABLE MAINTENANCE SPECIALIST SAYS
SO LONG TO THE BARN
OCTOBER 30, 2012

For roughly five years during my high school/college career, I was a table maintenance specialist at The Barn Steakhouse in Kinston.

Of course when I say "table maintenance specialist," I mean busboy. I was also schooled in food prep, which means everything on the salad bar was either sliced, ripped, smashed or poured by moi. Napkin folding was also under my purview, and not that lame old square to rectangle jive. We were taught to fold a napkin in a way that was a cross between a pirate hat and one of those paper pop guns that were popular in middle school. At Thanksgiving, we'd fold the napkins into the shape of turkey; at Christmas, we'd fold them to resemble Santa; on Election Day, they were folded to look like empty shirts.

In those days it was known as The Beef Barn, which gave my friends/acquaintances plenty of ammunition. To each his own, but after a while it got old having to explain to people that I did not work at a gay bar. If it had been a gay bar, I'd probably have a better sense of style than I ended up with. How anyone could think a gay establishment would have allowed me to wear $5 black pants, black shoes purchased from a hardware store and a white shirt that came free in a box of corn flakes is beyond me. It wasn't a revolt against being fabulous, but an adherence to practicality.

In all honesty, it made no sense to get my GQ on for a job that involved cleaning up the food remnants that escaped the mouths of total strangers. Sometimes a table could be cleaned and set back up in under a minute, while other times it took several minutes and some assistance from FEMA. Ironically, the people who came in dressed as if they'd just come from a taping of Jerry Springer's show were the best customers and the easiest to clean up after. The absolute worst customers were always dressed to the nines.

This customer was reportedly a man of the cloth, but to be honest he was probably a pretender who had a show on local TV for a while and ended up selling refrigerators to Eskimos. He'd usually come in with his two sons who were probably teenagers but not driving yet. As a little literary appetizer to illustrate how this guy operated, he routinely asked to be seated at the one table in the entire restaurant that wasn't ready. We could have five tables and two booths ready to go, but he'd always want the only one that hadn't been cleaned yet.

"Are y'all gonna clean that table tonight?" he'd ask as if I owed him a share of my check.

"No, sir, that is a living monument to President George Washington who ate here just after crossing the Delaware," I told him one night. "One of his wooden teeth fell out and we still have part of the toothpick he used to fashion a temporary tooth so as to finish his steak."

His insistence on having to have the one table that hadn't been cleaned was nothing compared to what this man did to our salad bar.

Usually, a fully stocked salad bar would have been enough to sustain 10-12 customers, but when this guy went through it made what Sherman did to Atlanta look like a pillow fight. If a rabid, vegetarian grizzly bear had busted through the front door and commandeered the salad bar, he would have made less mess and left more food behind than this gluttonous twit. This culinary commando would plop at least a pound of oysters onto his salad plate, which by the way was the first time I'd ever seen a ceramic plate buckle.

My other favorite was the guy who always demanded fresh lettuce.

"Excuse me, but could you put out some fresh lettuce please?" he'd say.

"Sir, this was put out just a few minutes ago. I believe the tray of ice it's sitting on has managed to keep it from wilting in a mere three minutes," is what I wanted to tell the guy, but my boss — Charles Andersen — adhered to the old "customer is always right" policy, so I did my best to make Tim Zagat Jr. happy.

At first this meant going into the back and adding more lettuce to the perfectly fine lettuce that was already in the pan. With time I learned that all I had to do was walk around the corner with the pan and stand in the kitchen for 30 seconds. I'd then walk back out with the same pan of lettuce and the little moron that probably couldn't never knew the difference.

I mentioned Charles Andersen earlier, and I have to say that he's earned his spot in the Hall of Great Bosses. Upon his arrival at the helm he noticed my rate of pay was out of phase with my level of work, and without prodding gave me a raise. With time we became friends; and, no, it wasn't because of the raise. We shared/share a mutual love for the band Rush and even saw them in concert together on the "Counterparts" tour. If a waitress had a sick child or someone had a family emergency, Charles was understanding and never cross. Everybody — following Charles' example — just cranked it up a little more to make it through.

My favorite part of our routine was the weekly Saturday night trip to Greenville. For his first few years at the restaurant, Charles was still working for the original owner. At the end of each week (Saturday night) we'd jump in his car and motor the receipts/paperwork over to the owner in Greenville. It probably doesn't seem like much to you, but it was (and is) incredibly cool to shoot down N.C. 11 in the dark of night with the windows down while listening to a Neal Pear drum solo.

As luck would have it, Charles was finally able to take over The Barn the very week two national chain restaurants opened within spit-ball distance of his parking lot. For many years Charles' work ethic, business acumen and dedication to putting out a high-quality product kept The Barn in the game. It wasn't uncommon for Charles to do his managerial gig, prep all the food and be the chef all in the same day. With all this in mind it was tough to hear The Barn was shutting down at the end of this month. I was glad to see Charles has landed on his feet with a new endeavor, and it won't take long for his new associates to pat themselves on the back for bringing him on board.

Along with Charles there was Lois — who to my knowledge was the longest-tenured Barn employee in its history. Becky and Donna, you guys were always fun to work with, as was Ray and his sweet sister who passed away about a year after I left. Thanks to all of y'all for sharing your Saturday nights and tips with me for all those years. As soon as Charles gets established at his new job, we should hit him up to spring for a reunion dinner.

THE REASON WHY WE PUT OBAMA ON THE FRONT PAGE
NOVEMBER 8, 2012

The elections are over — and half the population is madder than a Hindu at Golden Corral.

No matter who won Tuesday's presidential election, roughly 50 percent of the country was going to be upset with the outcome. Neither Obama nor Romney had a massive mandate, but rather a mosquito's chin hair chance of cobbling together 270 electoral votes.

I just took a shot at both candidates, but I'm sure some of you have already gotten out your little correspondence stock and your little half-gnawed crayons to let me know how biased you think I am. Take a deep breath, have a sip of your favorite beverage and read the previous paragraph again.

If you made it past the third grade in less than four tries, it should be obvious I'm saying neither candidate exactly set the world on fire. This is not an opinion, its math: if half the country voted for you, that means half of the country did not.

Over the past few days I've witnessed — in person and on social media websites — comments that range from the bizarre to the idiotic. One person threatened to start a riot if his candidate of choice wasn't elected. Another person wrote if his candidate wasn't elected, he was moving his entire family to Canada.

Sadly, both of these people will probably procreate at some point and make more people who will think and express themselves in the same boorish manner. A little loosening of those pesky toy warning labels would probably fix this problem in a few generations, but that's likely a pipe dream.

Local people took to the Internet claming The Free Press was trying to cover up the Benghazi attack in the weeks leading up the election. After reading this, I posted five examples of stories we'd run about Benghazi, only to be told I was "avoiding the question."

I finally realized this was the equivalent of trying to argue with a busted lawn sprinkler and gave up.

Thankfully, I had no emotional investment in Tuesday's presidential election. To be honest, my voting is motivated by guilt. As I type this, somewhere there's a veteran going through his or her sixth month of rehab just to be able to button a shirt. If you realize this is happening and still don't vote, then you're a waste of space.

Others were emotionally involved to the power of 10. Last night while attempting to (gasp) report on the election, someone got in a colleague's face and exclaimed, "The Free Press is the reason we lost! It's your fault!"

This is — of course — natural fertilizer obtained from a large male bovine, but I wonder if their side had won, would we have been given the credit for that as well? I don't remember receiving a gift basket when this group has done well in the past.

I'm trying to figure out how we helped one side over the other. We've allowed Republicans and Democrats to write columns stating their opinions, yet even when both articles have been printed side by side in the paper, we get complaints from both sides accusing us of showing favoritism. It's like giving twins $20 each for their birthday, and then having both of them complain the other got more money.

It's psychotic, but it happens.

A year or so back, one of our reporters shadowed Stephen LaRoque — a Republican — for a day in order to write a piece about — you guessed it — a day in the life of a state representative. Had Van Braxton — a Democrat — been in office, we would have shadowed him.

All of this sounds completely logical when spoken out loud, but several people went outhouse-rat crazy over the story. According to them, we were pushing a Republican agenda and were in the bag 100 percent for Stephen LaRoque.

I once had the grand idea of inviting the sources of these idiotic accusations to the office for a summit. Once behind closed doors, my plan was to pull out a comprehensive binder of our political coverage, point out it was straight down the middle, and then hold these people's noses in it the same way you'd train a dog to stop peeing on the rug.

This idea resulted in the first of my many suspensions.

Just this morning, the same colleague who had a finger shoved in his face by someone the night before suffered yet another humiliation in the name of political backwash. While standing in line at a gas station to pay for some Gatorade and a copy of "Cat Fancy" magazine, he noticed a woman rummaging through the newspaper racks in a rather annoyed fashion.

She then realized there was a guy who worked for The Free Press standing behind her.

"You work for The Free Press, don't you?" she asked.

"Yes ma'am, I do," he replied.

"Why in the world did y'all have to put Obama's picture on the front page today?" she breathlessly asked in a booming voice heard three counties away. "I usually buy The Free Press, but I ain't buyin' one with all that

Obama crap on it."

My colleague — and everyone within earshot — were too shocked to really say anything, so I offer the following retort:

Lady, who were we supposed to put on the front of the paper, Dwight Eisenhower? It's called a NEWSpaper, not a ONLYPRINTNEWSIFITFITSINWITHWHATIBELIEVEpaper. We didn't fabricate the story; Obama did win, okay? I'm not saying you have to be happy about it, but I am saying we have to report it.

If Romney had won Tuesday, he'd be on the front page, and I'm sure plenty of nut jobs on the other side would have reacted the same way you did. Putting Barack Obama's picture on the front page doesn't mean The Free Press is for or against Barack Obama — it's simply a case of stating a fact.

When you encounter people over the next few days, be careful of the way you talk to them. If you start whining or gloating about the election, chances are the person you're talking to could give a good bowel evacuation about your opinion.

If the person has their hand on the door and is leaning forward, that means they want you to stop talking so they can get going. If they give you a series of high fives and chest bumps, chances are you're speaking their language and you can blather till your tongue wears your teeth down to the size of a baby aspirin.

(That last comment was in no way intended to show favoritism to aspirin over Tylenol.)

ASSAULT OVER BARBECUE HAS HAPPY ENDING
NOVEMBER 13, 2012

Against the counsel of law enforcement, family and clergy, last Friday I set off on a road trip with Free Press Managing Editor Bryan Hanks.

What event could cause a seemingly sane person (me) to be locked in a petroleum-propelled motor vehicle with a man deemed incurable by the Bromidrosis Institute? A concert by The Who, that's what.

For many years, if I went to a concert there was a good chance I'd be alone. Aside from my father and long-time concert compadre Jon Hughes, the odds of me strangling the person riding to the show with me were 50/50 on a good day.

While inviting someone to a concert seems like a fairly casual thing to do, it is a deadly serious social contract.

Your average mook is going to show up at least a half an hour later than the agreed upon time of departure. Anybody that shows up late outside the umbrella of A) a family emergency or B) anything involving a really good-looking woman should be treated as a possible terror suspect.

Another potential power keg is food. Especially when heading to a show after work, time is of the essence. Even without the clarity achieved after a series of raps to the head with a tire iron, most people would realize it makes more sense to get something quick that's on the way.

Sadly, there is a chunk of the population that believes it's perfectly viable to visit a sit-down restaurant, take seven to nine hours to peruse the menu (to end up ordering a hamburger) and expect to get to the concert on time.

Then there's booze. Acquiring that rare import beer that was brewed in a hut by the Dalai Lama and kept cool by being stored in the hole where Perez Hilton's soul should be is to some people even more important than the concert itself. I once witnessed a guy get so schmammered in the parking lot before a Pink Floyd show that he passed out on the hood of his car and missed the entire show.

Years later when I encounter this guy, he talks about how awesome the show was. Instead of pointing out his lie I smile, nod and lift a few prescription pads from his desk while he's not looking.

This year, however, has been a time of rejuvenation. After a thoroughly enjoyable trip to see the Chris Robin-son Brotherhood with the aforementioned Mr. Hughes, I hit paydirt again with last week's Who concert. Joining me on the excursion were Hanks and my band mate Joe Gray.

I did most of the driving, so that meant I had control over the iPod — even over numerous protests from Hanks. While Hanks is a lifelong U2 fanatic, there are some things on his iPod that would make Helen Keller want to be cured of deafness just so she could go deaf again. You might think that was an insensitive thing to say, but the man has a hip hop song in his collection that uses "Visine" as a rhyme.

"Visine."

On the way up, we had time to stop and allow Joe to do a little shopping for his wedding anniversary. At the time, it seemed perfectly normal for two adult men to sift through racks of women's coats, gloves and scarves. Later on, Hanks brought up the fact that my very first column was about two guys shopping. It was a clear cut case of life imitating … art.

I'm happy to report neither of my travel partners felt the need to drink enough alcohol to float Rosie O'Donnell out of dry dock. All of us did OD on one thing — barbecue from Greensboro landmark Stamey's. We're spoiled with good barbecue around here, so I was skeptical. With one combined bite of barbecue/ hush puppy, though, we were all smitten. The barbecue was so good we took turns slapping each other.

Two of us proposed to the waitress; one of us proposed to the chef.

Once inside the concert venue, the line to get through security was long and slow. This didn't sit well with Joe since his teeth were about to start floating. The man was in need of a W.C. in the worst way. To help him out, I started talking about waterfalls, massive rain storms and gushing tidal waves.

At one point, Hanks used his iPhone to pull up a video of a plumber flushing a toilet over and over and over. Two of us thought this was hysterical; one of us did not.

The show was fantastic. It was inspirational to see Pete Townshend and Roger Daltrey — both of whom are approaching 70 — put it down in such an authoritative manner. Hanks may or may not have floated an air biscuit close in vicinity to the one person out of 20,000 who was sitting down as the band members were introduced.

Three of us thought this was funny; the guy in charge of shutting the fire alarms off did not.

Hanks drove a chunk of the way back home, so I begrudgingly relented control of the iPod to him. Thankfully, he pulled up U2's "Achtung Baby" and a sing-along of "Glee" proportions ensued. Turns out Hanks has one heck of a falsetto — especially when the seat belt malfunctions and performs an amateur vasectomy on him.

Long live Rock — be it dead or alive.

HUMANITY 1, BIEBER 0
NOVEMBER 29, 2012

Tax Deduction No. 1 and I spent all of last Saturday Christmas shopping.

To be more accurate, we spent several hours looking and about 15 minutes actually buying things. At a time when the economy is as stale as a Jay Leno monologue, it just seemed like the prudent thing to do.

I'm a firm believer in buying local — especially when it comes to produce and semi-automatic weapons. That being said, I thought TD No.1 would get a kick out of visiting an old school behemoth of a shopping center, so we pointed the Impala west and headed for the Streets at Southpoint in Durham.

Anyone that knows me at all knows I detest two things: Being late and sports memorabilia in any color other than the team's official colors.

I know this is America and people want choices, but pink Dallas Cowboy T-shirts are just wrong. Even Free Press Managing Editor and sports elitist Bryan Hanks special-orders pink adult-sized Virginia footy pajamas by the case.

Wanting to cram as much into the day as possible, we got started fairly early. The plan was to be pulling into the parking lot just as the stores were opening, which would be 10 a.m. We didn't exactly bring our A-game, but we made it there at a respectable 10:06 a.m.

If a certain 8-year-old weren't so nitpicky about things like breakfast, bathroom breaks and having to have BOTH shoes we could have made it by 10 — but I'm not bitter. Not one bit. Not at all. It's fine.

We entered the Streets at Southpoint and were greeted by a mass of humanity not seen since Rush Limbaugh and Rosie O'Donnell hooked up at Burning Man back in '06. Their love was brief, but at the time Moses couldn't have parted them.

The purpose of our trip was to find something for The Wife/The Mama. The Wife/The Mama never asks for anything or drops hints. Apparently being married to a man with the body of Adonis, the charm of Pierce Brosnan and the natural scent of hickory-smoked bacon has rendered the idea of any further gifts as mere piffle.

The only Christmas gift I've given that was an unabashed homerun was a novelty item purchased as a goof at the last minute. I was walking out of a store and noticed a stack of those odd concoctions that only appear in December. An example would be a frying pan/MP3player/label maker that can be folded into a pair of sunglasses.

The item stacked in a pyramid in the middle of the walkway this time was a jewelry washing machine. Supposedly all you had to do was dump your fine jewelry into the machine, squirt a little of the provided magic goo on top and hit a button and within seconds your jewelry would be restored to its original pawn shop luster.

I was hesitant to buy the jewelry washer for two reasons. For one thing I'd already purchase a home spa kit for The Wife/The Mama. This thing turned an ordinary tub into a Jacuzzi, so I just knew I'd struck pay dirt. Secondly, aside from a wedding ring and maybe 3 percent of a dinner ring I bought her when we were dating, most of The Wife/ The Mama's jewelry was as fake as Matt Lauer's left buttock.

For whatever reason, I ended up getting the jewelry washing machine. I figured if nothing else I could use it to wash the letters off of M&M's. They say the chocolate doesn't melt in your hand, but we all know that's not necessarily the case.

In short, that Christmas the Jacuzzi/spa thing was met with a polite thank you while the jewelry washer elicited a "wow" and a hug. It was this moment that led to several years of gift-card only Christmas shopping.

Over the course of a year the Jacuzzi/spa thing was cranked up maybe twice, while the jewelry washer caused a stir in the family. Women of relation near and far interrogated me about the jewelry washer. For months afterwards strangers would stop me on the street and ask for any information that could lead to the acquisition of the magical $20 machine that could clean $4 worth of jewelry in a matter of seconds.

TD No.1 and I plowed through the crowds to peruse gifts no wise man in his right mind would pay for. When we found a nice blouse that was priced at a mere $265, TD No.1 remarked that it should only cost about $5. I figured the woman who knitted the thing was probably paid $5 a week. We passed on the blouse.

With the help of Friend of The Column and Durham resident Correai Moore, we eventually found a few nice things for The Wife/The Mama. Later on we ended up at a Best Buy that — shock of shocks — still had a CD section.

I mention this because TD No. 1 went up to the Christmas music section and began a feverish search. Fearing the worst I stood stoically by as she passed over the insipid Justin Bieber, the apparently possessed-by-Perry-Como Rod Stewart and the blusterously nonsensical Trans-Siberian Orchestra.

What did that sweet, brilliant child eventually choose? She chose the Vince Guraldi Trio's "A Charlie Brown Christmas Soundtrack." This may seem trivial, but anytime quality wins out over well-promoted garbage it makes me happy. It did my heart good to see TD#1 choose something she genuinely liked instead of what the rest of the world is trying to tell her to like.

I forget where I was going with this. Free Tibet and Merry Christmas!

I have the day off; now I can get some work done.

'LETTERS TO SANTA' CONTEST WINNERS ANNOUNCED
DECEMBER 6, 2012

Hundreds of devoted Free Press readers entered our "Grown Ups Write Letters to Santa" contest, but only a select few could be deemed winners. We'd like to take this opportunity to thank everyone for their submissions and let you know that every person who submitted a letter will be receiving a complimentary Free Press 2012 calendar.

Please allow 4-6 weeks for delivery.

On to the top three …

Third place:

Dear Santa,

I've been a fan of your work for some time — even though I've been patiently waiting for a Hot Wheels City since 1980. We could continue to dance the same dance we've been dancing since I was 5-years-old, but who are we kidding? I haven't been a very good boy this year. Nothing major — just a citation for expired tags and a order to remain at least 1,000 feet away from Cloris Leachman. Our eyes met as we passed each other in a Denny's parking lot and I admit I was smitten. Her portrayal of Frau Blücher in "Young Frankenstein" gave me what one guidance counselor described as a "zestful appreciation" of discipline.

Anyway, if you could hook a brother up with an Xbox, I'd appreciate it.

Michael Gagliano, 41, Kinston

Second place:

Dear Santa,

Everyone is always asking you for something, but what about you? I'm concerned that in your quest to deliver toys to all the good girls and boys you've been neglecting yourself. I know you're supposed to be jolly, but I've noticed you've had to add a few extra reindeer to handle the extra tonnage as of late. Speaking of those two new reindeer, your publicist should really work up some decent stage names for them. I know we're not supposed to judge, but "Mortimer" and "Osama" don't seem to jive with "Donner" and "Blitzen."

As for your weight problem, I've sent a press release to every major news organization detailing the types of healthy snacks children should leave for you on Christmas Eve. Expect lots of spinach balls and artichoke cookies.

Correai Moore, 39, Durham

First place:

Dear Mr. Kringle,

Like the majority of Americans, my family has felt the impact of our stagnant economy. We've tightened our belts and let a few luxuries go, so for the time-being we're doing OK. We've also told both our children Walmart has changed its name to the Dollar Store.

It will warm the deep, dark cockles of your heart to see a child get excited over receiving a four-pack of Peter Pan batteries and a copy of Mr. T's 2006 fruit-based crime novel, "I Pithy the Fool."

A recent article in North Pole Monthly detailed the staff cuts you've had to make in order to keep the whole toy delivery thing going. Sometimes I think big corporations use a tough economy as an excuse to lay off workers and pile on those remaining, but I believe in your case, it was just something that had to be done.

Many of the elves that have been laid off over the last few years have found work through the "Elf on the Shelf" program. Parents love the "Elf on the Shelf" because their kids love it; furthermore, the fear of that little dude reporting any naughtiness back to you this close to the big day frightens many kids into good behavior.

I'm all for these unemployed elves earning a living, but the little guy that's currently residing in my house is starting to wear out his welcome. For one thing, he insists on having an entire glass of milk with each cookie. I know elves have different diets than humans, but I'm just before having to start milking the dog to keep up with demand. FYI, this dog doesn't even like it when someone tugs on its ear.

If you could call your boy and ask him to ease off on the cow juice, it would be greatly appreciated.

Also, while you were here last year, your reindeer left several "presents" on my tin roof. At first we didn't notice, but as the temperatures warmed, the "presents" started to thaw and roll off the house. It's quite disarming to be staring out a window at night and see a large "present" fly by the window.

Our little girl saw this one night and, to this day, wonders what kind of massive prehistoric bird could produce a "present" with such girth and pungency. What do you feed those deer, gun powder?

I've taken the liberty of hanging an industrial strength trash bag and shovel on the edge of my roof in anticipation of your visit on the 25th. If you could take just a moment to shovel any "presents" from your reindeer into that bag, it would be much appreciated.

My neighbor down the street is a card-carrying member of the ACLU and he's been having a hissy-fit over the manger scene in front of our town post office. I figure a giant pile of individually wrapped reindeer "presents" will be a big hit around his secular humanism tree.

Peace, love and soul.

Paulette Burroughs, 22, La Grange.

KINSTON MAYOR SUFFERING FROM RARE CONDITION
DECEMBER 11, 2012

Cough. Aches. Runny nose. Fever. If you're currently experiencing any of these symptoms, you've either got the flu or you've sat in a chair recently vacated by Paris Hilton.

With temperatures going up and down faster than Bill Clinton's pants, inevitably, germs will take advantage of the situation. Over the past month, everyone at my house has come down with a wet cough that sounds like a mule stepping in (and out of) a mud hole. Always thinking green, we collected enough used tissues to construct three floats in the Kinston and La Grange Christmas parades.

Scoff if you will, but we saved lots of money on glue this year.

While it's easy to make light of the flu season, it's not always a laughing matter — everyone reading this knows someone who is currently suffering from a potentially serious fever. The latest victim is someone well known, not only in Eastern North Carolina, but also to hundreds who've attended any of Newt and Callista Gingrich's austerity-themed costume parties.

The news broke Sun-day afternoon around 3 p.m. The following tweet was posted by Kinston Mayor B.J. Murphy: "@BJMurphyKinston: Love it or not, I'm a #Bieber fan. Mistletoe is a good song."

I was sitting in a chair when I read the news, but for some reason I felt the need to stand up and sit down again.

We've all read about political leaders suffering health problems while in office. President John F. Kennedy was apparently on multiple medications to combat Addison's disease, which many believe led to his cavalier actions during the Cuban Missile Crisis. President Ronald Reagan was rumored to have been suffering from a degenerative brain disorder that led him to invite Mr. T to play Santa Claus at the White House Christ-mas party in 1983.

The first documented cases of the so-called "Bieber-Fever" were reported in Canada in 2008 when Jus-tin Bieber's mother began posting videos of her son singing Ne-Yo songs on YouTube. Within a few months, these spore-like videos began to infect the minds of impressionable youth all around the world.

R&B icon Usher swooped into action, signed Bieber to a contract and has, to date, hired several dozen accountants to keep up with the massive waves of cash that have hit in a tsunami-like fashion ever since.

"This Bieber problem is similar to the Pat Boone/Little Richard situation of the 1950s," said Professor Link Wray of the Harvard School of Rock, Funk and Swing. "When Pat Boone covered Little Richard's 'Tutti Fruit-ti,' it was played off as a business tool used to sell rock and roll to white record buyers. This may have been the end result, but the idea to do this unquestionably came from a demented, feverish mind."

The professor continued, "I've looked at samples taken from victims of the Pat Boone incident in the 1950s and compared them to samples taken from people with 'Bieber Fever.' The strains are not identical, because — at least in the first instance — Little Richard had some killer songs. This Bieber kid is spreading a rehashed type of music that was lame to begin with."

Since the "Tweet Heard around the World" was posted Sunday, no public statement has been issued by Mayor Murphy or the Never Say Never Super PAC, although a few Murphy supporters agreed to speak to The Free Press under the veil of anonymity.

"I noticed something was wrong at a barbecue back in the summer," said a friend of Murphy's we'll refer to as "Buddy". "We had B.J.'s iPod plugged into my car stereo because I wanted to get my 'Hotel California' on — that's my jam. When that song ended, we all noticed this high-pitched, siren-like screech coming from the stereo.

"It sounded like a thousand tanks getting stuck in second gear at the same time while driving over a herd of elephants who were all in the process of passing stones."

Buddy continued.

"At first, I thought some little punk was trying to break into my car so I put my hand on my toaster with the intent of firing a warning shot in the air," he said. "Before I could actually get the gunpowder loaded into my gat, somebody told me nothing was wrong; the noise that caused seven non-pregnant women to go into labor was a Jus-tin Bieber song."

Murphy's supporters have rallied around him since the news broke on Sunday.

"I think he's done a terrific job as mayor," said a Murphy supporter we'll refer to as "Rita". "I don't know what would compel an otherwise savvy public servant to go public with his appreciation of Justin Bieber's 'music.' Remember, he said he liked the song 'Mistletoe' by Bieber. Just because he likes one song doesn't mean he's bought into the whole Bieber gestalt hook, line and schnoinkel."

In another interesting twist to Biebergate, local Democrats have not stepped forward to pile on the Republican mayor during his time of distress.

"The truth of the matter is there are plenty of people on our side who like Jus-tin Bieber too," said N.C. Sen. Ron Davis. "I don't really get it; I'm more of Brian McKnight/Toby Keith man myself. Murphy has a lot of support; I think he'll come through Biebergate a stronger, tougher politician."

Murphy is expected to address the public via Twitter early this morning. Stay tuned to this space for updates and/or deals on a new car or truck as they happen.

THE RETELLING OF A CHERISHED KINSTON HOLIDAY DITTY
DECEMBER 18, 2012

Usually, whenever somebody decides to improve on something that already works fine, the results can be disastrous: New Coke, pink John Deere hats or gravy-flavored Crest immediately comes to mind. Other times, the original can be improved upon: Peanut M&Ms, Doctor Who and Cher.

This little ditty was originally published in The Free Press on Dec. 11, 2008. The intervening years have been a bit of a roller coaster for my family. We've gained a Tax Deduction, lost a dog and replaced a couple of 18-year-old cars with a few six-year old cars.

Please don't bring us a dog, though. We're in the process of working the ninja out of this second Tax Deduction — one crisis at a time.

To date, Tax Deduction No. 1 and No. 2 have proven to be valuable members of our family — especially every year around April 15. Depending on which ravine we land in after going over the so called "fiscal cliff," they may become as relevant as a Beta max VCR.

They do have their moments though. A few weeks ago, the youngest one asked where biscuits came from, so naturally, I told her they came from hibiscus flowers.

Right now, I'm heading outside to stable bits of biscuit to my wife's award winning hibiscus flowers — all in the name of adding to a child's sense of wonder during the Christmas season. And now, our feature presentation:

'Twas the night before Christmas,
when all throughout Kinston The wallets were starving from money gone missing
The credit cards were maxed-out with nary a care
In hopes the Prize Patrol soon would be there
The children were nestled all snug in their beds
While their parents scratched lottery tickets till their fingers bled
And Mama in her bathrobe, and I in my chaps
Had just settled down for a long winter's nap

When out on the lawn there arose such a clatter
I searched through the house for a ball peen hammer
Away to the window I flew like a flash
Flung open the door and hid all my cash
The moon on the driveway of a midnight frost
Gave the luster of an oil leak from an oil pan of rust
When, what to my crustated eyes should appear
But a repo man, with car jackin' gear
With a scary old scalp, so slimy and slick
Surely he came for my treasured Crown Vic
More rabid than badgers the payments were due
With each payment, I wrote such a note:
"I don't have it all, but I'll get it soon!"
"My workman's comp case will surely balloon!"
To the top of the porch I sang with my all:
"Now go away! Go away! Go away all!"
But with a set of keys from the dealership on his finger
He drove off into the night, he did not linger
As I cried in my hands, and was turning around
Down the chimney, St. Holmes came with a bound
He was dressed in red spandex, from his head to his foot
His nametag read "Patrick," all covered in soot
He summoned me closer, to ask me a question
"Do you have any Tums? I've got indigestion."
With a cure in his tummy, he walked out of sight
With — to my chagrin — my kiddy's new bike.
If that weren't enough to steal our elation
On the door was a notice about annexation.
The council decided our land should be theirs
Which meant our taxes would climb like the stairs.
"It's time to move," Daddy said with a holler
"These people won't rest till they have every dollar!"

A quarterly publication should only cost 25 cents.

NUCLEAR MATERIALS DISCOVERED IN TOY VACUUM
JANUARY 3, 2013

Everybody have a nice Christmas? I sure did.

How many of you had your Christmas decorations put away before Santa made it back up the chimney? How many of you didn't realize until October your decorations from last year were still up and just rode it out the save the effort? How often do you see a paragraph made up entirely of questions?

We still get a real tree because there is nothing like the aroma of a Douglas fir in full stank. If I live long enough, I'm sure our decorations will devolve into a stolen poinsettia with a candy cane stuck in the middle for good measure, but for now I want whatever we stick our ornaments and lights on to have been killed with a chainsaw.

While we all know San-ta brings most of the toys at Christmas, he sometimes leaves the assembly of said toys to the parents. Anything beyond building a s'more is usually beyond my mechanical prowess, but a recent successful attempt at assembling a child's tent/tunnel set had artificially inflated my confidence.

Tax Deduction No. 2 always wants to help out when anyone is vacuuming in our house, which is cute until she tries to vacuum the toilet. With this in mind, San-ta brought her a toy version of a Dyson Ball vacuum. According to the instructions left by Santa, the Dyson assembly consisted of only two steps. Step 1: Attach handle to base of unit; Step 2: Insert four C batteries.

Upon reading the instructions, visions of sugar plums and getting to bed before midnight danced in my head.

Attaching the handle was a snap. Surely, inserting four C batteries wouldn't be a problem.

Before I could insert the batteries, I'd have to remove a plastic cover that was held in place by 37 amoeba-sized screws. After the screws were removed, I started placing the batteries in the provided slot. The first three batteries were no problem; it was that fourth one that repeatedly caused the first three to spring from the slot in a rather violent manner.

At one point I asked The Wife — who was working on her own toy assemblage project — to hold down the three batteries while I tried to convince the fourth battery to join its brethren. With all four batteries finally in place I slid the aforementioned cover over the batteries and proceeded to re-install the 37 microscopic battery cover screws.

While in the process of tightening the 37th screw, I heard the batteries shift from within the demon instrument of suction. I wasn't sure how batteries packed in tighter than a Kardashian's butt girdle could have possibly broken loose, but they did.

An hour and 40 minutes later, the batteries were finally in their final resting place. I hit the big red button expecting to hear a whir, but all I could hear was a deafening quiet and the intense throb of blood that was pulsating through my ears.

I started retracing my steps over the previous year, wondering what I'd done to cause that obese burglar in the red suit to do this to me. I'd given what I could to charity and helped a few elderly people with their groceries. Sure, I may have snapped on a few people who felt the urge to unload their grievances with the paper on me while I was out in public with my children, but stitches rarely leave a mark these days.

Maybe he was paying me back for the time the cashier was too busy blathering on his phone to realize he'd undercharged me by $12. Nah, I'd imagine Santa would be down with that.

As it happens, a family member had also awakened to find a Dyson toy vacuum left at her house by Santa. We got on the phone and explained the Ken Burns-style drama that we'd just gone through. Apparently, their Dyson toy vacuum was assembled in about one minute and fired up without incident.

I was so, so happy for them.

Admitting defeat, we finally got to bed around 2 a.m. True to form, Tax Deduction No. 2 called out for some hooch around 5 a.m. We wanted to let Tax Deduction No. 1 sleep till at least 7 a.m., so in a flurry of inspiration and ninja-like choreography, I set up my laptop computer on the floor of our bedroom so Tax Deduction No. 2 could watch Cinderella, thus buying us another 90 minutes of "sleep."

Before the movie was over, Tax Deduction No. 1 ambled into our room. Instead of trying to yank us into the living room, she crawled in bed and started watching the movie. For about 15 minutes, we were having a very Huxtablelike Christmas.

Tax Deduction No. 2 is prone to get excited and react physically to the movie when things get tense, but I didn't mind taking a Onesie-covered foot to the nose. Compared to the horror I experienced with the toy vacuum, it was almost pleasant.

Around 7:10 a.m., we marched down the hall to see what Santa had left. Tax Deduction No. 2 ran past several items and straight to the dreaded toy vacuum. Our intention was to let her push it around a bit that morning and search for a replacement the next day, but there would be no need.

Without any instruction from us, Tax Deduction No. 2 found the on/off button, pressed it and brought the vacuum to life. In a somewhat mocking manner, the motor in the toy vacuum revved as if it were being simultaneously powered by Shearon Harris and the Hoover Dam. That thing inhaled half of a foot stool before we could shut it off.

Be it a Christmas miracle or spiteful St. Nicholas, we all lived happily ever after. Lord help us all if I ever run into that British nob in the Dyson commercials.

You may think it's cruel, but watching a confused magician pull a hat out of a rabbit is just funny.

GOLDSBORO STORE PLAYS PROFANE
MATERIAL FOR CHILDREN
JANUARY 8, 2013

A few days ago a friend of mine hipped me to a Goldsboro record store that was going out of business.

When most people hear that a store is going out of business, their brains are immediately immersed in thoughts of bargains. The people who'll be losing their jobs don't usually come into play until you show up to pick the meat off the bones of their once flourishing business.

The store in question was an FYE (For Your Entertainment) CD/DVD store. Since they routinely charged $18 for a single CD, the FYE may have actually been an anagram for "Fork (Over) Your Earnings."

I had a few non-negotiable days off, so I peeled Tax Deduction No. 2 off the ceiling and forged a path down U.S. 70 West with visions of finding that ever-elusive Japanese import version of the Jim Nabors box set for cheap.

(The Japanese version is special because it contains tracks from the Jim Nabors/ Rock Hudson duets album "Rock Pyle" that were omitted from the U.S. pressings.)

Upon arrival, I immediately noticed what a consultant would refer to as "creative marketing" and a veteran dirt farmer would refer to as a crock of "bull fertilizer."

For example, a DVD copy of "Cream: Live at the Royal Albert Hall" (with a cutout mark on its side) would normally be priced at no more than $9.99. But now — with a giant "30% off " sticker slapped on it, the DVD is priced at $15.99.

You tell me, is this corporate skulduggery at its finest or just a fool catcher's holiday?

My buddy actually found a few genuine deals the day before, so I figured a little digging would be required. As TD No. 2 and I started rifling through the albums, a store employee started a movie on the in-store system.

Within a few minutes, some of the movie dialogue caught my ear. The words that were emitting from the speakers were the kind best left to locker rooms, fishing trips, band rehearsals and reactions to newspaper employee pay checks.

All of the old favorites ("s" and "f " especially) were on display for everyone in the store — including at least three children under the age of 5. Surely the employees at FYE wouldn't knowingly play a profanity-laced movie to people who couldn't legally see the film in a theater ... or would they?

The closest employee was a guy wearing a tobaggan who seemed to be trying to kick a hackey sack that wasn't there. In the nicest voice I could conjure, I asked the illegitimate son of Dobie Gillis and Drew Barrymore if he'd mind changing the movie to something that didn't involve cursing.

"Uh ... I ... don't ... think there's any cursing in the movie," Dobie Jr. said.

"Yes, there is," I said as I covered TD No. 2's ears. "There have been four s**** and one ***k in the three minutes I've been in the store. Do you think my kid or any of these others should be hearing this in your store?"

"Well, the other parents aren't complaining," Dobie Jr. said.

"That's because they're idiots," I replied.

After referencing his iPhone app for walking, Dobie Jr. eventually put one foot in front of the other and walked up to his manager to confer.

While awaiting the results of the summit between Dobie Jr. and his superior, I wondered if this sort of thing would have bothered the younger me. I think it would.

In fourth grade, I once kicked a classmate square in the onions for throwing spitballs at a group of kindergartners who were just trying to go to lunch. After telling the teacher what happened, I was pardoned from an almost certain paddling.

Today I would have probably been sued for millions of dollars and the teacher fired. The teacher and I could have eloped to France where the age difference wouldn't be such a big deal and sell overpriced junk to antique-hunting tourists, but I digress.

While Dobie spoke in a hushed tone to his boss lady, she assumed an exasperated demeanor and issued her ruling.

"We can't turn it off, but we can turn it down," Dobie said when he returned.

"Why can't you turn it off?" I asked. "Have you lost the remote?"

"It's store policy that once we start a movie, we have to finish it," he said.

Instead of allowing my skull to explode while holding my second-born I left the store, noticing that the profanities could be heard several feet outside the store. A little old lady who looked like she may have dated FDR in high school seemed stunned at what she heard as she walked in front of the store.

When I got home, I called the store and asked to speak to the manager. I asked why they played these kinds of movies in front of small children who couldn't legally buy them.

Manager: "Our store policy states we can play anything with a PG-13 rating."

Me: "So you're telling me a 7-year-old can't buy the movie you were playing, but they can view it in your store?"

Manager: "We play the movies so people will want to buy them; that's how business works."

Me: "I understand how business works, Mrs. Trump. I also realize if you tick off people in your store they don't buy anything. Were you out with rickets the day they covered that at Dunderpate University?"

Manager: "I've been at this store for four years and no one has ever complained before. Look, I'm a mother and both of my kids have seen that movie."

Me: "You must be proud."

Manager: (Click followed by dialtone).

Me: "Mmyellow?"

I left a message with the Berkeley Mall office and with FYE's corporate office, but haven't received any type of response. Desperate to find out if I was the crazy one, I called a law enforcement agency in Goldsboro and asked if it was legal to broadcast this kind of stuff to an audience that couldn't legally buy it.

"Well, it's not necessarily illegal but they could be fined for it," the officer said. "There's not a lot that can be done about it."

I thanked the officer for his time and peacefully gave up.

Initially, I thought the store manager was lying when she said no one had complained in four years, but she probably wasn't. All I can do is make sure my girls hear their first curse words the old-fashioned way — by accident the next time I hit my thumb with a hammer and forget they're within earshot.

FREE PRESS REPORTER RESIGNS AMID SCANDAL
JANUARY 10, 2013

After nearly six years on the job, a veteran Free Press reporter is resigning under a cloud of allegations and bandages.

"I really hate to see David go — especially under these circumstances," said Free Press Managing Editor Bryan Hanks. "It's a shame he let his schnoinkel cloud his shapat. The way he mingled with that goy was just not kosher."

According to several of his coworkers, Anderson's troubles began when he was introduced to Free Press Concierge Paulette Burroughs in 2007.

"She throws herself at every young guy that walks through the door," said former Free Press reporter Chris Lavender. "Usually after a few months, Paulette will get bored and move on to her next paramour. If you ignore her advances she'll stop throwing herself at you and start throwing staplers, phone books and printers."

Anderson and Burroughs allegedly began seeing each other socially in the summer of 2010.

"They coordinated their vacation days and followed the Molly Hatchet tour for two weeks that year," said former Free Press reporter Vanessa Clarke Shortley. "I think David was impressed when the band dedicated 'Flirtin with Disaster' to Paulette every night."

Shortley — who is now running a successful furniture-sitting business in Orange County — says it was only a matter of time before the Anderson/Burroughs romance went awry.

"David is a mild-mannered, introspective kind of guy, while Paulette is more of a 'kill 'em all and let God sort 'em out' kinda gal," Shortley said. "She never asked for my lunch money; I just surrendered it to her every day as a precautionary measure."

Burroughs celebrity skyrocketed to the realm of E-Listers when she appeared on the cover of my 2012 book "Making Gravy in Public." Talent scouts started booking the rising star at county fairs, federal prisons and boat shows.

By the end of the year, Burroughs was commanding double-digit appearance fees. Her highest profile gig came when Rick Ross cast her as "Shorty Washing Car No. 4" in the video for his song "Stay Schemin'."

Sadly, Burroughs' scene was cut because guest artist Drake felt her dancing was "too erotic for a rap video."

Burroughs didn't realize her scene had been cut until its simultaneous MTV and BET debut. This perceived slight sent her into a tailspin that friends and family say she's yet to pull out of.

"Mama crashes by design, that's for sure," said Burroughs' daughter, Kelly. "Her driving is fine; it's the parking her vehicle in the middle of U.S. 70 at 7:50 a.m. on a Monday that's a problem."

"Look, The Fuzz told me I had to stop puttin' mustard on my biscuit while I was driving and Tweetin' about Kimya's baby, so I put the car in park," Burroughs said. "It's like Otis sang, 'I can't do what 10 people tell me to do.' "

Incident reports obtained from the La Grange Police Department indicated Burroughs routinely assaulted Anderson whenever her beloved Tar Heels lost a basketball game during the 2012-13 season. He is currently recuperating at an undisclosed location in the greater Kinston area.

With his speech encumbered by a series of facial bandages and stitches, Anderson has to choose his words carefully these days.

"They lost four of their starting five," said Anderson through a flag semaphore interpreter. "Whenever people start blaming it on Roy, it gets her blood boiling. For some reason when she's been drinking, she thinks I look like Mike Krzyzewski.

"Let's just say my ability to duck a Chinese throwing star isn't nearly as strong as her ability to throw a Chinese throwing star."

Instead of pressing charges, Anderson has decided to take a job with the Baltimore Sun. Along with covering local politics and education, Anderson will also be in charge of explaining the complicated plot line of "The Wire" to confused tourists.

We'll miss you David. If you see Gee or Bolander up there in Baltimore, tell them we said, "Howdy."

CITY OF KINSTON TO ANNEX TRI-COUNTY ELECTRIC
JANUARY 15, 2013

Many City of Kinston utility customers are still fuming over the recent Rouse Road substation failure that left thousands of customers without electricity. Those who weren't fuming described themselves as "steamed," while those who were stoned at the time didn't notice anything out of the ordinary.

Officials with the city have narrowed the problem down to a piece of equipment known as an "arrestor," which — in laymen's terms — is a surge protector on a grand scale. This device is not to be confused with the equally popular surge scale on a grand protector or its lesser-known cousin, the scale surge on a protected grand.

According to a story written by Free Press reporter Wes Wolfe, these arrestors would normally last between 30 and 50 years. As it turns out, the arrestors that have caused the two most recent blackouts are only about 16. An unnamed source at the City of Kinston confirmed the faulty pieces of equipment were still under warranty.

"This equipment came with a 30-year warranty, but somebody forgot to clean his pants pockets out before he put them in the wash and the receipt was ruined," said the unnamed source. "For a while, I'd check his pockets before they were washed, but after so many years you just get tired of treating a grown man like a little boy.

"I reckon he thinks his mama is gonna keep cleanin' up after him, but his mama don't live here — although there may be room for her soon."

Wolfe's story went on to say officials plan to replace all of the arrestors at the problematic substation in question. As for the current faulty equipment, minutes from a 1993 Kinston Council meeting reveal that a heated debate led to a 3-2 vote in favor of purchasing electrical equipment from a new vendor at a cheaper price.

"Looking back on it now, buying electrical equipment from Hasbro may not have been the wisest decision," said a former Kinston City Council member who wished to remain anonymous. "Them Cabbage Patch Dolls were hot as fire at the time. They agreed to throw in a few dozen cases of them dolls if we bought our arrestors from them. Everybody on the council that year had Cabbage Patch Dolls to give to their youngun's and grandyoungun's; I didn't have children at the time, so I sold my share and went to Cabo for a month."

The unnamed council member continued, "A little Old Spice and a wad of money goes a long ways down there, although I brought something back that penicillin nor Ajax could run off."

While most citizens realize it's pointless to blame the current administration (no pun intended) for the city's electrical woes, a combination of rising bills, lower income and spotty service has them screaming for solutions.

To that end, the Kinston City Council held an emergency meeting during last week's power outage.

"We met by candlelight at the courthouse," said one council member. "The mood was much more relaxed than our usual meetings. At one point someone turned on a battery-powered radio and Andre Crouch's 'The Blood Will Never Lose It's Power' was playing.

"I'd be lying if I said we didn't get a little emotional."

The meeting — which didn't adjourn until 4 a.m. the following day — yielded what may be the most controversial decision ever reached by the City Council.

"We're going to annex Tri-County Electric," said a Kinston City Council spokesman. "They're not burdened with this ElectriCities thing, it'll be less of a burden on our utility workers and they stopped buying parts from Hasbro back in the '70s. As far as ElectriCities go, we're just going to stop sending in payments. What are they gonna do, turn off the electricity?"

Just as this edition of The Free Press was about to go to print, a small but spirited rally broke out in front of the Rouse Road substation in Kinston. Out of a group of 17 in attendance, 15 were holding up signs demanding better service and lower rates, while two individuals who appeared to be under the influence of marijuana were seen clutching the chain link fence and repeatedly asking for help.

"We've been hearing about this sub place all week, so we came down to get a sammich," said Tommy Marin of Brewster Place, Kinston. "The dude has been on like a bathroom break for hours, man. Having access to all that cheese is probably harshing his mellow right now."

Is anyone angrier than a bald barber?

DANE COOK, COMMON TAKE ON AGING LOCAL MAN
JANUARY 17, 2012

Tomorrow will be Jan. 18 — or as the Mayans refer to it Oops Plus 28.

Many significant things have happened on January 18:

• Jan. 18, 0532: Nika uprising at Constantinople fails, 30-40,000 die

• Jan. 18, 1896: The X-ray machine is exhibited for the first time

• Jan. 18, 1903: Cher is born in El Centro, Calif.

• Jan. 18, 1973: John Cleese appears in his final episode of "Monty Python's Flying Circus"

• Jan. 18, 1973: Jon Dawson is berfed

• Jan. 18, 1974: "The $6 Million Man," starring Lee Majors, premieres on ABC

• Jan. 18, 1975: "The Jeffersons," a spinoff from ""All in the Family," premieres on CBS

• Jan. 18, 1979: Rerun, Raj and Dwayne are finally told what was happening: Cancellation

If, like me, you went to ECU, get a friend to help you with the math. If nothing untoward happens between now and 11:42 p.m. tomorrow, I'll be turning 40.

Mid-life should be a time of reflection, but for better or worse, I've always attempted to live in the now. Cher's torso was still a spry 79-years-old when she tried to "Turn Back Time" in 1989. If she could have turned back time, she might have thought twice about getting that life-sized tattoo of Hervé Villechaize on her back.

Luckily, Cher's current beau is a Corinthian leather salesman from Newark.

Aside from brief dizzy spells that cause me to wander off topic from time to time, turning 40 isn't turning out to be as traumatic as I've been led to believe it would be. I wasn't cool when I was 18, so growing older hasn't necessarily made me feel older.

I've yet to have the urge to eat supper at 4:30 p.m., unless we're talking Early Bird Special and then all bets are off.

Physically, I don't feel that much different. The other night, Tax Deduction No. 2 (age 2.5) walked up to me and said "whee whee", which means she wants to be tossed in the air while yelling "WHEE! WHEE!"

Seeing this, Tax Deduction No. 1 (age 8) requested the same treatment and I obliged. I was happy with the knowledge I could still throw 4-foot, 3-inch TD No. 1 up in the air without breaking any of her bones or — more importantly — mine.

As of this writing, my advancing years haven't resulted in any signs of baldness. However, as a precaution, I've never made fun of the follically challenged.

After typing "follically challenged" just now I thought it might make a good bumper sticker, T-shirt or novelty comb. I typed the phrase into the Google search engine only to discover that Seinfeld/ Curb Your Enthusiasm creator Larry David apparently claimed "follically challenged" a few years ago.

Since I came to it on my own, I think I should be able to use it, because frankly, Ol' Larry is doing OK with the Benjamins.

On second thought, since Larry David is bald, he should probably reap the rewards of the "follically challenged" empire. If I received any royalties from "follically challenged," it would be like Michael Bolton making money off "When a Man Loves a Woman."

(For the record, I realize the Michael Bolton scenario has already happened; I just choose not to acknowledge or accept it.)

Although my rather bulbous head is still covered with enough hair to get a herd of alpacas through a Wisconsin winter, a few gray hairs are starting to mix in with the predominantly lush, auburn locks. I told God a long time ago I wouldn't complain about going gray as long as the hair didn't fall out.

Also, I see a lot of commercials about guys who — for some reason — need to take a pill just to be able to sit outside in a tub. I'm more of an indoor shower guy myself, so — as for now — I'm not worried about going bald or being able to sit on the edge of a cliff in an antique tub while the sun sets.

As for my friends who've already gone over to the other side, it's about a 50-50 split between those who handled it well and those who gave up and started buying John Mayer albums. Maybe the best way to figure out how I'm handling 40 is to compare myself to some famous people who are also turning 40 this year:

Me vs. Dane Cook: We both have giant foreheads and look like a petty thief who got off on a technicality, but he's turned his mediocre talent into a lucrative career. Advantage — Cook.

Me vs. Common: We both know how to spit on a mike, but I've got hair while he's cultivating a "Hangin' with Mr. Clean" kind of look. Still, he's loaded so … Advantage — Common.

Me vs. Wayne Brady: I have this man beat on hair and street cred, but he once took Dave Chapelle's sammich and made him cry. Advantage — Brady.

Me vs. Gwenyth Pal-trow: I'll concede she's slightly better looking and more successful. On the other hand, she's married to that clod from Coldplay and named her kid "Apple." Advantage — Me.

Getting older is OK … so far. The way I feel, 40 is the new 39.

SILENT CONDITION MAY BE AFFECTING
HALF OF POPULATION
JANUARY 22, 2013

If you're a moron, idiot, dumbbell, dullard, imbecile, dunce, halfwit or addle pate, this could be the most important story someone will read to you all year.

According to a recent study by the Le Pew Research Center, 50 percent of all Americans encounter morons on a daily basis. Of that 50 percent, nearly 67 percent are, in fact, morons themselves.

"That's one of the tragedies of the moronic condition," said Mel Blanc of the Le Pew Institute. "When someone has a full-on case of moronossis, they believe everyone else is stupid. It would be the equivalent of a penguin chastising his girlfriend for wearing the same outfit every time they go out for seafood."

How do you determine if you or a loved one is in fact a moron? According to the Le Pew study, adults who chew with their mouths open or manage to sound like a gravel truck even if eating marshmallows are at the top of the list.

"Believe it or not, open-mouth chewing is still a problem in the 21st century," said Chuck Jones of the Le Pew Research Center. "At one time the scientific community believed it would become more difficult for the open-mouthed chewers to mate and reproduce. These people have not only fought off extinction, judging by the eating habits observed in most restaurants, but they're also making a comeback."

The smacking sounds emanating from your larger mall food courts have been blamed for causing migrating geese to mistakenly fly further north for the winter.

"Our theory is the geese would rather freeze to death than have to listen to people yammer about 'America's Got Talent' while simultaneously chomping on an unholy mixture of pizza, soda and saliva," Jones said. "It's despicable."

The study also concluded people who type with the force of a steam hammer are probably suffering from a full-blown case of moronatosis.

"For some reason, millions of Americans feel the need to pound on their computers as if the keyboards owe them money," Blanc said. "Based on our findings, many morons believe hitting the keys harder will make the words appear onscreen faster and emails travel faster. In fact, pounding on the keys with such force only annoys coworkers and dramatically shortens the life of the moron's computer. When the 'Enter' key on the moron's computer ceases to function, the moron will blame the foreign computer assembler instead of himself."

On the bright side, morons have done their part to prop up our sagging economy.

"The success of home delivery/streaming movie services owes a lot to the moronic film goer," Jones said. "Between people who can't shut up during the movie and parents who bring their kids to a horror film and get offended when the disembowelment scene makes little Billy barf like a Crayola sprinkler, it's no wonder Netflix became a success."

While identifying the behavior is no longer a problem for the scientific community, a cure may be problematic to come by.

"If we loosened some restrictions, the moron tide would probably subside in a few generations," Blanc said. "The world has been moron-proofed to the point that people who would have just a century ago overdosed on chalk now simply bounce off the bubble-wrapped world we've created on their way to a high-paying job."

Blanc is quick to point out that many people are routinely misdiagnosed as morons.

"That guy who leaves his car stereo blaring while he walks into a gas station — he's not a moron," Blanc said. "He's a jerk and most likely an impotent jerk at that. Parents who beg their children to behave instead of disciplining them — those folks are spineless.

"Oh, and the people who walk at normal speed on the sidewalk and then slow down to the pace of a snail with a gait problem when crossing the street? They're 100 percent a******s; they Wish they were morons."

CONTROVERSY SURROUNDS LA GRANGE
STEW CONTESTANT
JANUARY 24, 2013

On Saturday, La Grange Boy Scout Troop 114 is sponsoring Stew Fest, a contest which will allow local culinary artists to paint on a public canvas.

The event — which is being held at the La Grange Rotary Club on 201 S. Caswell Street — is expected to attract roughly 20 chefs. One of the confirmed participants is La Grange resident and "Bachelorette" semifinalist Paulette Burroughs.

"I've been throwing random items into pots of hot water for years," Bur-roughs said. "One night when I'd got my pills mixed up I mistakenly dumped the contents of my purse into a stew I was fixing for church. Thankfully, the Quaaludes counteracted the amphetamines, although our bell choir did spontaneously launch into 'Truck-in' during the benediction."

Burroughs continued, "Along with cooking a few pots of stew, I'll be selling other things at the festival as well. If anybody wants me to shake their hand, it'll cost $5. Hugs are $10, kisses are $15 and a prolonged embrace is $25. For the more adventurous types, $50 will get you what is referred to in certain parts of Deep Run and Seven Springs as a 'Tallahasse Moon Pie'."

Burroughs' reputation as a rabble rouser, haranger and open-marriage propagandist has made her a folk hero to some while others view her as a villainous reprobate with an insatiable appetite for younger men and fried okra. Since the late 1970s, Burroughs has been charged with dozens of misdemeanors including aggravated assault, relaxed assault, selling counterfeit sausage biscuits and indecent liberties with a toaster.

"I've done my best to calm down here lately," Burroughs said. "I haven't been arrested since I beat up Dog the Bounty Hunter and Montel Williams at a charity golf game in Myrtle Beach last summer."

Since her grandsons Kevin and Josh are members of the La Grange Boy Scout troop, Burroughs says she just wants to help out an organization that means so much to her family.

"Those boys have learned so much stuff in the Scouts," Burroughs said. "They've started showing me all of the fancy knots they've learned how to tie, which really comes in handy for me on the weekends."

While most participants are expected to base their stews around beef, chicken, fish and deer meat, Bur-roughs plans to improvise on the day of the event.

"Whatever I happen to encounter on the way to the contest is what I'll cook with," Burroughs said. "If I find a possum on the side of the road that's just lost a fight with southbound Peterbilt, it'll give my stew a unique flavor and it'll already be tenderized."

Event organizers are hoping Burroughs' reputation will encourage people who would otherwise sit at home under their bed with a loaded musket and a copy of Al Gore's autobiography to join in the festivities.

"We're resigned to the fact that Paulette will probably eat a big bowl of chili and then spend the rest of the night floating air biscuits near lit matches," said Roy Smith of the La Grange Volunteer Fire Department. "We'll have a foam truck on standby."

Although not confirmed, live music is tentatively set to be provided by Taboo Stu. Children under the age of 26 get in for half price with a $5 donation to whoever is working the door.

Four out of five dentists agree that fifth dentist is just a contrary jerk.

AFTER 26 YEARS, BELOVED ZENITH BITES THE DUST
JANUARY 29, 2012

I've now been 40 for about two weeks. As for now all is well, and I'm still confident enough in my health to buy green bananas.

One thing I've learned with age is that it's not always best to solve every problem immediately. Sure, if an agitated co-worker partially disembowels you with a stapler, you may want to get to an emergency room within 24 hours. Otherwise, sometimes problems will solve themselves if given the proper room to breathe.

For example, the television in my living room is a 1987 Zenith. Against the wishes of family, friends and clergy, I've refused to get rid of the TV just because it's not the width of a credit card. The picture on the thing is clear as a bell, and I believe if the job is being done there's no reason to make a change.

Does anyone reading this believe one of these newfangled slim TVs will last for 26 years? That's longer than the average lifespan of the child labor now assembling the current fleet of anorexic, gutless televisions.

According to RadioMuseum.org, the phrase "clear as a bell" was originally used by the Sonora Phonograph Company as an advertising slogan for its line of radios and record players. One branch of the company eventually morphed into the Magnavox Company. Sharing is caring.

Recently my cherished TV has shown signs of wear. Every so often, for no reason, the picture will go away. This is easily remedied by turning the power knob ever so slightly to the left. Whenever a family member blacks out in the middle of the day, we don't throw them away, do we? We adjust their medication, unplug the microwave and get on with our day.

Although I had to cram my heart with steel wool to do it, about three weeks ago I decided it was time to get a new television. Ol '87 has been blacking out upwards of three times a week lately — most recently near the end of an episode of "Columbo," when Peter Falk was halfway staring a suspect in the eye and explaining how it was possible for him to kill his business partner with a stick of celery.

Ol '87 was with me for "Miami Vice" — the two good years at the beginning and the three so-so years that followed. When "Twin Peaks" came along and reinvented what a television show could be, Ol '87 was there. I was about to become one of those lying liars who claim not to watch TV, but Ol '87 pulled me back in with "Seinfeld," "Arrested Development" and "30 Rock." Ol '87 duct taped the once crumbling umbilical cord between myself and pop culture back together.

I'd gone so far as to price new televisions. As it turns out, it's possible to get a decent set without having to sell any of your toes to medical schools — although, if you're interested, the dough is pretty good. Many of my friends are obsessed with television-al terminology, such as resolution, frame rate speed and high definition. As long as I can tell who is saying what to whom, I could care less.

Besides, do we really need to see a close up of Honey Boo Boo's mama in high definition? Will being able to see the Dorito dust stuck between the mom's jowls make the experience more enjoyable? Okay, I guess that would be pretty cool; one point for technology.

I've never seen the "Honey Boo Boo Hour," or whatever the show is called, but I'm assuming the cinematography isn't a sticking point for most viewers. I just looked up some information on the show and found out Honey Boo Boo's family is allegedly paid $50,000 per episode. If you created 10 of me in a laboratory and rolled them in gold dust, I wouldn't be worth $50,000. Maybe I should euthanize Ol '87 out of respect.

Other people want me to get a smart TV or a plasma TV. First of all, no TV that's fed the current stream of stupid shows will ever be smart, and plasma should be in a local blood bank or black market organ drop-off Igloo cooler. I want a TV with some guts in it — not some slim, tofu-eating TV that thinks meat is murder. Had you rather board a plane with big, hefty engines or an ultralight powered by two AA batteries?

While this debate of one was going on in my slightly oversized head, I got a call from a family member asking if I'd be interested in a 4-year-old TV that was perfectly fine.

"This isn't a new thin one that can be hung on the wall," I was told. "It's about a foot thick and is the same weight as Delaware, but the picture is clear as a bell."

"You had me at Delaware," I said.

Turns out it was smart not to run out and plunk down my hard earned money on a TV I didn't really want. Ol '87 has led a good life, and it's my hope that it'll find a home in a friend's shop, basement or erotic dungeon. There's something cool about a TV that still has a knob on it in an era when most of the shows are full of knobs. My new TV will sadly be knob free, but at least it'll be heavy enough to give anyone trying to steal it a hernia.

'TIS THE SEASON FOR SELLING STEAKS FROM A TRUCK
JANUARY 31, 2013

Jobs of any kind are turning into a rare commodity. Whenever I see a grown man dressed as the Statue of Liberty in front of a Rent-A-Center I don't mock — I salute. I salute not out of some jingoistic obligation, but because that guy has a job.

Maybe he's being paid in Skittles instead of money, but a gig is a gig and Skittles are dang tasty.

Earlier this week while in the middle of trying to synthesize Elizabeth Montgomery, a couple of entrepreneurial knuckle-draggers drove up to my front door and blew their horn as if to summon their date for the evening. A wormy little dude exited the passenger side of a 1991 Toyota truck featuring a giant cooler in the back and what appeared to be a former David Allan Coe roadie behind the wheel.

"I promise I'm not crazy or anything," Wormy said as he approached me.

"Well, I am, so that's close enough — what do you need?" I asked.

Wormy held up what was allegedly a license to sell meat door to door.

"I used to be in your line of work," I told Wormy.

"Oh, you sold meat door to door?" Wormy asked excitedly, as if he thought he'd run into someone from his old fraternity.

"Naw, I was a door-to-door door salesman," I quoted from an old column. "I'd knock on the door and then hold up a brand new one before the pigeon opened their old door. I only got punched two or three times a week; you look like you've been punched a few times today already, rookie. What are you selling?"

"I'm selling steaks and..." but before Wormy could crank up his pitch, I pulled him off the mound.

"We're not interested in buying any meat," I said.

Wormy looked confused.

"An old Brahman bull pulled me out of a burning building when I was a little boy," I explained. "The old bull pulled me to safety and went back into the fire in an attempt to save the family cat. The cat nor the bull survived but the fire department said it was the best barbecue they ever had.

From that moment on, my entire family became vegetarians out of respect."

"Is that true?" Wormy asked.

"No, but since you're taking up my time I thought I'd take up some of yours," I answered.

I then pointed to a house about a mile away from mine.

"You see that house over there? Don't go to that house. An elderly uncle of mine lives there and doesn't need to be bothered," I said.

With that, Wormy and The Roadie headed off. I stood in the yard to see where they'd go, and sure enough, they went straight to the house I asked them not to. I did my best John Schneider scoot across the hood of my car and barreled down the road to my relative's house.

I pulled into the driveway behind the little Toyota and pulled to within an inch of its back bumper.

"Why are you guys here? I just told you not to come up here," I said.

"Well, this is a free country and we can go wherever we want," Wormy said.

I ducked in to make sure my uncle was OK. He was a little ill about having to get up out of his chair in the middle of Dr. Phil's show, but otherwise, everything was good.

I went back outside to deal with Wormy.

"Do me a favor," I said to my uncle. "About every minute or so, holler like something's got hold of you; I want to mess with these idiots outside."

I put on my best worried look and headed back outside.

"Here's the deal," I said to Wormy. "That old guy in there fell while trying to get to the door when you knocked. He's lying on the floor in terrible pain; I think he broke his hip."

"OHHH!!!" my uncle yelled from the house. "THIS IS THE BIG ONE, ELIZABETH!!"

Wormy's splotchy complexion suddenly took on a more intense kaleidoscopic plaid quality. Being the brains of the operation, The Roadie beckoned Wormy back to the truck.

"We need to go," Roadie whispered to Wormy.

"JESUS, COME ON AND GET ME NOW!!" my uncle screamed from the house.

"Can you move your car so we can go?" Wormy asked.

"Nope, this is a free country and I can go wherever I want," I retorted. "Besides, the sheriff will probably need to get a statement from you two anyway."

"What sheriff?" Wormy and The Roadie asked in almost perfect unison.

"The one that's going to be called out here after I call an ambulance to get my uncle to a hospital," I calmly answered. "Is your employer bonded or will he or she lose the entire company once we get the lawyers involved?"

"I SEE A BRIGHT LIGHT!!" my uncle shrieked.

"Man, please; I need to keep plenty of space between me and law enforcement," Wormy said. "What can we do to make this go away?"

"I don't know — my uncle's insurance will cover the new hip, but his pain and suffering needs to be accounted for," I said. "How much money do you have on you?"

Between Roadie and The Worm, they produced $27, a pack of Nabs and a coupon for $3 off a box of Doral cigarettes.

"That's a good start but won't nearly be enough," I said while cutting my eyes toward the cooler full of steaks in the back of their truck.

"Does your uncle like steaks?" Wormy asked.

"Shoot yeah!" I said. "Half the time he doesn't even bother thawing or cooking them anymore; he bites into 'em like they're Nutty Buddys."

Suffice to say, my uncle's dogs will be having steak for supper from now till Easter. I jotted down Roadie and The Worm's license plate number before they drove away. I told them if so much as a Kleenex went missing over the next few months, I'd turn them in.

This is America and you can eat any kind of meat you want — be it cow, pig, chicken or cat. If you decide to eschew your local, health-department-inspected meat market to buy what is allegedly dead cow from two future wards of the state driving around in a truck that's more Bon-do than metal, then I salute you.

If you end up in the hospital with kangaroo poisoning, don't fret; I hear the pouch ends up being quite useful once you get used to it.

First day of hunting season and just counted 23 shots in 1 minute. Are you guys shooting at ants?

LA GRANGE MAN WAKES UP WITH BODY ON HIS FACE
FEBRUARY 7, 2013

According to Stevie Wonder, superstition ain't the way. Far be it from me to question the guy who wrote "For Once in My Life," but he might have been wrong about the superstition thing.

When Tax Deduction No. 2 started preschool last year, our household was under siege. We weren't dodging bullets or Leroy Bin Laden's collard bombs; we were under constant biological attack. Seemingly, every week, some new strain of cold, flu, or diphtheria showed up at our door with a sack of clothes tied around the end of a stick.

The weeks leading up to preschool this year were scary ones for me. I feared months of hacking, sneezing and wheezing were in our future. Even if the preschool of your choice is cleaned by Felix Unger and Hyacinth Bucket (pronounced "Bouquet"), it's still a giant Petri dish filled with germ-carrying agents disguised as cute little bags of cytoplasm.

This diapered army masks their germs with Cheerio breath and grape juice, which makes being sneezed on in the middle of a yawn palatable but still deadly.

This school year has been relatively calm in the sickness department — which is OK to think but not verbalize. After a couple of months free of thermometers, doctor visits and castor oil smoothies, I had to open my big mouth on Monday.

"Man, it's been nice not having any sick people in the house for a few months," I said as The Wife looked for a fax machine to throw at my head.

"DON'T TALK ABOUT IT!" she whispered in a strained tone.

Sure enough, within 24 hours, Tax Deduction No. 2 came down with a hacking cough reminiscent of someone trying to crank a flooded Packard Phantom.

That night, TD No.2 tossed, turned and barked incessantly. She'd sleep for 10 minutes or so before waking up to request "rrrrback" (translation: "Get up, step on the miniature but sharp toy I left in the hall — without cursing — and rub my back until I go back to sleep").

This back rubbing I speak of usually took a good five minutes to take effect. If you tried to phone it in by only doing it for two minutes, TD No.

2 would miraculously stop coughing long enough to look up at you like a horse who knows you've never ridden a horse before.

The second night — last night — was worse.

The hack remained the same, but now little, if any, sleep was being had. We put TD No. 2 in the bed with us thinking having Mama and Daddy close by might calm her down a little.

During all of this, TD No. 1 continued to populate the reservoir of drool she'd amassed on the left side of her pillow. We're in talks with officials from Iowa to build a pipeline from the edge of TD No. 1's pillow all the way to their drought-stricken farming communities.

Based on TD No. 1's 2013-14 nocturnal drool forecast, the USDA predicts rice production in the Midwestern U.S. to quadruple by March.

TD No. 2 tried to settle down by burrowing into my rib cage. After several minutes of trying to find just the right angle, she came to rest on my left shoulder. After about 20 minutes of this, my arm started to go numb. I attempted to ever so gently remove my arm from under her head but she was having none of it.

Eventually, my left arm went completely numb, which either meant TD No. 2 had cut of all blood flow or I was experiencing a cardiac event. When she sneezed directly into my armpit at 4:15 a.m., I realized I was still alive.

After a luxurious 21 minutes of sleep, TD No. 2 started flipping and flopping again. The demonic cough returned and offers of water or juice were met with what was surely some type of toddler profanity. This time, TD No. 2 laid her head at the foot of our bed, which meant from 1 a.m. to 3 a.m., I was kicked in the face with a cute but lethal pink footie-covered foot. Around 5 a.m. — an hour before I had to get up — she finally dozed off.

I awoke an hour later feeling as if my entire body had been used to Swiffer all of New Orleans after the Super Bowl. I opened my eyes but saw nothing but darkness. My entire face felt as if the weight of the world was bearing down on it.

As I pulled my hands to my face to rub my eyes, I realized TD No. 2 had shifted during the wee hours of the morning and her tummy was pressed up against my face like a bug on a windshield.

I now faced a dilemma. Should I remove her and risk waking her up, or do I burn a sick day and risk being suffocated by OshKosh B'gosh?

Eventually, The Wife pulled TD No. 2 off of my face and with about an hour of sleep under my belt, I went to work. I don't think the quality of my work will suffer, although those poor people who saw me walking around the courthouse before I realized I'd forgotten to put on pants this morning may need some grief counseling.

THE WAR ON VALENTINE'S DAY CONTINUES
FEBRUARY 14, 2013

Smell that? That's the smell of a million men breaking into a flop sweat over Valentine's Day.

The origins of Valentine's Day have nothing to do with chocolate covered diamonds or edible socks. The Orthodox Research Institute describes St. Valentine as "a priest (who lived) near Rome in about the year 270 A.D, a time when the church was enduring great persecution. His ministry was to help Christians escape persecution and to provide them the sacraments, such as marriage, which was outlawed by the Roman Empire at that time."

According to History.com, St. Valentine was eventually imprisoned by the Romans and sentenced to death. Before his execution, he supposedly wrote a farewell note to a girl he'd healed and signed it "from your Valentine."

Now how did we go from this to the buy 10 wings/get 10 wings free Valentine's Day special at Hooter's? Nothing screams tribute to a wrongly murdered holy man like a bunch of guys eating fried chicken parts delivered to them by buxom ladies who wouldn't be seen on the same planet with them if tips weren't part of the equation.

I haven't always been a Valentine's Scrooge. In kindergarten, I had two girlfriends at once, and they both knew about it. It was a groovy scene, man.

The other boys thought it was strange that I'd want to spend recess trying to play "McMillan & Wife" with Girlfriend 1 and Girlfriend 2 instead of kicking a stupid ball around.

I gave both of the girl's Valentine's cards, but it all went south when we started first grade. The other boys eventually realized kicking a half-inflated gym ball left over from the Reconstruction Era wasn't nearly as fulfilling as having a girlfriend. Not being the competitive type, I had no interest in jumping through hoops to win anyone's affection, thus beginning The Great Drought of 1980-89.

While in high school, some friends helped me construct a Valentine's Day road sign for The Girlfriend (who is now The Wife). The sign did not include any syrupy teenage sentiment and I didn't cover it with lyrics from a Night Ranger power ballad. The sign simply said "Happy Valentine's Day" with her name written under it. We attached the sign to a tobacco stick and placed it alongside the road on her route home from school.

It wasn't as grand a gesture as standing outside her window in the rain with a boombox blaring a Peter Gabriel song, but it got the point across.

The sign now rests in a cardboard tube in the Dawson Family Archives next to my Monsanto belt buckle, the suit James Brown wore on the Ed Sullivan Show and Michael Jackson's original nose.

When The Wife and I were dating, we were both usually working on Valentine's Day. I was a table maintenance specialist at a steak house, which meant on Valentine's Day, it was all hands on deck. The tips were fantastic on Valentine's Day because these putzoid men would leave big money in an attempt to show off in front of their dates.

The Wife was an in-demand baby sitter so she usually had a gig on Valentine's Day, as well. You may think this is unromantic, but we thought of it as a way to make the system work for us. The candy tastes just as good on Feb. 15 and its 50 percent cheaper, so take that, Whitman's.

As for the now, wasn't everyone was supposed to be tightening their belts? Aside from necessities such as food, clothing, shelter and smartphones that can perform mammograms, who has the disposable income for a big Valentine's Day woopty-doo? The National Retail Federation recently reported Americans will be spending nearly a billion dollars on Valentine's cards alone, not to mention $1.9 billion on flowers and $4.1 billion on jewelry.

Has this multi-year recession we've been going through just something Pamela Ewing dreamed?

I'm not against sending flowers; I'm just against the social pressure to do so. If I get my wife a flower, I tend to pick a random day when it's not expected. Notice I said "a flower," not "bushel of flowers." A single flower conveys the same sentiment as a barrel of them; everything need not be super-sized.

Just so the florists in our readership don't bust a vein, I'm not anti-flower. I just believe instead of spending $70 on flowers one day per year, why not spread that $70 out over the course of a year?

Surprise your sweetie with a flower on the anniversary of the pencil sharpener — just to keep her off guard. Send her a nice assortment of tulips on June 10 for no reason at all. You think L.L. Cool J's wife waits till Feb. 14 to send him a Chapstick bouquet? The man is going to lick himself to death.

If you want to join in with the rest of the lemmings (but just enough to get by), here's what you do: Stop at the gas station on your way home from work and buy a Snicker's bar the size of a small dog. Once home, place the candy bar in your freezer.

Later that night, light a few candles and carve the Snicker's up with a fork and steak knife. Dial up something romantic on the stereo like Marvin Gaye or Boxcar Willie and make a night of it. Candlelight, fine dining and romantic music.

If that doesn't work, pretend there's a crisis at work and sleep on your desk. It's nearly as comfortable as the couch and it'll save you some time the next morning.

O.J. SIMPSON OFFERS OLYMPIC MURDER SUSPECT SOME ADVICE
FEBRUARY 21, 2013

Double amputee and Olympic sprinter Oscar Pistorius can now add murder suspect to his resume.

On Feb. 13, Pistorius shot and killed his girlfriend at his South African home, alleging he mistook her for an intruder. Pistorius was subsequently charged with murder.

According to excerpts of an affidavit published by the Associated Press, Pistorius told the court, "I fail to understand how I could be charged with murder, let alone premeditated murder, as I had no intention to kill my girlfriend; I deny the aforesaid allegation in the strongest terms."

Pistorius claims he shot the would-be intruder through a closed door because he believed his girlfriend was still in bed. While investigators, a good portion of the public and two out of three kinder-gardeners believe these claims to be dubious at best, one expert on the subject has spoken out in support of the Olympic star.

"It really sounds like the local police have it in for Pistorius," said O.J. Simpson via telephone from the Lovelock Correctional Center in Nevada. "Just because he admitted to knowing she was in the house before he pulled the trigger doesn't mean he's guilty. If there's no sign of intent, you must acquit."

Simpson — currently serving a 33-year prison sentence for stealing his own sports memorabilia at gunpoint — doesn't believe the Pistorius episode will eclipse the lunacy of his own murder trial. When asked how difficult it's been adjusting to prison life, Simp-son unveiled the smile that launched a million Hertz rental cars and charmed Los Angeles domestic abuse investigators for years.

"I just look at it as another chapter in the book of my life," Simp-son said. "The first 400 times the cafeteria guy looked at me during breakfast and asked 'Does the Juice want any juice?' was tough. Thankfully for all of us, the knives in here are plastic."

After Simpson was acquitted of all murder charges in 1995, he spent much of the following decade searching the golf courses of Florida for the person or person(s) responsible for the death of his wife and her friend.

"I searched those golf courses high and low but couldn't find any tangible evidence related to the case," Simpson said while a fellow inmate slipped him a pack of smokes and half a bag of Skittles. "I did a lot of research for my role as Det. Nordberg in the 'Naked Gun' movies. I dusted every ball from Bay Hill to Mangrove Bay for prints but never found a match."

Although never formally charged, authorities labeled Simpson "a person of interest" in the 2010 death of "Naked Gun" star Leslie Nielsen. Nielsen's official cause of death was listed as pneumonia.

"O.J. once poured a cooler of Gatorade on Leslie's head during the wrap party for 'Naked Gun 3'," said co-star Priscilla Presley. "Les-lie subsequently caught a cold that he was never able to completely shake off. I'm pretty sure O.J. bumped off Elvis too, and probably Dan Rather."

Just as The Free Press was going to print, the Associated Press reported needles containing what may be testosterone were found in the bedroom shared by Pistorius and his girlfriend. Sounding excited, Simp-son called The Free Press to recant his earlier statements.

"He's as guilty as the day is long," Simpson said in an almost jubilant tone. "In fact, I believe he's the real killer I've been looking for all these years. He's all hopped up on testosterone and my wife had a habit of falling for the angry, athletic type. Yep; it was him!"

He continued, "Could you give me a ride? I've got reservations at The Sizzler with Greta Van Susteren."

THINGS ARE ABOUT TO GET SO BAD,
THE LAST DECADE WILL LOOK GOOD
FEBRUARY 26, 2013

Do not throw away this newspaper. By Friday, you may need it to insulate your clothing once the heat has been turned off or a tax on the sun has been enacted.

The bad news is the much talked-about mandatory federal budget cuts are on the way. The good news is things are about to get so bad, the drudgery of the last decade will be looked back upon as the good times once we're all living off government cheese and gas station lasagna.

The following is a partial list of services that will be affected throughout the United States if the sequester is allowed to fester:

TRANSPORTATION: By the end of March, all traffic lights could be reduced to only two colors — yellow and red. The Department of Transportation estimates eliminating the color green from traffic lights will save millions of dollars and produce a less amorous conglomeration of drivers.

Additionally, interstate highways will no longer feature painted lane markers. When asked how motorists would know if they were veering into another driver's lane, a DOT spokesman remarked, "That's what horns are for."

SENIOR CITIZENS: The old folks will continue to receive their medications, but not in the form to which they've become accustomed. The FDA has announced it will begin delivering the raw materials needed to manufacture popular medications such as Accupril and Diovan to all seniors, along with a detailed recipe book.

While most senior women enjoy baking, the government admits there could be some casualties among aging feminists who avoided the kitchen as if it were an STD.

EDUCATION: Schools will most likely be the hardest hit by the upcoming budget cuts. Instead of each student having his or her own books, each classroom will be given one book in each subject for the entire class to share.

To save money on school lunch programs and physical education courses, students will be required to hunt and dress wild game that will be released on their schools' playgrounds each day at noon. The energy the students burn while chasing down a deer or wild boar is expected to equal or surpass the amount generated by an entire year's worth of dodgeball.

Instead of selling candy as a school fundraiser, most elementary school students will now be selling timeshare rentals. The child who books the most condos will receive a pizza party while the child's underachieving classmates will be allowed to gnaw on any leftover crusts.

MILITARY: The brave men and women who allow us all to live in a moderately free society will no longer have access to the world's top weaponry. Soldiers will be required to relinquish all guns and tactical gear in exchange for a bag of sharpened sticks and rocks.

No longer able to pay for the fuel necessary to power jeeps and tanks, all military personnel will be required to use their own personal vehicles in combat situations. This loss of vital transportation and weaponry will be difficult to overcome, but the Pentagon believes the shock of being attacked by a batallion of soldiers throwing rocks and sticks from Honda Civics will at least confuse the enemy for several minutes.

TWO-YEAR-OLD HAS TO POTTY TRAIN
40-YEAR-OLD PARENT
FEBRUARY 28, 2013

Have you ever tried to teach a squirrel how to knit? I'm guessing it's easier than potty-training a 2-year-old.

I love my children and thank God for them daily, but every year around tax season my love for them reaches a fever pitch. Tax Deduction No. 1 and Tax Deduction No. 2 just seem a little bit cuter when we get to their section on the ol' 1040. I was so happy about it this year I let them stay in the house rent free for an entire week.

Along with the federally mandated financial benefits of having children, there are also occasions that make you think the life of a monk might not be all that horrible. Monks all wear the same clothes, so there's no pressure to keep up with fashion. Every monk I've ever seen in a movie has a shaved head, so you don't have to worry about going bald.

I'm also pretty sure most monks didn't spend nearly two hours of their Monday night in a bathroom trying to potty-train a child that's more stubborn than a pack of mules refusing to use email.

Around Thanksgiving, we'd actually strung a few potty successes together with TD 2, but by Christmas she was off the program. At the beginning of the process, a small bribe of a solitary Sweet Tart would get her to sit on the apparatus without a knife fight.

The dangled reward of another solitary Sweet Tart was usually enough to get the proper gears and pipes to present the product we needed. Apparently the kid has integrity, because as soon as she discovered she was being bribed, she shut the whole project down.

Over the last month, we've reorganized our efforts to get this kid in line with the water closet. To describe TD 2's attitude towards this new campaign as unenthusiastic would be an understatement of Herculean proportions. There has been much pulling of hair and gnashing of baby teeth over this potty situation.

If you take incident reports from local law enforcement at face value, you'd be led to believe this kid threw a television at me in protest. Bottom line: She ain't happy about it.

I'm happy to report that we've successfully worked through TD 2's anger issues, which leaves us with our last obstacle — her stubbornness. She'll sit on the old loo without a fuss, but that's all she'll do — sit. That's only one letter away from what needs to happen, but it might as well be the entire alphabet.

On Monday night TD 1 (8 years of age) convinced TD 2 (nearly 3 years of age) to sit on the potty. A lollipop may or may not have been used to entice cooperation, but either way it got done. After 10 minutes, I popped in to make sure everyone was still alive, which they were.

Another 10 minutes went by and I checked in to find TD 1 and The Wife now holding vigil around TD 2. Wanting to help, I sat on the edge of the tub and joined in the festivities.

I don't know how many families as a whole spend a large chunk of time together in the bathroom, but I'm hoping it counts as bankable penance. You haven't lived till you've sat on the edge of a tub for the majority of an evening waiting for a kid whose teeth are by this time swimming to just let it go.

If it were the good old days when we were on the well system, I would have turned on the faucet for a little encouragement. Someone in the room — not me — floated the idea of the "hand in warm water" trick, but knowing our luck, if it worked the kid would insist on using that method until she was 46.

Around the one hour mark, it was just me and TD 2. I fetched my laptop and pulled up some Three Stooges clips on the internet, thinking laughter might shake something loose. She laughed as expected but kept all the machinery on lock-down.

I stood up to see if I still had functionality in any of my limbs, and in doing so knocked a wash cloth on the floor. The cloth was still damp from the bath, so on a whim I balled it up and tickled the top TD 2's foot with it. Miracle of miracles, the floodgates opened and the drought was over.

Feeling prideful that I was a good parent or at least still more stubborn than my offspring, I went outside to get some fresh air. I stood at the edge of my carport and gazed at the stars that had decided to make an appearance after a few hours of rain.

It was pitch dark outside, but the breeze blowing through the trees was comforting. After a good minute or so of this, what sounded like 17 deer galloped through the tiny pond that formed at the edge of my yard.

Hearing those deer thunder through the yard with such violence and then burst into the woods as if a repo man was after their schnoinkels did more than break my contemplative mood … it honestly nearly scared me to death. Also, it pretty much undid the previous 40 years of potty training I'd undergone. In an instant, I went from semi-pro to T-ball.

Maybe TD 2 can help me get my mojo back. The student has become the master.

THE DEVIL REALLY EXISTS — AND HE
MADE ME A SAMMICH
MARCH 5, 2013

I don't know if it's the roofing insulation in the chicken nuggets or the hormones added to the milk, but something is turning our populous into a country of imbeciles.

For the record, I'm not pretending to be immune to this condition. Just now, I had to check the spelling of two words in that opening sentence and neither of them were "populous" or "imbeciles." In my defense, that type of stupidity doesn't affect anyone but me. Thanks to spell-check, no one has to know that I tried to spell "milk" with a "q."

What I'm talking about today, brothers and sisters, is the kind of stupidity that cannot be contained. I'm talking about the type of stupidity that causes an otherwise functional human being to wear a short sleeve shirt and Bermuda shorts — even when his Eskimo neighbors won't leave their igloo without putting on an extra layer.

I'm talking about the kind of stupidity that drives a person to post a picture of themselves smoking a joint the size of a fire hydrant on the Internet and then wondering why no one will hire them.

Saturday, I found myself in the middle of a large department store in the tri-county area. I won't say which store it was, but they seem to believe it's perfectly normal to paint a red circle around a dog's eye and film him frolicking with models in their commercials.

Interestingly, the dog is actually red and they have to paint his entire body white except for the ring around his eye.

Before I drove to the store, I visited the store's website to make sure the item I wanted was in stock — which it was. When I get to the proper department, the 'roided-up Doogie Hows-er behind the counter seemed to be generating electricity for the entire store through his open-mouth gum chewing.

I haven't heard that much smacking since Tom and Roseanne Arnold's honeymoon video went viral.

After doing everything short of throwing a shopping cart through the glass display case he was standing behind, I got Chewbacca's attention. I told him what I was looking for — and he did something that will probably land me in the electric chair one day: he started talking over me before I could finish the sentence.

"We don't (smack) carry that (smack) brand," Chewy said.

I didn't have any gum, but I attempted assimilation.

"I checked (smack) your store's (smack) website this morning and (smack) it says this store has four (smackity-smack) in stock," I said. "(Smack smack)."

Chewy then rolled his eyes and let out an exasperated gush of air from his Wrigley's spearmint-flavored pie hole. In an attempt to prove I was mistaken, he pulled his "smart" phone from his pocket while grinning like a young Jedi who was about to kick Yoda in the head with his knowledge.

But wouldn't you know it, Chewy was wrong. His little phone told him the same thing I did, which somehow made it easier for him to accept. That poor phone looked like the guy had been dating it exclusively for a number of years.

I made a mental note to write a letter to Amnesty International as soon as I got home.

On the way out of town, I stopped at a fast food restaurant in order to take advantage of a buy one/get one free coupon on a chicken sammich. The plan was to give the guy at the drive-thru window the coupon and $4.26 (exact change, because I'm good like that) and deliver the sammiches to the wife and assorted Tax Deductions back home.

Try as I might to lead a clean, uncluttered life, it doesn't seem like it's in the cards. Charles Baudelaire said "the greatest trick the devil ever played was convincing the world that he did not exist" — but I know he exists. The devil's most recent choice of earthly vehicle is a skinny little dude working the drive-thru at a tricounty restaurant.

Immediately after handing the wormy but well-groomed kid my coupon and exact change, I was thinking I'd made this guy's day a little easier. Thanks to my thoughtful gesture, he wouldn't have to waste any time or brain power on coming up with the correct change for a $5 bill. As he reached to hand me the bag of food with a sparkle in his eye, a smile on his face and not an ounce of trepidation, he said the following:

"Here ya go, big guy."

My automatic response was to smile, but within a second or two a rush of heat flew up my neck and out to my ears. Without changing my facial expression, I looked back at the wormy kid who had probably just started bathing without assistance that week.

"Big guy?" I said back to him.

"Uh, er, I didn't mean to make fun ..." he said.

"Were you making fun of me?" I asked.

"No I mean, you know, I was just thinkin' ..." he said, his voice trailing off again.

"You mean, you actually put some thought into that before you said it out loud?" I asked.

"Oh, I'm sorry, I just meant you could be, I don't know ..." he said, as sweat started to bead along his wormy forehead.

"You think it's fun to goof on people with a glandular problem?" I asked.

"Oh my gosh ... I didn't know you had a glandular problem!" he said.

"Who said I have a glandular problem? I just asked if you made fun of people who did," I said.

By this time, the kid is starting to cry a little, so I drove off. On one hand, it was fun to deflate whatever air of misguided confidence was coursing through that little demon's veins.

On the other hand, it made me realize I need to abstain from comfort food for the next few weeks.

Confidence in the hands of a genius like the guy who won on Jeopardy for six months straight or the guy who successfully landed a plane in the Hudson river a few years back is a great thing. Confidence in the hands of doltish, oafish skull-renters is like a deadly missile with a busted guidance system.

If you or someone you know is numb from the neck up, please contact a clergyman, police officer or trusted family member. Only you can prevent someone from trying to fax a $100 bill to the utility company as payment.

New Gallup poll shows 4 out of 5 Americans don't care about being apolitical.

LENOIR COUNTY CHOOSES NOT TO OBSERVE DAYLIGHT SAVINGS
MARCH 7, 2013

"Spring forward, fall back/tell me where the hoochies at," sang Clay Aiken on his 2004 hit "This Is The Night," a song inspired by Aiken's missed audition for "Rambo: The Musical."

Aiken reportedly missed that audition because he forgot to realign his clock with daylight-saving time. While depriving the world of the chance to witness Aiken don military garb and sing "I'm No Tourist" and "He'd Do It for Me," many people still believe daylight savings time serves a purpose.

According to www.usuallyaccurate.com, daylight-saving time was invented by a guy in New Zealand who wanted more daylight for his work involving telescopes. As time went on, governments around the world implemented the practice under the auspices of saving energy and making the attendance of after-work activities tied to retail more palatable to the masses.

Retailers have embraced the daylight-saving system with open arms, while animal rights groups continually call foul. Citing the annual admittance of thousands of roosters to psychiatric wards immediately following daylight-saving time, animal caregivers believe the idea is outmoded.

"Those roosters are used to people milling around shortly after their sunrise crowing is finished," said Dr. Drew Thompson of the Nick Searcy School of Veterinary Medicine in Cullowhee. "They think people can't hear them, so they crow louder and louder until their vocal cords shut down. One guy brought in a bantam rooster last year that strained so hard he laid four eggs and a cup of coffee."

While most of the United States will be moving their clocks ahead one hour at 2 a.m. on March 10, Lenoir County leaders have decided to bow out of this year's observance.

"We've done it for years, and all it does is make people cranky and late for a few weeks every March," said Chris Blizzard, chairman of the Kinston/Lenoir County Department of Buying and Selling. "If I don't get my full eight hours of sleep every night, I'm just not The Blizz."

Blizzard recently oversaw an emergency meeting of the Kinston/ Lenoir County Dept. of B.S., which yielded a 5-1 vote in favor of amending the county's daylight-saving policy, along with a 6-0 vote in favor of crunchy over smooth.

"We weren't able to totally abolish daylight-saving, but we put a good dent in it," Blizzard said. "To pacify the one politically correct priapism on the board, Lenoir County will be observing daylight saving on a rotating schedule of one day per week."

According to a Dept. of B.S. press release, the first four dates all Lenoir County businesses and government institutions will observe daylight-saving are March 11 (Monday), March 19 (Tuesday), March 27 (Wednesday), and April 4 (Thursday).

"This sounds like a fantastic idea," said no one representing Lenoir County Schools. "We don't think altering the sleep time of our students, staff and parents by one hour will have any negative effects on our day-today operations. We're sure we won't see a spike in the number of parents who decide to home-school their children."

Residents who believe they'll have trouble remembering which days to spring forward, fall back or kneel are invited to download the free "Lenoir Time" app at thirdofnever.com. The app will automatically adjust all timekeeping mechanisms such as clocks, televisions and pacemakers to current Lenoir County time.

Those who do not use any type of smartphone are encouraged to join their local Boy or Girl Scout troop and learn how to tell time by scratching a rock with a stick and holding it up to the sun.

GROWING DEER POPULATION TO BE
THINNED BY U.S. DRONES
MARCH 19, 2013

Walter Clemmons of the Piedmont Wildlife Association says the instances of deer trespassing on military bases have quadrupled over the last decade.

"Last year, a deer made its way onto a Seymour Johnson landing strip," Clemmons said. "The deer collided with a jet just as it was about to take off. The pilot was OK, but the plane and the deer were totaled."

The Seymour John-son incident is just one of dozens, according to information obtained from the State Department. A recently declassified memo stated that back in a December a deer found its way into a Cobra helicopter at Cherry Point. Apparently, the helicopter door was left ajar, and a deer that was seeking shelter crawled in and laid down in the back.

The flight crew didn't discover the deer until they were flying several thousand feet over the White Oak River in Swansboro. Once the deer realized what was going on, it reportedly kicked and bit everyone in the helicopter with extreme prejudice, all the while voiding its bowels in an explosive yet impressive manner.

"I was out on the river that morning with my grandson," said Jack Dawson of Kinston. "When he saw that deer fall out of the sky into the river, he was really confused. I told him it was a reindeer that Santa had caught stealing toys. I also told him chocolate milk comes from brown cows, and that the crowd that collects stray cats turns them into Vienna sausage."

The declassified memo states a plan to allow unmanned drones to shoot any deer located within two miles of any military base. Although portions of the memo have been blacked out, the remaining text seems to indicate the drones will be spraying doe scent from the sky in an attempt to draw bucks into clear view.

Although it may seem pleasant enough, the thought of a flying robot firing deer urine upon the earth doesn't sit well with everyone. Groups such as PETA (People for the Ethical Treatment of Animals) and HARP (Humans Against Raining Pee) believe this is just another example of the government sticking it's nose where it doesn't belong.

"Being an avid hunter, I never thought PETA and I would be on the same side of an argument," said Dewey Crowe of Snow Hill. "Those little bottles of deer scent I buy every year are expensive; I can't compete with Optimus Prime spewing out gallons of the stuff from the sky. This economy is so bad that even with a degree I can't get a job that pays more than $11 an hour, but the government has enough money to fill Robbie the Robot with deer urine and let him water the entire tri-county area like it was the 12th hole at Augusta?"

During her 2008 vice presidential campaign, former gubernatorial babe Sarah Palin received much criticism from Obama supporters for shooting bears from a helicopter in Alaska. Asked why her detractors seem to have no problem with unmanned drones doing essentially the same thing to deer, Pal-in's answer evoked the ghosts of William F. Buckley and George Will.

"Geez, ya know using drones to kill deer is very un-American," Palin said. "The deer should be killed with a Chinese-made SKS rifle by a person flying in a helicopter that was made in Canada."

Operation Rain Deer is scheduled to begin Oct. 27.

LOCAL BUSINESS ACCUSED OF DISCRIMINATION
MARCH 26, 2013

A local gym has been accused of discrimination — and the accuser is an Olympic medal winner.

"Between endorsements and speaking engagements, I've done well over the years," said Matt Splitz, 63. "My wife and I recently moved to the area, so I figured the best way to meet people was to get a part-time job at a local gym."

Splitz says he responded to a help wanted ad posted by Dumbbell's Gym of Piles Boulevard in Kinston.

"According to the ad, the gym management was looking for a part-time trainer with a sports background," Splitz said. "If having won eight gold medals and one bronze in the 1972 Olympics for swimming wasn't enough, I also worked as a personal assistant/ bong loader for Michael Phelps in 2008 and 2012."

While most Olympians tend to stay in shape after their glory years, Splitz decided he loved pancakes more than squat thrusts.

"I had the most sadistic swim coach on the planet," Splitz said as he held out a mirror to see if he was wearing pants. "If I even looked at a bowl of ice cream he'd make me swim an extra five laps. I swore that if I ever got out of the swim game I'd eat whatever I wanted, whenever I wanted."

And eat Matt Splitz has. As of this writing — from a raw tonnage perspective — Splitz is hovering around the 515-pound mark.

"I figure anyone coming into Dumbbell's looking for a trainer would rather be led by someone who identifies with their struggle," Splitz said. "Being a tad on the heavy side myself, I'd rather work out with someone who's put a few railroad cars of cookies away in his day. Those skinny little trainers with their perfect abs, shaved backs and clipped nails don't know what it's like to be rolled back into the ocean by a bunch of meddling do-gooders when you're just trying to soak up some sun."

"SOME sun? That dude could soak it all up and have room for the moon and a few rings of Saturn too," said Richard Little, manager of Dumbbell's Gym. "If Matt Splitz does so much as a jumping jack in here, we'll have a new fault line within the hour."

Little said he initially thought he was being set up for a prank when Splitz applied for the job.

"I just knew I was on one of those hidden camera shows," Little said. "I kept looking to see if Ryan Seacrest was hiding under Splitz's shirt."

While researching Kinston, Splitz heard stories of college graduates being turned away from potential employers because having a degree meant they'd want to be paid a living wage. He says he never thought his weight would keep him from getting a job.

"Not only did they not give me the job, they wouldn't even let me in the building," Splitz said. "That smarmy manager said he was afraid one of the moons that was orbiting me might damage their building."

Splitz said American society is constructed to keep people overweight.

"From an early age, we're told to get an education so we can get a good job," Splitz said. "Once we get that job, the ones of us who are lucky enough not to be laid off will get slammed with work, thus only giving us a few minutes for meals. What's the solution? Just look to the hundreds of fast food commercials we're inundated with on a weekly basis.

"After we've ballooned up to the point someone is tying a rope to our ankles outside a Macy's on Thanksgiving, they shoot a few gym commercials our way."

When asked who "they" were, Splitz was vague in his response.

"I heard it on a radio talk show," Splitz said. "The Bilderberg's and Kanye West are tied up in it somehow."

Nowhere in the Dumbbell's employee handbook is an employee's weight, girth, circumference or ability to clap their hands mentioned. When presented with this information, the Dumbbell's corporate office deferred comment to their attorneys, who in turn issued the following statement:

"No comment."

WOMAN DENIES PLACING LINGERIE, CIGARETTES
IN EASTER EGGS
APRIL 2, 2013

All Julee Cruise wanted to do was host a nice little Easter egg hunt for the neighborhood children.

"Our congregation was supposed to have an Easter egg hunt after church on Sunday but it was rained out," Cruise said. "When the sun peeked out later that afternoon, I decided to put together an impromptu egg hunt."

Cruise sent her husband Angelo to the store to pick up all the Easter candy he could find, although the pickings were slim.

"It looked like a crime scene in there," Angelo said. "There were a few hints of that green Easter hay strewn on a few shelves and maybe one chocolate bunny with its tail bitten off, but that was it."

When her husband returned from the store with only a Larry The Cable Guy/Git-Er-Done rabbit ear bottle opener and a pack of Peeps lemon-flavored hair extensions, Julee swung into action.

"I called the parents and grandparents of every child that was coming to our Easter egg hunt," Cruise said. "I told them whatever candy they had — be it a bowl of peppermint that's been in the living room for six years or a bag of Werther's that currently being used as a door stop — to bring it over immediately."

Within minutes, people started showing up at Cruise's door with candy.

"Everyone came into our kitchen and started filling plastic toy egg shells with their candy," she said. "The sense of community that permeated the room was almost overpowering."

Several of the parents in attendance told The Free Press they were touched by the kindness of the Cruise family.

"This was a great gesture," said Sheryl Lee, 41, mother of 5-year-old Donna. "Our daughter was disappointed when the church festivities were canceled, but this event has cheered her up."

Will Munson, 52, said, "My kids are off at college; I'm very lonely."

Putting on the egg hunt changed up the Cruise's Sunday routine, to say the least.

"Usually on a Sunday afternoon I put on a pair of sweatpants and watch a ballgame on TV until I pass out and wake up four hours later in a pool of my own drool," Angelo Cruise said with an unsettling smile. "But this ... with the kids screamin' and causing hundreds of dollars worth of damages to our landscaping to find $4 worth of candy? This is much better.

"No, really, it's great."

The only hitch in an otherwise successful endeavor came when the parents of few children who attended the Easter egg hunt called Cruise to complain about some of the items found in their eggs.

"A woman called in and said her kid's toy eggs were filled with dyed cigarettes and frozen shrimp," Cruise said. "Another mother fought back tears as she recounted the numerous questions posed by her 5-yearold son after he pulled a garter belt from a green plastic egg. They told him it was a slingshot, so now he's running around the neighborhood trying to fling rocks at birds with women's lingerie."

The offensive items have been traced back to Paulette Burroughs, 39, of La Grange.

"They invited some of my crowd to the festivities so I just wanted to help out," Burroughs said. "They shouldn't be upset about the lingerie. That garter came in a pack of 10 I bought at South of The Border back in '86, and it's made from a type of poly/cotton/asbestos blend that's illegal in the United States now, so it's quite valuable."

Along with boasting of the garments rare pedigree, Burroughs says it's also durable.

"That garter was part of my wardrobe rotation during the years I dated Porter Wagoner and Martin Lawrence at the same time," Bur-roughs said. "That thing has seen more action than a trampoline in a kangaroo preserve."

Cruise said clergy from all over the country were flying in to counsel the 5-year-old boy who found Bur-roughs' inappropriate items on Sunday.

"He's started wearing his robe around the house all day," the little boy's mother said. "Just a few minutes ago, he told me he wanted a subscription to 'Maxim' for his birthday."

KINSTON RANKS THIRD IN WORST DRIVING
CITIES IN AMERICA
APRIL 4, 2013

The American Auto Club has released its annual "Worst Cities to Drive In" report — and Kinston made the top five.

"We take every city in the nation and divide them into regions, and Kinston came in just behind Atlanta and Charlotte," AAC president Roger L. Darvacet said. "Our formula is based on road conditions, the layout of the city and — most importantly — the driving demeanor of the community as a whole."

When it comes to road conditions, Darvacet said most areas are feeling the effects of budget cuts.

"Most of the cities we studied are broke or, at the least, not signing their name on outgoing checks to buy a little time," Darvacet says. "One of our surveyors lost a Honda Accord to a pothole on Herritage Street. The driver was able to climb out, but the insurance company said it would be cheaper to replace the vehicle instead of bringing in Halliburton to lift the car out of the hole."

While the report suggests the local level of street/road disrepair in the K is on a par with other southern cities of the same size, it also praises the layout of Kinston.

"Many members of our team reported being able to leave one Bojangles', make only one turn and end up at another Bojangles' in under 40 seconds," Darvacet said. "Also, the members of our team who were robbed or assaulted during their Kinston assignment found the hospital and police department easy to find with ample parking at each."

The AAC data suggests Kinston's drivers are what set the city apart.

"Our team observed several dozen cases of people diddling with cell phones at stop lights," Darvacet said. "This is probably the reason Kinston has more reported cases of sprained middle fingers per capita than any city outside of Salt Lake or Detroit. We observed one elderly lady — riddled with arthritis — who had taped a picture of an elongated middle finger and placed it on the back of a paper funeral home fan.

"She raised that thing to more drivers than a hooker working the

NASCAR circuit."

The report also describes legions of small cars with intensely loud mufflers being a particular problem.

"We found many drivers in the area favored small cars that were only large enough to hold the driver, a cheap static-laden stereo and a muffler that emitted the noise of a thousand mosquitoes mating," Darvacet said. "The drivers of these cars like to drive erratically and rev their vehicle's little sewing machine engines while stopped at red lights.

"This means they either want to race the 69-year-old grandmother in the minivan next to them, or they want to be sure everybody notices their vehicle's Rorschach pink/green/ orange paint pattern."

One phenomenon that seems to be specific to Kinston is the dreaded "two-car drag."

"A two-car drag occurs when two vehicles each drive 47 mph — side-by-side — in a 55 mph zone, thus blocking anyone trying to drive like a normal person," Darvacet said. "This was observed multiple times on U.S. 70 and N.C. 11 — usually at 7:50 a.m., when people were trying to get to work."

He continued, "We've found the majority of these people to be mentally unstable or part of the aggra-fetish community, which is a group of people who can only achieve physical stimulation if they've somehow done something to aggravate everyone around them. David Lee Roth and Kanye West are the group's charter members; Lady Gaga is in charge of refreshments."

Although a vehicle's decor was not part of the formula used in the AAC's calculations, Darvacet's team mentioned several items in the report's footnote section.

"You could glean a person's life story by reading the stickers on the back of their vehicle," Darvacet said. "Many people spent money on stickers to make sure the whole world knew where they stood on subjects such as drug legalization, politics, what not to do if the vehicle was a-rockin', gun control, sports, ladies sandals and — most importantly — which brand of truck young boys should relieve themselves on in public."

SUIT WORN IN MOVIE FOUND AT SPCA THRIFT STORE
APRIL 9, 2013

On Saturday, the SPCA Thrift Store held a yard sale. No, they didn't sell their yard, but anything you could fit into a bag was yours for $5.

There is something about thrift stores that has always fascinated me. To me, thrift stores are museums for the working class. Just think of the sociological data that can be gathered by taking a stroll though the discarded clothes, furniture, books and music of previous generations.

In 2013, where else could you purchase a medium sized "Where's The Beef?" T-shirt, a Milli Vanilli cassette single and a copy of "Breakdancing Two: Electric Boogaloo" on VHS tape?

Up yours, Walmart.

By all accounts the yard sale was a success, thus allowing the poorly-funded SPCA to keep their hostel of dogs, cats and kangaroos housed and fed for a little while longer. The usual crop of psycho bargain hunters were on hand ("Hey, is 25 cents the absolute lowest you can go on this couch?"), but one smart shopper walked away with an antique that could end up being worth several thousand dollars.

"I bought it for my husband," said Con-stance Hollowell of La Grange. "He's into all types of music, be it blues from the 1920s, jazz from the 1960s or experimental rock music from last week. His collection is out of control, but since I have more shoes than Thom McAn, I don't really have a pump to stand on."

The item in question is a suit believed to have been worn by one Francis Albert Sinatra in the original "Ocean's 11" movie, released in 1960.

"There's a tag sewn into the inside pocket of the jacket that reads, 'heist scene, Ocean's 11, Frank Sinatra'," Hollowell said. "The suit is grey and smells like Jack Daniels, so I'm pretty sure it's authentic."

Other items found in the suit include a poker chip from the Sands Hotel and Casino, a room service bill signed by Ava Gardner, and an invitation to the 1959 bris of Sammy Davis Jr.

Miller Gaffney is known to millions as the trollop with the short skirts and ability to turn one-syllable words into Shakespearean sonnets on the PBS series "Market Warriors."

"Conservatively, I'd say this suit would go for $50,000 at auction,"

Gaffney said. "If I were buying this item from a man with no backbone, he'd probably let me talk him down to $6. Then I'd pretend I was made of glass, pooch out my bottom lip a little and ask him to carry it to my car for me. He wouldn't even notice that I was carrying a purse that weighs more than the suit would if Sinatra were in it."

While no one seems to be questioning the authenticity of the item, just how a suit worn in a movie by Frank Sinatra over 50 years ago made it to the little slice of purgatory known as Kinston is a mystery. Fortune cookie writer and former car cranker for the Bonanno crime family Benmont Tench believes he has the answer.

"Sinatra was tight with Sam Giancana of the Chicago outfit," Tench said from his home in Jones County. "When they brought Giancana back to the United States in 1974, he became an informant for the FBI. According to the FBI, Giancana was assassinated while cooking sausage and peppers — just before he was supposed to testify about what part the mob and the CIA played in the Kennedy assassination. That story was a hoax."

Tench contends the feds put Giancana in the witness protection program and hid him in Deep Run.

"Giancana was a store greeter at Walmart," Tench said. "Sinatra would send him care packages filled with food, booze and clothes. He probably sent the 'Ocean's 11' suit without even knowing what it was."

Tench says Giancana died in a stand collapse at a 1992 tractor pull in La Grange.

Hollowell says her husband plans to sell the suit on eBay at some point, but right now he's wearing it around the house.

"The Sinatra Capitol Years box set has been on rotation in our living room ever since this suit came into our lives," Hollowell said. "He slept in that suit the night I brought it home."

As The Free Press prepared to leave the Hollowell residence, from behind a closed bathroom door a flush was followed by the refrain, "I faced it all, and stood tall, and did it MYYYYYYYYY WAAAAAAY!"

MAKING A BUCK OFF OF THE BOSTON BOMBING
APRIL 18, 2013

On Monday, I had an important conversation with The Wife and Tax Deduction No. 1. We talked about dandelions — or more specifically — the gamma ray-laden strain that are currently overrunning my yard and apparently couldn't be killed with a flamethrower.

"Now if I cut the grass while they just have the yellow flower on top, it won't spread the seeds when it's cut, right?" I asked.

"They only spread when they have the poofy things on top and you blow on them," said Tax Deduction No. 1.

"You have to dig them up by the root; that's the only way to stop them," said The Wife.

"Can't I just douse the area with Roundup and kill them before they get the poofy things on top?" I said.

The poofy thing discussion went on for a few minutes with no real resolution. We decided to use the excess dandelions as pillow stuffing. Our first shipment should go out to all the organic stores in early May.

After we broke huddle, I turned on the computer and saw photos of what happened at the Boston Marathon. Within minutes, video of the explosions was all over the Internet and TV. For the rest of the night, the same information was repeated over and over again.

The following day, everyone in the journalism business was hit with a deluge of emails from public relations firms trying to grab air time or ink for their clients. Before we go any further, you should all know that I have no issue with anyone making a dollar. I believe those hippies who demanded to be let in to the Isle of Wight Festival for free should never been allowed to reproduce.

Anyone who thinks all you need is love should see the face of the usually nice woman at Kinston Public Utilities when I try to pay my electric bill in hugs.

All that being said, the crass jackassory that was on display by the media and those who feed it this week makes the coverage of the O.J. Simpson trial look subtle. The following are excerpted examples of the actual emails that were sent to members of the press on Tuesday:

Email No. 1:

Two explosions near the finish line of the Boston Marathon on Monday have resulted in deaths and injuries to runners and spectators at the event that draws crowds of 500,000.

Gregory Jantz, Ph.D. is a nationally recognized psychologist and mental health counselor with over 25 years experience who specializes in emotional counseling, depression, stress disorders and grief recovery. He is a go-to media source for commentary on national as well as international traumatic events in the news. Dr. Jantz is the author of several mental health books including, Healing the Scars of Emotional Abuse and Moving Beyond Depression.

Dr. Jantz is available immediately for interviews via phone or email if you're interested — just let me know!

Email No. 2

Hi Jon,

In light of the tragedy which occurred in Boston yesterday, Michael Finkelstein, M.D. wanted to personally offer his guidance and counseling for any stories you might need insight on. He is camera ready and is available immediately for interview.

Camera ready? I can't think of 10 profanities that could accurately describe the ugliness of that statement.

I didn't make either of those emails up. Someone in an office somewhere makes their living waiting for catastrophes to happen so they can get their clients some air time and hopefully sell a few books.

Listen, I felt a bit queasy putting my own book out so close to Christmas as I don't think the original intent of the holiday was commerce-based. After seeing these jackals at work in the wake of the Boston tragedy, I'm beginning to feel almost saintly.

Somebody somewhere needs to be slapped with a muddy shovel for allowing this sort of thing to become commonplace. Since the news is now on 24 hours a day, I guess they need something to fill the time.

Ted Turner and his mustache could probably be blamed for this non-stop news culture, but then again, maybe the people who are happy to watch the same story repeated more than "The Contest" episode of Seinfeld should be held accountable as well.

Camera ready. The doctor is camera ready. In my heart, I've got to believe if some twit said this to Edward R. Murrow, he'd lean over and put out his cigarette on their forehead. Then again, during a live newscast Murrow asked Liberace when he was going to find a nice girl and get married, so what do I know?

New cover band Ringo Unchained performs Beatles songs in the style of Van Halen.

DEER TICKS, FELONIES ALL PART OF
BIRTHDAY CELEBRATION
APRIL 23, 2013

I never thought I'd live to see it, but Tax Deduction No. 2 turned 3 on Monday.

I arrived at TD 2's preschool a few minutes early, so I peeped around the door to see how she acted away from her parents. To my amazement, as other parents showed up to pick up their kids, TD 2 picked up each kid's book sack and handed it to the corresponding parent.

At home if we hand her a few pairs of socks and ask her to put them in her room, they end up in our mailbox.

That she has the wherewithal to memorize the face of each child's parent and their book sack tells me she's ramrodding us on the whole sock deal — although it was funny watching our mailman pretend to like the size 3 pink butterfly socks he thinks we gave him for Christmas.

When we ask her a question at home, TD 2 usually responds in a series of clicks and clacks — sometimes tapping out a message with a stick upside down on the dining room table. Today at school I saw her explain to a classmate why it's better to get any and all felonies out of your system before turning 16.

Being that it was the kid's "berfday," I stopped at the Dollar Store to procure her one of them helium-filled aluminum foil balloons. I let the girl of honor pick the one she wanted, and as I'm sure I don't have to tell you she got into an altercation with the balloon within seconds.

I broke up the fight by holding up a copy of the latest Guns 'N Roses album that was sitting on a nearby shelf. Just looking at the album made TD 2 cover her ears in fright, thus freeing the balloon to take its rightful place on the store ceiling.

I could have held up a James Blunt CD, but I didn't want the poor girl to be sick on her birthday.

There was only one cashier on duty, but mercifully the store was bereft of customers. In fact, the only other customers in the place were shopping for a kid's birthday as well — and they were in front of me in line at the check-out counter. The old me would've immediately started dreading whatever chunk of check-out hell was about to come my way, but over the last few months I've had good experiences at cash registers.

Recently at Aldi, an older gentleman who had enough groceries in his cart to feed a Kardashian's ego for a week saw me standing behind him with one lowly pineapple and waved me ahead of him. To pay this act of kindness forward, I walked up to an elderly lady and asked if she'd like me to carry her groceries for her.

Apparently the poor woman's hearing aid was on the fritz, but her canister of Frontiersman Bear Attack pepper spray was firing on all cylinders. After explaining to the woman and the responding officer and EMS personnel that I was just trying to help with her groceries, the remorseful woman apologized and gave me a piece of Werther's candy. Nothing says "I'm sorry" like a piece of caramel-flavored granite.

Back to my current check-out line situation ... the people in front of us were apparently buying items for a kid's birthday party as well. These people had five of those helium-filled aluminum foil balloons, a 3-liter jug of carbonated punch imported (I'm guessing) from Bogota, and some party hats. Also in their cart were five large glass items that were either giant candle holders or brandy snifters.

I once drank some ginger ale from a brandy snifter and being inexperienced with that type of delivery vessel accidentally inhaled two nostrils worth of Canada Dry. I covered the faux pas gracefully, but the resulting sneeze did result in chunks of Gouda and Conran Christmas crackers being embedded permanently in a nearby curtain.

I'll give the Dollar Store employee credit for thoroughness, because she meticulously wrapped each piece of glass in old newspapers as if it were chunks of the Maltese Falcon. I've seen newborns handled with less care than these pieces of $1 retail glass, of which I have no problem. The problem came when the total due was $38.14 and the customer decided to pay in $1 bills.

In the middle of counting the stack of $1 bills for the third time, the customer looked at me as I gnawed on the edge of my shopping cart as if I was somehow annoying her.

"I'm sorry, OK, I just got paid and I have a lot of ones," she said. "That mean look on your face won't get me to count any faster."

"I'd hoped that those three years you spent in fourth grade would have handled that," I said. "I've always wondered: Does an employee of the strip club re-coat the pole with Pam at the beginning of each shift or do the dancers have to do it themselves?"

Eventually the cashier is handed the stack of ones and determines she needs 14 cents more from the customer.

"I think I have 14 cents," said the customer who then began to give herself a full-body cavity search that would shame a Tijuana border agent. After four minutes, all she found on her person was a pair of salad tongs and a deer tick. She then handed the cashier another $1 bill to cover the 14 cents. Of course the cashier then discovered she was out of change and we had to stand there until an armored truck from Fort Knox showed up with a stack of dimes, but at least we got our balloon.

Tonight we'll temporarily lift the fruit/ vegetable policy and treat TD 2 to a feast of macaroni and cheese with chicken tenders, topped off with a birthday cake depicting her hero, defense attorney Johnnie Cochran. Between the presents, the carbs and the sugar, we'll be lucky if we don't end up in the holding cell.

LA GRANGE MAN ATTENDS GEORGE W. BUSH LIBRARY OPENING
APRIL 30, 2013

Through several twists of fate (and an uncle who works at Southern Methodist University), I was invited to attend the opening of the George W. Bush Presidential library last week

Save for the occasional sojourn to the great state of New Jersey to rock and/or roll a little bit, I don't like being away from home. But, when given the chance to be in the presence of five U.S. presidents, I jumped — or at least hopped — at the opportunity.

Also, Billy Gibbons from ZZ Top owes me money, so I figured, two birds/one stone.

Being a Methodist myself, I was impressed with the facilities at SMU, although I was a little disappointed by the absence of a covered dish dinner. How you can have 12,000 Methodists on one piece of land and not have a plate of chicken at every water fountain is an abomination. At least show me something in a dumpling.

Having worked at Joyner Library at ECU during my college days, I consider myself to be fairly knowledgeable in all things Dewey Decimal. The fact that several friends and I moved up through the ranks at Joyner with excellent performance reviews but weren't even allowed to interview for any full time positions upon graduation in no way made us bitter.

That we had to train the person they brought in from Minnesota — who'd never actually worked in a library — facilitated the bitterness quite nicely, though.

The GWB Library periodical section was filled with articles from The National Review and The Weekly Standard. To anyone believing the reading materials were biased towards publications deemed conservative, many issues of Mother Jones and The Progressive were easily attainable by prying up every third floor tile in the library's lobby. Patrons wishing to pull up the tiles will need a rotary hammer, which are available for purchase from the Halliburton Gift Shop for $7,500.

On the second floor were several rows of classified intelligence documents labeled "Bin Laden, 2001" that were in pristine condition and don't seem to have ever been opened. In a nod to the banking crisis that occurred near the end of George W. Bush's presidency, an audio recording of Janeane Garofalo calling members of the Tea Party "racists and rednecks" during a Stop The Hate Rally in Starched Shirt, Wyo., plays as patrons enter the artifact room.

Watching the presidents shoot the Shinola was the most interesting part of the day. When Barack Obama looked George W. Bush straight in the eye and said, "You know, George, my policy on terror is totally different from yours," the two men exploded into a fit of laughter that even caused Ted Kennedy's eavesdropping liver to chortle a bit.

"Hey, and we're a transparent administration, too!" Obama exclaimed before doubling over at his own rapier wit.

At one point, Bill Clinton drew the ire of Obama when he complimented Michelle Obama's dress one too many times. The conversation got contentious enough that at one point, Clinton resorted to biting his bottom lip for emphasis and gesturing with his thumb. Jimmy Carter stepped in to make peace, which resulted in George Bush Sr. asking Carter to go convert the square footage of the building into meters.

Former Vice President Al Gore apologized for being a bit gassy after a three-bean burrito lunch. To compensate, Gore vowed to purchase enough carbon credits to cover the damage he'd done to the ozone layer by floating a series of air biscuits that reportedly singed nose hairs at 50 paces. He then hopped in an SUV, which drove him to a private jet. When asked if he believed in Gore's carbon credit system, Bush Sr. said he preferred Glenn Miller.

Always the rapscallion, former Vice President Dick Cheney egged on a group of college students who were demonstrating outside the building. Cheney bragged that due to hip, heart, lung and knee replacement surgeries, he was now legally deemed a cyborg and no longer required to pay income taxes.

In conclusion, Cheney threw a ball of yarn at Vice President Joe Biden, who playfully but tactfully spent the rest of the afternoon untangling under a nearby statue of Larry The Cable Guy, which Cheney later mistook for a quail and shot in the face.

N.C. State fans chanting N.I.T. at UNC? Isn't that like George Costanza making fun of a bald guy?

3-YEAR-OLD FOUND HAPPY, HEALTHY IN MAILBOX
MAY 9, 2013

Last Saturday morning, I boarded a GMC Denali with Free Press Managing Editor Bryan Hanks and headed to New Jersey. Our mission: Retrieve 10 cases of CDs, a guitar, an amp, go to a Yankees game — and try to avoid murdering one another in a Denny's parking lot.

I've got several musical irons in the fire, but the main gig is still Third Of Never — a New Jersey-based endeavor. Having just wrapped up our second album (details available at www.thirdofnever.com), it was time to pick up the discs from the pressing plant as the label wanted the discs in a week.

While up there, I wanted to bring home a guitar and an amplifier to use in a local endeavor, and Hanks wanted to hook up with his old buddy and former Free Presser Drew Loftis for a Yankees game.

To accomplish these tasks, we determined it would require the rental of a vehicle. Being a seasoned deal-maker, Hanks jumped at the opportunity to display his scheisterly prowess. After all, I once witnessed this man spend 40 minutes talking a Girl Scout down to $1.25 on a box of Thin Mints, so I knew he'd show up to play.

After a bit of research we huddled around his computer to bask in the glow of the deal he'd put together. According to the terms of the rental agreement, we could save $10 on the additional driver fee if he listed me as his "domestic partner." To me, $10 is $10 so I told him to put us down as a couple and I'd go register at Belk just to make it look authentic, but Mr. Ethical wussed out.

The rental agreement also stipulated that if the car was driven outside of North or South Carolina, there would be an additional fee. I leapt into action and showed Hanks that a fictional route to Asheville, Charlotte, Columbia, Charleston and back would be about the same mileage as our real trip to New Jersey and back. This little white lie would save $80, which, to anyone making all or even part of their living writing for a newspaper, equals (before taxes) roughly a month's salary.

Hanks never really got on board with my idea to restage the Lufthansa heist of '78. After reading about the GPS devices these paranoid, nontrusting car rental companies install in all their vehicles, I gave up as well. All that being said, when Hanks showed up at my house with a nicer car than we'd signed up for at a smaller price, I realized I was a mere mortal traveling with a bargain hunting deity.

Hanks showed up at my compound at 9 a.m. sporting a Ralph Sampson muumuu and a Washington Redskins cap. He already had his iPhone plugged into the car stereo, so I shuddered a bit wondering what infernal Drake ditty was headed our way.

To my credit, I was on my best behavior, even though I really wanted to pummel the L.L. Cool J track coming out of the speakers with my James Brown box set. Eventually, Hanks requested to hear a podcast from my iPod and for some reason, we couldn't find his iPhone for the rest of the trip.

I have no idea how it ended up under my seat, duct taped to a spring.

Once on the road, Hanks decided to sync his phone up to the vehicle's Blue-tooth system. To me, Blue-tooth is what you get after eating too many Smurf sammiches, but apparently, it's a service that allows you to talk on the phone without having to use the phone. Once it was hooked up, Hanks was able to talk to Siri — the woman who lives in his phone. Here's an excerpt from one of their conversations;

Hanks: Where is the nearest Starbucks?

Siri: Redd Foxx was born in St. Louis in 1922.

Hanks: No, Siri, where is the nearest Starbucks?

Siri: "Buck Rogers" was first published by Amazing Stories in 1928.

Hanks: NO! You stupid (censored)! I'm trying to find a Starbucks!

Siri: You ain't gonna come up in here talking to me like that. I make my own money.

A few seconds later, a Virginia State Trooper pulled us over; Siri apparently reported Hanks for making a threatening phone call. Thankfully, the trooper was a University of Virginia grad; after seeing Hanks' Ralph Sampson muumuu, he let him off with a warning.

Eventually, Hanks found his Starbucks. When he pulled into the parking lot, I informed him that I've never set foot in a Starbucks and had no intention to do so. My lovely wife had packed a small cooler for me that was packed with ice and plenty of fruit and carbonated refreshment.

I pointed out that if any of my dearly departed ancestors who'd gone through the Depression got wind of me paying $8 for a cup of bean water, they would rise from their graves to smite us both.

Hanks pleaded for me to go in, eventually offering to pay for whatever I ordered. Apparently he really wanted me to experience Starbucks, so I ordered a cup of iced coffee, which came to $2. Hanks ordered a triple venti caffeine-free, no foam, extra caramel, with whipped caramel macchiato, a sliver of soap used by the Dalai Lama, three pumps basil, one pump Mountain Dew, an inch of non-fat milk, with a strand of Lindsey Lohan's mustache hair on the side, which cost $36.

I did a little research, and for the amount of money spent on our two cups of coffee, you could buy a barrel of Sanka or the Charlotte Hornets.

Once we made it to New Jersey Saturday afternoon, my business went smoothly and we motored over to the home of Loftis, who, after securing his valuables, graciously agreed to let us crash in his basement.

On Sunday, Hanks and Loftis took in a Yankees game while I opted to lay on the couch in a cool, dark basement and do absolutely nothing … and it was glorious.

On our way home, we hit some road construction in Richmond at 3 a.m., moving only about 1 foot per minute for 45 minutes. When the logjam finally broke, I put the hammer down, intent on making it to my bed before sunrise.

At 5 a.m., after an Iliad-like journey that spanned hundreds of miles, gallons of soda and two Kasabian albums, I made it back home. Hanks helped me stack my gear on a couch in my office and I bid him adieu.

I tippy-toed into the house with the intention of becoming one with my Serta mattress, only to discover Tax Deduction No. 1 was in my spot. The Wife told me TD No. 1 woke up with a stomach issue about an hour earlier, but with the storm now passed couldn't get back to sleep in her own bed.

Not having the strength to slam the bedroom door on my head repeatedly, I walked down to TD No. 1's room and attempted to catch some sleep in her empty bed. This would have been fine if not for the fact that everything from my knees down hung off the end of the mattress. Dikembe Mutombo could use this mattress as a napkin.

My last option was the ancient couch in my outside office. It's a durable piece of furniture that allegedly once sat in the living room of Mussolini's summer house in Rome.

In all my agony, I took all the stuff I'd just stacked on the couch and piled it on the floor. I collapsed into a drooling, snoring heap and awoke two hours later to take TD No. 2 to preschool. I took one step away from the couch and tripped over four boxes I'd moved the night before. Thankfully, the guitar amp I fell face-first onto broke my fall.

Having been up for 24 hours straight with only two hours of sleep didn't affect me all that much, although my wife was perplexed when a woman from the post office called to say a disoriented man had just dropped off his daughter thinking it was a day care. Thankfully, they gently placed her in our mailbox with the Piggly Wiggly circular that afternoon.

FAMILY FORCED TO SELL CAR WHILE ON VACATION
MAY 14, 2013

"If you cannot get rid of the family skeleton, you may as well make it dance." — George Bernard Shaw

I've never spent much time researching my family tree. Once while slapping a genealogy project together for a school assignment, I did a little digging and found one interesting tidbit. Apparently, a few generations back, a relative of mine in England — last name "Bonham" — took revenge on someone who wronged his family by sealing the guy up in a barrel and rolling it off the end of a pier.

To paraphrase Mark Frost, was this a case of vigilante justice or just clean country living? Aside from the fact I might be related to a famous English drummer, it gave me chills to realize I share some DNA with someone who killed a guy via Tupperware.

The funniest bit of family lore to come my way in a while involves one of my great uncles. Many of my great uncles have nicknames such as Duck or Pomp, but this story isn't about either of them. Seeing as this guy had an animal nickname, for our purposes, he will be referred to as "Uncle Squirrel."

Whenever the family killed hogs, Squirrel would be given some meat in exchange for helping out. Curiously, whenever Squirrel would go out to his smokehouse to select some meat to have with supper, he always chose the absolute highest quality specimen he could find. Most people would use the good meat for an average meal and save the great meat for a special occasion — but not Uncle Squirrel.

After a time, someone finally asked Uncle Squirrel why he always started with the best meat he had.

"I want to know I'm always eatin' the best I've got," was his reply to more than one relative. Uncle Squirrel always knew how to straddle that fine line between Zen and psychotic.

The most epic dose of Uncle Squirrel came when he decided to take his family to the Grand Ole Opry. At the time, it was a big deal to leave the county, so a trip to Nashville might as well have been a trip to the moon.

Having never been in a hotel before, Uncle Squirrel's family took to the then-new Holiday Inn like ducks to water. Being a hardworking family with a rural background, the air conditioning and swimming pool were considered true luxuries. It took the hotel manager 20 minutes to convince Uncle Squirrel's wife that she didn't have to clean the room herself.

The biggest revelation, however, was this thing called "room service." For people who grew up having to raise, plant, pick and kill whatever they ate, the idea of simply calling someone and having prepared food delivered to your room was astonishing. Not since he found out "Gunsmoke" wasn't a documentary had Uncle Squirrel been at such a loss for words.

For starters, Uncle Squirrel ordered a bowl of butter-pecan ice cream. A few minutes later, Aunt Squirrel ordered a tuna salad sandwich and a Pepsi. It got so good to them that eventually the kids ended up ordering one of everything on the menu just to see what everything looked like.

After seeing Loretta Lynn and Roy Acuff perform a duets of "Hello Darlin', " "Louisiana Woman," "Mississippi Man" and "Cold Sweat" at the Grand Ole Opry, Uncle Squirrel and his family packed up the car and prepared to make the long trip back to Kinston. Uncle Squirrel turned in the key at the front desk and turned to go, only to be called back by the hotel manager.

"We need to settle on your bill," the manager said.

"No, I paid for the room in advance, you see," Squirrel said.

"Yes sir, you paid for the room in advance, but there's the matter of the $348 room service bill," the manager said.

When Squirrel came to, the manager explained that room service wasn't included in the cost of the room. Faced with a bill he couldn't pay and a family he needed to get back home, Squirrel knew what he had to to. He sold the car to pay off the room service bill and bought bus tickets to get his family back home.

For years, a cloud of mystery hung over the events that took place during that weekend in Nashville. Squirrel told everyone back home his car had been stolen. That story stuck until one of his children let slip at a Christmas gathering why her father always threw any trash that was in his truck into the local Holiday Inn parking lot, or why he insisted on stopping in to take advantage of their free continental breakfast even though he wasn't staying at the hotel.

"Mathematically, he figured he'd get that $348 back if he knocked 'em off for a couple of donuts and some orange juice every couple of weeks," his nephew said recently. "When they switched over to bagels, he just said to hell with it."

Ramification: The process of becoming a UNC fan.

INTERNAL REVENUE SERVICE RAIDS THE
FREE PRESS OFFICE
MAY 16, 2013

At 8:01 a.m. on Wednesday, agents from the Internal Revenue Service and the U.S. Department of Justice executed search warrants on The Free Press building at 2103 N. Queen Street.

"Based on information obtained from confiscated Associated Press phone records, we saw fit to kick in the front door of The Free Press offices and have a look around," said U.S. Attorney General Eric Holder. "Also, the writer with the funny hair keeps inferring that I'm actually Oprah's boyfriend Stedman Graham, which has caused me all kinds of trouble back at the house."

When asked why the door was kicked in even though it was unlocked for business hours, Holder declined to comment.

"I held the door open for them," said Free Press Chief Photographer Janet Carter. "They asked me to shut the door so they could knock it down. I told him to tell Gay-le 'hey' for me."

The explanation for the "Kickdown heard 'round Queen Street" was simple.

"Our team was there because The Free Press had previously published an article about local Tea Party activity that presented the facts and was unbiased," said IRS Commissioner Steven T. Miller. "That's a definite red flag."

He continued, "Also, the income these reporters listed on their tax returns seemed ludicrously low. As it turns out they were telling the truth about that, too; my bust."

Connie R. Hill, spokesperson for Independent Voters of America, says this level of corruption is rampant on both sides of the aisle.

"The previous administration was lambasted for doing this kind of thing," said Hill, who recently completed a six-week stay at the Betty Ford Center for caffeine and run-on sentence addiction. "Now, the current administration who lambasted the previous administration is doing it while the remnants of the previous administration that also did it are shocked and appalled that the current administration is doing the same shady stuff they themselves did."

Holder — who has ironically never been seen in the same room with Oprah's boo Stedman — said information obtained from a phone tap gave them plenty of reason to execute a search of the premises.

"One Free Press employee — Paulette Burroughs, 39, of La Grange — was overheard ordering knives, hand grenades, swords, anti-aircraft missiles, crossbows, ear daggers, Gatling guns and Kenny Chesney albums on more than one occasion from her desk phone," Stedman, err, Holder said. "That makes this a matter of national security and questionable taste in music."

When asked why she ordered so much weaponry, Burroughs response was succinct.

"I was out," she said.

When contacted by the Associated Press, former President George W. Bush declined to comment because he thought Stedman might be eavesdropping on the call. Vice President Joe Biden eluded reporter's questions by throwing an imaginary ball and running away to fetch it.

While the Obama administration is now being criticized for doing the same sort of things the Bush Administration did — such as outing CIA agent Valerie Plame and filling Kanye West's tour bus with owl guano — former Vice President Dick Cheney doesn't believe the comparisons are fair.

"Neither President Bush nor I ever had any knowledge of inappropriate … oh man," Cheney said, as he busted out laughing. "I used to be able to say that with a straight face (laughing while clutching chest). I have been out of the game too long (wiping tears from his eyes). But seriously, do you have any triple-A batteries? One of my pacemakers is about to blow and I've got an appointment to blast a guy in the face with bird shot in a few hours."

President Obama scoffed at the notion that he was as seedy as George W. Bush.

"They'll warn that tyranny is always lurking just around the corner," President Obama said. "You should reject those voices. But, if something unconstitutional does occur — like targeting the tax records of a political group or confiscating the phone records of a news-gathering organization, just remember this: gay basketball star Jason Collins is a brave American and that should be our sole focus for the foreseeable future."

Late Wednesday afternoon, the DOJ announced they will be pre-opening everyone's Christmas presents this year. Operation No Child's Toy Left Behind is set to commence Dec. 20.

FREEDOM OF SPEECH NO EXCUSE FOR
SPEAKING STUPIDLY
MAY 23, 2013

We've all been in this situation: You're at a party and you run into an old friend you haven't seen in ages. You ask how her husband's doing, and she tells you her hubby hooked up with the baby-sitter, bought a mid-life crisis sports car and moved to Tijuana.

You vow never to start a conversation with any human ever again. People chastise you for being distant and anti-social, but you're just trying to avoid shoe polish breath.

The devastating storm that eviscerated an Oklahoma town this week brought out the best of what's left of our diluted humanity. Legions of people have volunteered their time, skills and money in an attempt to be a small bandage on a massive wound. It's impossible to believe every human on the planet would react in the manner these volunteers have, but thankfully there seems to be more of them than the two twits I'm about to tell you about.

Usually, there's at least one jerk out of every 10 people. In the old days, the 90 percent who were deemed moderately decent would drown out that 10 percent jerk factor. Now, with everyone hunched over their smart phones trying to absorb every thought of every human with a social media account, any random jerk can broadcast their jerkdom to the masses.

(Side note: Who has more Twitter followers? Perez Hilton — an Internet troll who recorded a song about gonorrhea and figured out how to make millions by criticizing people who actually have careers, or the American Red Cross — a group known for helping the needy, those devastated by disaster, and members of the military and their families? If you guessed American Red Cross, then you are absolutely wrong.

As of this writing, Perez Hilton has 6,123,353 Twitter followers, while the American Red Cross currently boasts 972,440. Maybe my 90 percent theory a few paragraphs up was incorrect after all.)

The afternoon of the Oklahoma tragedy, Lizz Winstead, co-creator of Comedy Central's The Daily Show and noted stand-up comedian posted the following on her Twitter account:

"This tornado is in Oklahoma, so clearly it has been ordered to only target conservatives."

Now what she's doing there (I think) is lampooning something Pat Robertson said about God sending hurricanes to Florida because of a gay pride parade that was going to take place in Orlando. Obviously, what Robertson said was stupid, but I'll get to him in a minute.

Lizz Winstead has every right to say whatever she wants, but to paraphrase an Adrian Belew lyric, it doesn't mean you should just because you can. And what's even worse than the initial statement is her half-buttocked attempt at an apology:

"Made a political joke, Twas before devastation revealed. In hindsight, had I understood, I would have refrained. Beyond sorry."

Based on my top-notch edumacation at a fine public university, Lizzy seems to be saying it would have been okay to make the joke if only a few lives were destroyed. This woman identifies herself as a liberal — a group who, according to all the bumper stickers on the SUVs I sit behind in traffic, are supposed to be compassionate and understanding. This chick makes Rush Limbaugh look like Arthur Godfrey.

Shortly after Lizz Winstead lost all her stand-up bookings at the Laugh Hut in Oklahoma City, we heard from Pat Robertson. Patty Pat Pat — The Patster. I thought by this time in your life you'd have squeezed all the crazy out of your system, but apparently, the guy who loads up your pill caddy has been using placebos to save some money.

Here's what Alfred E. Neuman's grandpa said about the Oklahoma tornado:

"If enough people were praying, He (God) would intervene."

In other words, Pat Robertson believes God would have canceled the tornadoes but decided not to because the people of Oklahoma weren't praying enough.

Robertson is based in Virginia Beach, an area that Hurricane Sandy beat like a rented mule back in November. Either Rob- ertson wasn't praying enough, or maybe the Big Man wants Robert-son to — I don't know — shut his pie hole. By Robertson's math, the people of Virginia Beach shouldn't get so much as a sunburn, much less millions in storm damages.

Being a moderate myself, I think I can safely say that neither true liberals nor true conservatives want anything to do with Lizz Winstead or Pat Robertson. Some will chastise them publicly but in their hearts agree with their craziness, but anytime a bunch of humans form a large group, something is eventually going to go wrong.

As of 2009, I refuse to even participate in discussions about where the office should go for lunch. I once suggested going to a place that had several different kinds of food so everyone would have a choice and everyone looked at me as if I'd used their lip balm as a bidet.

Right now, Winstead is probably waiting for a train full of orphans to plunge into an active volcano so she'll have something to write jokes about, while Robertson will blame the train's engineer for not excommunicating his gay son from the family.

These two are prime examples the unabashed, pseudo-intellectual idiot that serve no other purpose than to divide and rile. Jerry Clower nailed it on the head when he said some people are educated beyond their intelligence.

To donate to the Red Cross, visit www.red-cross.org.

WAR REENACTMENT DOESN'T SPOIL
SCHOOL SPELLING BEE
JUNE 4, 2013

Tax Deduction No. 1 participated in the second-grade spelling bee on Monday. Judging by the number of auto-corrects the ol' laptop has thrown at me during these first two sentences, you'd think she didn't stand a chance.

As a matter of fact, I won the spelling bee when I was in third grade. It was down to me and a pretty redheaded girl, and the word was "gurgle." When she spelled the entire word correctly — except for the "e" on the end — I knew glory and a gift certificate for a free hamburger at King's were just seconds away.

When it was my turn, I spelled "gurgle" correctly, and for whatever reason a couple of guys in class hoisted me on their shoulders and walked me around the room as if I'd won the Superbowl. One of the guys who paraded me around the room is now a successful politician, and the other went to prison a few years back for trying to kill someone. It's going to be an awesome class reunion.

After years of reflection, I've determined they weren't necessarily happy that I'd won, rather that the redheaded girl who'd repeatedly rejected them had lost. These rubes actually thought they'd win this girl's heart by giving her their school cafeteria-issue square peanut cookies, or by performing some Twyla Tharpe-esque routine on the playground jungle gym.

I'd had girlfriends since kindergarten, but I wasn't giving up a cookie nor a healthy spine for any dame. That I ended up being a chubby kid with scoliosis helped me stay focused on my studies.

The Wife won the spelling bee when she was in fourth grade, although she claims not to remember her winning word. I spent some time rummaging through her school records and discovered the word she spelled correctly was "andro-phobia." After I looked up what androphobia meant, it concerned me that A) she had that in her pocket at such a young age and B) she always talks about how comfortable she is around me.

The days leading up to TD No. 1's spelling bee were tense. Not a moment went by that someone wasn't hurling a random word at the child and demanding she rattle off the correct order of its contained letters. She was doing well with most of the words, so every few minutes I'd throw in something like crudivore, donnybrook or gaberlunzie just to keep her humble.

For nights on end, I woke TD No. 1 from a deep sleep and made her spell 10 words correctly before she could go back to sleep. Most fathers wouldn't take the trouble to wake an 8-year-old at 3 a.m. and ask her to spell snollygoster, but I'm old school. One day we'll get paddling back in the schools, but one step at a time.

As I pulled up to the school, it appeared Noah was gearing up for a summer tour as the clouds voided themselves with extreme prejudice. The one, sad little umbrella that hadn't made its way into The Wife's car was sitting in the back seat of the car begging for some playing time.

The umbrellas that used to be in my car could repel hail, locusts and process servers. Over time, these umbrellas always end up migrating to my better half 's conveyance, thus leaving me with the brittle, bent and tattered umbrella that was purchased at the Dollar Store in 1993.

I have to say that beat up little umbrella did a heck of a job keeping my right hand completely dry as I walked across the school parking lot. Once inside, I was able to use that dry right hand to squeeze seven gallons of water out of my clothes.

After identifying myself at the front office, school officials went against their better judgment and let me in. Once inside, I sat at what was undoubtedly a durable cafeteria table that was not built for a 6-foot-tall man. After reattaching my knee cap to my leg, I waited for the festivities to begin.

The kids eventually came in and took their places on stage. The moderator went through several rounds of words before the participants (who had to win in their classes to get this far) started to be thinned down. Most of the words were of the "paste" or "smile" variety, although the inclusion of the word "onomatopoeia" was deemed cruel by many in attendance.

After several rounds, it came down to two kids: TD No. 1 and her best friend, Mary. The drama of two best friends going into battle was almost Shakespearean, but there was something else to consider. TD No. 1 had just attended Mary's birthday party the week before, and their friendship was stronger than ever. I worried that being thrust into competition on such a public stage might tear their friendship apart. This could rob them of the chance to have a falling out over a boy, only to later reconcile during a chance meeting at the concession stand on field day.

TD No. 1 and her best buddy seemed calm and collected onstage — even when a teacher yelled out "BABABOOEY!" during a quiet moment. Except for the low creak of the air conditioning system and the barrage of violent crashes and explosions emanating from the cafeteria kitchen, you could here a pin drop. It would have to be a pretty big pin to be heard over the civil war re-enactment going on in the kitchen, but you could have heard it.

Eventually, TD No. 1 tripped up but made us very, very proud with a second-place finish. She received a certificate, a cup full of goodies and a trophy that will no doubt have its lettering rubbed off before the weekend is here.

CAN THE PEOPLE OF KINSTON BE QUIET IN A MOVIE THEATER?
JUNE 13, 2013

I live by a code — many codes in fact. If a driver pauses to let you into the traffic flow, by God, you give that person a "thank you" wave. If you accidentally dial a wrong number, be a man or whatever Wendy Williams is and apologize to the person on the other end of the line.

While it's impossible to believe all of humanity will ever develop a singular belief system, there is one thing all sane people from the Toulambi Tribe to the White House know: You need to shut up in a movie theater.

For years, people have been wondering why box office numbers are down. Some say it's because the quality of mainstream movies is off. Others say it's the proliferation of services that allow people to watch movies in the comfort of their homes. I say these theories are symptoms of a bigger problem.

The problem? People don't know how to act in a movie theater anymore.

Why would anyone want to pay $7 to $12 to go sit in a dark room full of drooling knuckle-draggers who act as if they've never had first-hand experience with furniture before?

How about the couple that's been together all day, yet wait until they're in a movie theater to start hashing out their marital issues via a series of loud, Dr. Phil-esque conversations? Lord help us all if this unholy union has already produced offspring, for they will undoubtedly be allowed to incessantly caterwaul while the movie is playing.

I've repeatedly written to my congressman asking him to introduce a law that would allow moviegoers to pummel, subdue and remove people who disrupt the movie viewing experience for others.

To his credit, the congressman wrote me back. He said he appreciated my initiative but thought it would be unfair to single out the hammerhead section of the population. He also noted these people made up most of the voting bloc, so I guess you gotta dance with who brought you.

Before the politically correct crowd began their quest to ban testosterone, it was socially acceptable to pour soda on the head of anyone caught yakking their head off during a movie. I'll admit that on more than one occasion, I've thrown ice and/ or roofing nails at people in movie theaters who thought they were in a public speaking course.

In college, one of our professors told a student who was nervous about speaking before the class to imagine she was in a movie theater; it calmed her right down.

With all the hoodoo going on with the IRS and little G-men hiding under the sink with a microphone, why am I so fixated on people acting like twits at a movie theater? It's because I've broken one of my codes and agreed to accompany some friends to a screening of the new "Man of Steel" movie this week.

Before you folks with the Lois Lane tattoos and Jimmy Olsen hair weaves get your Underoos in a knot, I have nothing against superhero movies. OK, honestly I could care less about them, but there are plenty of things I enjoy that most of the population would yawn at, so I have no qualms with you. The way I see it, anything that helps you get out of your own head for a few hours and helps stimulate the economy is a great thing.

I was into the Superman movie franchise back when Christopher Reeve and Richard Pryor were in the mix. I had a Superman lunch box in grade school, and whenever I sat at a table with someone who had that school lunch/tater-tot shaped okra on their plate, I'd pretend the okra was kryptonite.

Anyway, my buddy Prozac owes me a few shekels so he offered to pay my way into the movie as recompense. I told him I wasn't really into big movies with lots of 'splosions and whatnot, but when he offered to throw in an LTD 225-sized bucket of popcorn and a drink big enough to swim in, I agreed to his terms. If nothing else I could have a good time making inappropriate noises during the movie's quiet moments*.

(*Note: Replicating flatulence noises during a boring movie is not considered boorish behavior and is encouraged. Raspberries are always funny and are encouraged. If at any point Clark Kent holds his stomach, you'd better look out.)

Since this little expedition has been thrown together, Free Press Managing Editor Bryan Hanks has been added to the guest list. There's only one thing that keeps Hanks from being a perfect moviegoer: The man is a Twit, and by that I mean he loves Twitter.

On more than one occasion, I've caught the man tweeting during weddings and funerals. Most recently while attending a bris, Hanks tweeted, "That's gotta hurt" to his thousands of online followers. The rabbi threatened to make it a double ceremony if Hanks didn't knock it off — no pun intended.

To all you boneheaded, dopey, cloddish nitwits out there, if someone "shushes" you during a movie, they're not trying to violate your rights. What they're trying to do is let you know that you're acting like a lobotomized squirrel. Just take a deep breath, realize the earth doesn't revolve around you, and SHUT UP.

Enjoy the show.

ILLNESS, INJURY MARS FATHER'S DAY FESTIVITIES
JUNE 18, 2013

If you have a Facebook account and at least one functioning eye, you've probably seen upwards of 46,000 images of fathers, dads, daddies and pops over the last 48 hours. Everybody looks happy in all the pictures and the smiles rarely look coerced.

I've been a father coming up on nine years, and with the increased level of daditudinal fortitude I've had to drum up as the years go passing by, I assumed the Father's Day festivities would get ramped up accordingly.

When the kids are 3 or 4 years old, a homemade card is perfectly acceptable. When the little scamps reach a point where they can program the DVR and access NASA launch codes with a Gmail account, then it's time for them to wheel in the Rolex watches and gold tooth caps.

Even though I believe myself to be a bling-worthy father, I haven't worn a watch in 20 years and gold tooth caps make Pepsi taste funny. Instead, Tax Deductions 1 & 2 came up with a very nice shirt and two pairs of shorts as a gift. Since the shorts I wear most of the time are hand-me-downs that were out of style when they were turned over to me around a decade ago, these new editions were right on time.

In addition to the great presents, The Wife prepared my favorite dinner: breakfast. There is nothing like dining on bacon, eggs, biscuits and fruit in the middle of the day — except for maybe a peanut butter and cabbage sandwich.

Some of the woe surrounding my Father's Day was self-inflicted. After several months of misfires and house fires, we decided to delve headlong into Tax Deduction No. 2's potty training. We knew this mission would be a difficult one, but it was also one that had to be done. Many hours have been spent sitting on the edge of the tub while TD No. 2 was perched on a little plastic training potty with the collected works of Walter Elias Disney by her side. I kept asking her if she needed to go, and she just kept saying, "It's stuck!"

After a rocky start a few weeks back, we'd gotten TD No. 2 to a good place in all matters water closet. To be fair, we did ask her if she needed to go every six minutes for several days straight, but after a while, she started charging into the facilities with vigor — and on more than one occasion, a flawed sense of depth perception. With a rousing chorus of "GOOD JOB," hugs galore and the promise of two shiny new M&Ms with every successful launch, we were one step closer to not having to spend a king's ransom on diapers.

While potty training was entering the home stretch this week, TD No. 2 came down with some sort of virus. I wrongly assumed that once both of the TDs were away from school and its army of smarmy, walking Petri dishes with flashing-light sneakers, we'd be in the clear. The doctor told us it was a virus and would probably last for three days. During those three days, much of the potty progress we'd made eroded at an alarming rate. Between her sore throat and headache, TD No. 2 was in no mood to perform for M&Ms.

On Sunday — Father's Day — TD No. 2 finally gave up the ghost and realized she needed to bond with the facilities. In her panic to get to where she needed to go, she got a little tangled up in her big girl draws. Hearing her distress call — which resembles a giraffe with vertigo — I walked into the bathroom to find her in the toe-touching position. She'd somehow gotten tangled up in her undergarment and was hobbling around the bathroom like a tall crab yelling, "It's stuck, it's stuck!"

While she was still tangled up in her skivvies, TD No. 2 kept trying in vain to sit on the little plastic potty. A couple of times she missed by a good 2 feet; a few other times she'd glance the side of it and come to rest on the cold, unforgiving bathroom tile. I saw a guy do the same little dance at the CBGB bathroom in New York once, but I was under no moral or legal obligation to help him.

Eventually we freed TD No. 2 from her flowery cotton shackles and she was able to complete the transaction with seconds to spare. After her hug/ M&M tour, we noticed TD No. 1 was lying down in the living room. After a thermometer check, it was determined that whatever TD No. 2 had just about gotten over had now infected TD No.

For a brief moment, a job as a weather station janitor in Antarctica sounded mighty inviting.

With the whining and the twitching and the squealing and the moaning seemingly under control for a few seconds, I decided to take my father (actually, my Daddy) his Father's Day present. I believe spending time with your father on Father's Day is spiritually rewarding. It also had the added benefit of being several miles away from the twitching, squealing, whining and moaning that has wallpapered my existence going on four days.

I walked into my parents' house and — to my amazement — many of the same sounds I'd just escaped were there to greet me. Apparently, The Parents had come down with some sort of sinus/achy/fever of the bubonic variety themselves.

My father opened his present — a book on Bobby Jones written by Mark Frost — and sneezed a sneeze that could've put out a California forest fire. This sneeze actually showed up on the Doppelganger radar on the local news that night.

After trying unsuccessfully to un-stick the pages from each other, my father now owns a Bobby Jones door stop.

I eased back to the house and caught a segment on CBS Sun-day Morning that profiled comedian Jim Gaffigan. Gaffigan and his wife have five children, and even though he is one of the top touring comics in the country, he/ they have decided to reside in a small New York City apartment. All of his children — living in dirty old New York City — were free of fever and seemed a general delight to be around.

Gaffigan said he and his wife were having such a good time with the kids that they may have another one.

Sorry, but I'm having to cut this column short. I'm about to board a plane headed for NYC. I have a Monday morning appointment to slap Jim Gaffigan with an old fax machine.

LA GRANGE MAN HIRED AS KANYE WEST'S ASSISTANT
JUNE 20, 2013

A chance meeting with an international superstar at an airport has changed a La Grange man's life forever.

"My sister Nicole got us tickets for 'The Price Is Right'," said Kelvin Morgan, 41. "She won an all-expenses paid vacation to Detroit on the show."

After the taping of the show, Morgan and his sister headed to LAX airport. While in line for a security check, Morgan noticed a couple with a newborn traveling with a huge entourage.

"Even though we were in Los Angeles, I didn't expect to meet any famous people," Morgan said. "I once met the woman who played Ms. Garrett on the 'Facts of Life' at a tractor pull, but that didn't prepare me for what happened at the airport."

As it turns out, the couple with the newborn and the entourage was Kanye West and Kim Khardashian.

"I couldn't believe it!" Morgan said. "At first, I thought it was just someone who looked like Kanye, but when I noticed the baby was acting more mature than the father, I knew it was him."

According to Morgan, security personnel at the airport believed Khardashian may have been trying to smuggle something onto the airplane.

"They kept waving that X-ray wand over Kim Khardashian's buttocks area," Morgan said. "They went through four wands before they found one that wouldn't start overheating midway through scanning the entire area."

Morgan says an exasperated Kanye threw his sunglasses, iPod and Strawberry Shortcake coloring book up against a wall in protest.

"Kanye went off," Morgan said. "He fired his entire entourage on the spot — including the woman in charge of alerting the press to his whereabouts and the guy in charge of writing Kanye's tweets about how much he hates the press."

After the dust settled, Kanye took a seat next to Morgan in the waiting area.

"He sat down and started talking to me as if he'd known me for years," Morgan said. "He said he felt guilty for becoming rich selling albums even thought he can't sing and can't even play a triangle. He's apparently felt this way for a while, and the pressure of becoming a parent with a woman who is even less talented than him just caused him to snap."

As Morgan and West chatted in the waiting area, the two became fast friends.

"When they called his flight, he asked if I wanted to go to work for him," Morgan said. "Without even asking what I'd be doing, I said yes. Being a manicurist at a funeral home is rewarding work, but 20 years is enough."

Now settled into the Kanyashian compound in California, Morgan says he's enjoying his new job.

"Kanye is a great boss," Morgan said. "So far, all I've had to do is remove the peanuts from his peanut M&Ms. I asked him if I should just buy the plain M&Ms instead, but he said plain M&Ms are just out-of-date Skittles the U.S. government is using to brainwash its citizens. What can I say? The man is profound."

Morgan's other duties include donning a blonde wig and reenacting the Taylor Swift speech interruption and watching "The Bachelorette" and explaining it to Kanye at breakfast.

"The plot tends to confuse him," Morgan said.

Although he wouldn't comment on Khardashian, Morgan believes she and Kanye have a strong bond.

"They kid around a lot," Morgan said. "Just the other day he sat a drink on the top of her rump — while she was standing. She walked around the house with it up there for around an hour before she realized it was there; never spilled a drop. Whenever there's an earthquake, we all take cover under that thing."

For the most part, Morgan says he just does what Kanye asks him to do, although he did recently try to broaden his employers' horizons.

"He walked by my room while I was watching a James Brown DVD," Morgan said. "He asked me who all those people were on stage behind Mr. Brown, and what were those strange objects they were holding. I told him those people were called 'musicians,' and those things they were holding were called 'instruments.'

"He laughed and accused me of pulling his leg — which he often will ask a staff member to do — but eventually, he believed me."

Morgan continued.

"Later, we watched an Anthony Hamilton concert, and Kanye asked what Mr. Hamilton was doing in front of the microphone," he said. I told him that was called 'singing.' He then looked at me with that look of an astronaut that's just locked himself out of the space station and busted out laughing."

"You almost had me that time, Kelvin!" Kanye reportedly said. "Singing! Hey Kim, come listen to what this fool just tried to tell me!"

Due to a fitting for custom made extra wide diapers, the child of

Kanye and Khardashian was unavailable for comment. The baby's publicist said she would be available after a two-week stint filling in for Joy Behar on "The View."

The baby's new fragrance for infants — Le Poo Noir — hits stores on June 28.

How many of you were upset when you found out what a Ham radio actually was?

FREE PRESS LOSES ANOTHER LONGTIME STAFF MEMBER
JUNE 25, 2013

To the millions of people who read the Kinston Free Press on a daily basis, Ryan Herman is known as our sports editor, sports writer and sports department. To his coworkers, he'll be forever remembered as the guy who tried to use White-Out on his computer screen.

As of June 30, Herman will no longer be a member of the Free Press staff. He has decided to take a job at his hometown newspaper in El Segundo, CA. While most everyone at the Free Press is towing the company line and saying "we'll miss him greatly" and "he was a valued member of the team" and "so what if he stole a few purses here and there," I refuse to take part in this politically correct hoodoo.

When Herman first arrived at the Free Press, he had that optimistic look they all have when they first get here. His desk was impeccably organized, with complaints that certain schools weren't being covered enough on one side and complaints about the non-coverage of retirement community checker tournaments on the right. Young Herman even used a carpenter's level to make sure the Post-It notes on his computer were aligned symmetrically in the 2-1-2 defensive pattern.

In the beginning, Herman attacked his job with the gusto of a bean taster with irritable bowel syndrome. If more than two people gathered to throw, kick, putt or filet a ball, Herman was there. No matter if young Herman was only getting four hours of sleep a night and a paltry Pop Tart from the break room for lunch, his desire to publicize local community sports was insatiable.

"I was raking leaves in my yard one night after work and Herman showed up out of the blue," said Paulette Bur-roughs, 39, of La Grange. "He mistook the leaf raking for Jai alai and wanted to make sure he wasn't missing anything. He played tough to get, too. I invited him inside for a chitlin' mimosa but he said he had to go."

As time went on, the grind of putting out a daily newspaper began to take its toll on the golden boy from El Segundo. His once vibrant game descriptions ("the two teams stalked the field of battle as if control of the

TV remote depended on it") eventually regressed to the bare minimum ("uh, a couple of guys took the ball and ran that-away, then the other guys took it and ran the other way").

Once while listening to an irate parent curse him out for not publishing photos from a hackey sack tournament, the usually affable Herman curled up in the fetal position and laid down in the parking lot. When the profane parent walked closer to see if Herman was alright, Herman bit the man on the ankle.

Luckily, the person Herman bit was into it.

"I'm just burned out," Herman said on Monday. "It's time for me to return to my hometown and recharge the batteries. Also, the local library redid their computer system years ago, so that copy of 'Heidi' I've had out since 1990 won't be a problem anymore."

"I'm going to miss all the friends I've made during my time in Kinston," Herman said. "It's been great working for Bryan Hanks. His insistence on giving me a deep tissue massage every morning during our staff meetings took a while for me to get used to, but every boss has their own way."

Herman will take over as the sports editor at the El Segundo Tribune on July 10. On July 13, he'll be reunited onstage with the El Segundo hip-hop legends Cypress Hill, a group he co-founded in 1985 with Q-Tip, Phife Dawg, Jarobi White and Ali Shaheed Muhammad.

Herman's original stage name was M.C. Hermtasia, but in recent years he has sporadically performed under the monikers C-Nugget, WD-41 and Ann Francisco.

"I left the group after we cut our first demo," Herman said. "We parted on good terms, but when 'Insane In The Brain' became a hit, they didn't take my calls for a few years. Hopefully, when we get to spit again, the magic will return."

Ryan Herman/WD-41 will be performing with Cypress Hill at Fours-E-Nuff in El Segundo on July 13 at 10 p.m.

SURVEY THAT QUESTIONS KINSTON'S
INTELLIGENCE IS STUPID
JULY 4, 2013

According to a survey by a web-based service dedicated to neuroscience research, when it comes to smarts, Kinston/Lenoir County ranks 476th out of 478 metropolitan areas.

Laredo, Texas, and Lumberton are the only cities ranked lower than Kinston. Even if in some alternate universe this survey was worth a hill of fully digested beans, of the bottom three cities on the list, Kinston would be No. 1.

The web service in question — Lumosity — has been online since 2007. According to their site, they "believe in improving brains." To achieve this goal, the doctors behind Lumosity have developed a series of online games that are supposed to improve your cognitive abilities.

Being the Mayor of Simpleton, I have no grounds to attack the wisdom of Lumosity's founders. I'm sure the walls of their offices are covered with Ph Ds, degrees and STDs. Could playing tic tac toe on the Lumosity website help ward off Alzheimer's disease, or is this snake oil for smart phone zombies?

I signed up for a free account but quickly learned that if I was serious about Ziplocing my brain for freshness, it was going to cost me. Lumosity offers several payment plans, but the best option seems to be the one-time $269.96 Lifetime package; NOT $270, but $269.96. They used three more characters to point out a 4 cents difference from a round number, so they're bound to know what they're doing.

Lumosity also offers a family plan, but I'm not so sure being surrounded by mentally sharp people is a good idea. It's worth the aggravation of being the only one who can change the clocks in the car if it means you'll have an advantage when it comes to dividing an estate. If your brother thinks 15 acres of swamp is more valuable than 10 acres of timber, who are you to argue? Make the man happy and buy him a nice helmet with all your pulp earnings.

The survey that purportedly determined we're all a bunch of dunderpates relied on people who had the free time to take an online test. I ask you, how many people reading this have time to take an online test that doesn't involve a free football phone?

Could the people of Kinston/Lenoir County be too busy trying to scrape out a living to devote a chunk of their day to an Internet survey? If anything, the results of this test should probably be flipped. Laredo and Lumberton came in below Kinston, which means they're the only other metropolitan areas with enough people smart enough not to waste their time on the Internet equivalent of magnetic bracelets.

It would help to know how the data was collected. Were area doctors, engineers and architects included in the survey, or did they pay a mime college dropout $7.25/hour plus a Hot Pocket to email people at random? Did Lumosity advertise their survey on "Face The Nation" or during an episode of "Big Brother?"

Some may deem this a radical thought, but what about the people who detest social media and the Internet in general? Were socially awkward teenagers armed with clipboards and $8 khakis sent into the wilds of Lenoir County in an attempt to attain an accurate reading?

You know who has time to play Internet games? People who drive around trying to sell steaks of indeterminate origin from the back of their pickup truck; people who take up two parking spaces; people who block two gas pumps just so they can have a shorter walk to buy a honey bun; the person in your office who bangs on their computer keyboard as if it was having an affair with his or her spouse; the person who has a swastika tattooed on their forehead and 2 feet of underwear sticking out of their pants who can't understand why they can't get a job.

Also, the tests on the Lumosity site are biased towards Northerners. More than one-third of the test questions were related to bagels and sidewalk urination.

In an attempt to be fair, I called the phone number listed for Lumosity on the San Francisco Better Business Bureau website. At 10 a.m. West Coast time, their mailbox was full. Apparently, no one at Lumosity has figured out how to check voicemail.

AN OPEN LETTER TO KINSTON'S REGGIE BULLOCK
JULY 9, 2013

Reginald. Reggie. Reginator. Regatola. Reg … It's time we had a little talk.

You're obviously a talented athlete with the potential to go far in the NBA, but it's interesting to me that a team named after a barber's instrument drafted a rising star with one of the most unique haircuts in all of basketball. A clipper can also refer to a fast moving ship, but other than a few wooden leg jokes, my nautical repertoire is rather limited.

Without even knowing it, your haircut has enriched my life.

For years, I caught guff for my haircut or lack thereof. Once while leaving the Lenoir County Courthouse, a man muttered something under his breath to the effect of "that's the jack**s from the paper; he needs a haircut." I turned around and discovered the guy giving me a hard time was wearing a toupee that had apparently been purchased from the Titanic's gift shop the day it went down.

I pointed towards his head and asked if he had a permit for it and could it eat solid food after midnight.

Reggie, thanks to you and your decision to rock that tribute to B.A. Baracus, I no longer have the most famous hair in Kinston. Encounters such as the one I described above have ceased and, for that, I'm truly thankful. I look forward to your haircut yielding more endorsement money than Chris Andersen's. If you know of a mop or angel-hair pasta company looking for a spokesman, you know where to find me.

Years ago, when the media started pronouncing "Bullock" as "Bull-ock," I wanted to cash in with a line of Reggie Bullock Bull-Lock Padlocks. For the commercial, we'd zoom in to see you guarding a defender on the court, then we'd jump to a scene of a frustrated criminal (in a Duke shirt, of course) unable to break into a storage building locked tight with a Reggie Bullock Bull-Lock Padlock.

Your high school coach Wells Gulledge quickly hit me with an injunction, which means I now have a 10x10 storage shed full of Bull Lock Padlocks. Ironically, someone broke in a few weeks back and stole most of them.

To get to the NBA, you had to leave my beloved Tar Heels one year early. Many people yammered till they were Carolina Blue in the face about your decision to forego your senior year and turn pro. While some critics of your decision were truly knowledgeable about the sport and more specifically your career, the vast majority of these people haven't touched a basketball since Jimmy Carter chewed his own food.

The coaches, mentors and friends who cared about you had a right to voice their opinions, and one would assume you appreciated their concern. Everyone else who chastised you for going pro would sell their heads to science for the kind of money you're now making. To paraphrase a scene from "MASH," if I were offered that kind of money I'd be out of here so fast my underwear would have to catch up with me.

Why should you believe anything I'm telling you? Because we've dueled it out on the basketball court. Frankly, I'm a little hurt that our epic basketball battle hasn't been brought up in any interview you've given over the last four years.

It all happened back in 2009. Free Press Editor and and My Little Pony collector Bryan Hanks begged/bullied me into participating in a charity basketball game. I told Hanks I hadn't played basketball in many years, but he assured me this game was just for fun, and that if I was a little rusty, it wouldn't be a big deal. About 10 minutes into a practice the day before the game, my jumper came back and with it, a modest amount of confidence.

On game day during the shoot around, the vibe was loose and it looked like it might be a fun day after all. I grabbed a loose ball and sank a 15-footer, so my teammate threw me the ball and suggested I try a 3-pointer. You were standing in front of me talking to a friend, but when you saw that I was about to take a shot, your instincts kicked in and you attempted to block my shot.

To my surprise, the shot rattled in. Since that fateful day, I've told a few hundred people that I made a 3-pointer while Reggie Bullock was guarding me. As soon as you have your first 30-point game for the Clippers, I'll start figuring out how to fit that story on my license plate.

Others present for "The Shot" contend you were just waving to someone while I was shooting, that your feet never left the ground and that you only looked up because you were afraid you might trip over my hair. To those naysayers I say, horseradish.

Also, the contest that took place that day was not friendly. The 1992 Duke/Michigan national championship game was friendly compared to the game played in Kinston that day. I showed up expecting to shoot a little hoop to benefit a charity, but ended up participating in some sort of Mad Max Olympics.

I've seen people get less worked up over the birth of a child — on an airplane.

I guess what I'm trying to say is that even though we've only met briefly while I was dominating you on the court, there is a bond between us that can't be broken. You're going to need someone in your organization who is honest, forthright, and not afraid to tell you you're wrong — of course, if that's OK with you.

I'm worried about an earnest North Carolina guy being transplanted into seedy old Los Angeles. Reggie, those people in L.A. don't even know what biscuits are, but obviously, I do. Plato once said "The man who foregoes a biscuit will foresaketh his soul; also, he'll always leave the toilet seat up."

Don't become a guy who leaves the toilet seat up, Reggie. For only 10 percent after taxes, I'll look after your money and the toilet seat.

Call me.

LEAKED MEMO SHEDS LIGHT ON NEW
FREE PRESS EDITOR
JULY 16, 2013

Despite being the person who suggested I should have my own column, last month Bryan Hanks was named editor of the Kinston Free Press.

To the general public, Bryan Hanks is an affable, civic-minded do-gooder who drives a military surplus Jeep that's riddled with bullet holes from the Battle of Gettysburg. The behind-the-scenes Bryan Hanks is a maniacal Svengali who terrorizes his employees with threats of termination and mandatory Neil Sedaka karaoke lunches.

One of the first things Hanks did after taking over the editor spot was send out a memo to the rank and file. Here is an excerpt from that memo:

Dear Sycophants,

The purpose of this memo is to let you all know how I intend to run things around here. Anyone not willing to kneel before Hanks and obey my every command is welcome to pick up their consolation bag of fun size M&Ms from the bucket in the lobby on your way out the door.

For starters, no one is to make eye contact with me at any time. Eye contact gives the false impression that a conversation is about to take place, and I can assure you that's not going to happen. If you wish to compliment one of my columns, my cologne or my choice of shirt, you can obtain an Eye Contact Permission Application from our human resources director. If your application for eye contact is approved, you may look me in the eye and compliment me during my weekly 4:56 to 4:58 p.m. office hours on Friday.

Secondly — and I can't stress this enough — once a massage schedule is finalized, IT'S FINAL! If it's your turn to administer my daily, two-hour deep tissue and corn massage, it's locked in. Schedules will not be altered for graduations, pre-planned vacations or unplanned funerals. Employees with standing restraining orders against me are exempt.

Corporate is cracking down on non-work related internet usage, and as some of you know I start my day with a few hours of Dungeons and Dragons online role playing. I'm currently immersed in a campaign to retrieve the remnants of Harry Truman's speedo from the caves of Lonely

Mountain. If anyone gets wind of an IT person coming in to check our computers, you have my permission to delete everything off of my office computer. The username is "Anderson"; password is "Cooper."

Also, on occasion I may ask some of you to perform certain tasks for me such as co-signing on a loan, searching dumpsters for furniture/foodstuffs, checking me for ticks or offering candy to any male employees who show signs of usurping my status as the handsomest man in the office. If Frank in advertising shows signs of slimming down, I better see a steady stream of biscuits, brownies and biscotti flowing from your desks to his thighs.

By all accounts, Hanks led a solitary life in high school. A former girlfriend says the brash, upwardly mobile Bryan Hanks of today is still trying to outrun his less than stellar past.

"Due to his acne, halitosis and rickets, for most of his high school years, Bryan Hanks was lonelier than the guy manning the fruit section at a Golden Corral breakfast buffet," said former girlfriend Peggy Lipton. "We thought he might grow up to become a super-hero or something; apparently he's taken the Joker/Lex Luthor route instead."

Former Free Press writers David Anderson and Chris Lavender corroborate Lipton's depiction.

"I didn't like having to clean his apartment on my day off, but it prepared me for my current part-time job as zoo janitor," Anderson said.

"Sometimes I still wake up screaming thinking it's my turn to loofah his elbows," Lavender said. "He simply refused to moisturize."

FUNERAL FOOD AIN'T WHAT IT USED TO BE
JULY 18, 2013

Kinston may not have a thriving job market, decent infrastructure, strong tax base, affordable utilities, well-funded schools, courteous drivers or an art/music scene, but it does have food.

It's a popular misconception that "Kinston" was derived from the word "Kingston" in an attempt to sever ties with England. Actually, "Kinston" is a Latin word that means "buffet." According to 2009 U.S. Census data, there is a buffet per every 4.7 people in Lenoir County. The phrase "Riding the Gravy Train with Biscuit Wheels" was the official Lenoir County slogan until it was changed to 'Stop Here for Gas on the Way to the Beach" in 1968.

One thing we Kinstonians do have going for us is the ability to comfort loved ones after a death in the family. While cards are nice and flowers are OK, nothing says "we're going to get through this" like a table full of fried chicken.

There was a death in the family this week, and afterwards a few people gathered at my parents' house to discuss funeral arrangements. As soon as I walked in the door, I was asked if I wanted a piece of pecan pie. The question was offensive, and I felt as if my manhood or citizenship were being called into question. Of course I wanted a piece of pecan pie. What am I, an idiot?

I'm at the point where desserts are only part of the equation at birthday parties and during the holidays, which truth be told is probably enough — but this pie was special. You could look at this thing and tell it hadn't been picked up from the gas station on the way home from work. There was a bit of a glow around it, as if ordained by the big guy himself. I'm not sure what heaven looks like, but one would assume it tastes like this fantastic piece of pie.

This pie was so good it felt wrong to be eating it. It was the culinary equivalent of cutting the Mona Lisa into six pieces and handing it out with a napkin and fork. Something with the ability to bring such joy to a person should never be destroyed, yet it would be a waste not to eat it.

Being the youngest person in the room made it easy to grab the rest of the pie and overpower those who tried to block the door. Once outside, I started running and didn't look back. I woke up the next morning in a Wayne County corn field with crows pecking pie crumbs off of my face.

The pie was made by Mrs. Ruth, a woman from a generation that weathered such storms as the Depression, World War II and the Happy Days spin-off "Joanie Loves Cha-chi." I don't know what she put in that pie, but its addictive powers frankly make crystal meth look like a bland sugar cookie.

Maybe this will start a movement to get people off drugs and onto pie. Wouldn't you just love to see pumpkin pie labs sprouting up all over the county? Flour would overtake cocaine as the white powder of choice, and junkies could move away from the needle and the spoon and onto the Easy Bake Ovens.

While attending funeral services in La Grange as a teenager, I began to notice a man who seemed to be at every funeral. I know La Grange is a small town and everybody sort of knows everybody, but this guy had his mail delivered to the funeral home. Everybody knew his name but never knew his association with deceased.

Finally, one of my uncles hipped me to the fact that the guy attended the funerals so he could go to the house afterwards and eat like a king.

Apparently, someone eventually tried to bust the guy by asking how he and the deceased were connected.

"Old Jasper let me pull in front of him when I was trying get out of a parking lot one time," the Funeral Food Marauder said. "We bonded over that."

I'm worried that future generations will be clueless when it comes to comfort food or even food in general. Over the last few decades, the feminist movement has tried to shame women out of the kitchen, and most of the men who are open-minded enough to help with meals insist on grilling an entire goat or consider microwaving a TV dinner "cooking." This scenario is probably what produced the worst/greatest dessert I ever witnessed being delivered after a funeral: A plate of Tootsie Rolls cut up into little squares.

Friend of the Free Press Jonathan Massey walked into my office today holding a jug of Gatorade. He tried for five minutes to get me to take a swig. He'd for some reason removed the label from the bottle, which immediately made me think it was air conditioner run-off or antifreeze.

To put my mind at ease, Massey picked up the jug and took a swig, but I still refused. I asked Massey point blank if this was Free Press Editor Bryan Hanks' way of getting me back for the harmless little tribute to him that I wrote for the July 16 edition of the paper. Massey refused to answer.

Turns out young Massey had purchased a jug of lime/cucumber flavored Gatorade. That someone in the Gatorade research department thought a lime/cucumber flavored beverage would be appealing to Massey's demographic is telling. Some genius over at the Gatorade company has figured out that combining two flavors that should never be in contact with each other — be it lime and cucumber or saffron and Quaker State — is appealing to a 25-year-old male with disposable income and a facial tick.

When the people of Massey's generation start funeralizing their dearly departed, I don't think people will be crashing the services for the food. Then again, Cajun-flavored Q-Tips might catch on.

RENTAL CARS NOW COME WITH GUNS, MARIJUANA
JULY 23, 2013

Right off the bat, let's get one thing straight: I'm a UNC basketball fan.

At a young age, I watched Michael Jordan, James Worthy and Sam Perkins do their stuff in Carmichael Auditorium. I've sent Roy Williams a loaf of Amish Friendship Bread for Christmas every year since 2006. I've joined militant vegetarians who eat nothing but Hardee's hamburgers for months on end because UNC radio legend Woody Durham said it was the official sandwich of the UNC Tar Heels.

My love for Tar Heel basketball is not, however, unconditional.

This mess P.J. Hairston finds himself in (or not in) is a bit disturbing. According to various media outlets, Hairston was arrested at at a license checkpoint on June 5 while driving a GMC Yukon that was rented to someone by the name of "Fats" Thomas. At the time, Hairston didn't have a driver's license in his possession, although he later produced it. USA Today reported Hairston was issued a speeding ticket in 2012 while driving a car rented by someone with the same address as "Fats" Thomas.

Apparently, car rental agencies are so hard up for business they're now offering complimentary Mary Jane and munitions with each vehicle.

"Many of our customers are into guns and ganja, so we just leave them on the seat now like soap in a hotel," said Larry Manet-ti of Hurtz Rental Cars. "All of our cars are equipped with four trap doors that make disposing of incriminating evidence a snap. Hurtz, nor its parent company, are responsible for any customers who are too stoned to tell the difference between a trap door and a policeman's shirt pocket."

According to NorthCarolina.Scout.com, the June 5 incident report stated 41 grams of marijuana and a loaded 9mm handgun were found in or beside the vehicle Hairston was driving. Hairston and his two passengers were charged with misdemeanor possession of marijuana. Hairston later completed a drug assessment and the possession charge against him was dropped.

Now to be fair, haven't most people found ourselves in a rented car with a bag of pot and a loaded gun? As for a driver's license, I haven't bothered getting one of those things since I was 16. What am I, a nerd?

Maybe this was all a big misunderstanding. Maybe Hairston volunteered for the Meals on Wheels program and he thought the bag of weed was paprika. He probably thought "Fats" was the name of the chef cooking all the food, and the 9mm was mistaken for a flare gun from the Yukon's safety kit.

Boy, am I glad we cleared that up. Bring on Duke!

Wait a minute; there's more.

According to the News & Observer and SportingNews.com, "Fats" Thomas said he doesn't know Hairston, while Hairston said he knows Thomas. Hairston also allegedly said he didn't smoke marijuana to get high, but occasionally would take a hit or two.

I'm a firm believer in deniability, so I have no problem with Thomas distancing himself from the situation. There is no "we" in "case dismissed."

What's worrisome is Hairston's alleged statement about not smoking marijuana to get high. Unless glaucoma runs in his family and he's trying to get way out ahead of it, what other reason is there for smoking marijuana? Does the guy who drinks a six-pack of beer per day do so in order to tighten up his physique? That's like saying I mow my lawn every week just to keep the blade on the mower from getting too sharp.

When I was 10-yearsold, I knew not to get in a car that contained weed and a loaded pistol. Hairston is an adult who has completed a few years of college at a prestigious school, but apparently, his orientation packet was missing the "Pros/Cons of Driving A Rented Car Containing Weed and Guns While Unlicensed" handbook that most college freshman in the UNC system receive when they first set foot on campus.

It was a mere clerical error.

Never mind what kind of message this sends to any impressionable children that might look up to Hairston. If this whole fiasco is an example of his decision-making skills, we in Tar Heel Nation could be in for a long season. If we've got a guy wide open under the hoop, will Hairston pass the ball or run into the parking lot and look for a rental car with weed and a gun in the glove compartment? Is Roy going to have to run gun/weed avoidance drills during practice this year?

Right now, deep in the bowels of Cameron Indoor Stadium, that legendary coach with the record for most wins and gallons of Grecian Formula applied to one head is plotting. He's meeting with student leaders to devise a way for those face-painting dunderpates who refer to themselves as the Cameron Crazees to exploit Hairston's troubles.

I'm sure some of them will be wearing jail-door glasses or hanging plastic bags of oregano from their ears during the game, and as Tar Heel fans, we'll have to sit there and take it … don't whine, just take it.

Stay strong, Roy.

STATE BUDGET CUTS LEAD TO THREE-DAY
SCHOOL WEEK
JULY 25, 2013

The latest North Carolina budget has sparked much discussion and drawer-knotting. Between tax reform, teacher tenure and Gov. Pat McCrory's decision to make the McRib the official state sandwich, there has been no shortage of vitriol.

Since the N.C. budget comes in just under 400 pages, journalists have understandably been focusing on the big issue items that will affect the most people. Changes to the number of cardinals bird watchers can shoot per season are of little interest to most citizens, but other overlooked items may cause dissent among the rank. Ranks.

To save money on electricity, effective Sept. 12, all N.C. traffic lights will only feature yellow lights. Eliminating the red and green lights will save an estimated $1,119,187 for the state annually.

"No one really pays attention to traffic lights anymore," said Peter Farrelly of the N.C. Department of Transportation. "If it were up to me, the yellow light and those annoying white lines on the road would be gone too."

While taxes will reportedly be going down for corporations and some individuals, new taxes on the arts have some people up in arms.

"On page 276, paragraph 4, it outlines a plan to tax anyone caught singing/ talking along to the songs 'Wagon Wheel' or 'Thrift Shop'," said Martin Landau for Citizens For Responsible Government. "It's bad enough these songs get more airtime than a flock of migrating geese, but when every Joe and Jane 24-Pack starts singing them at the top of their lungs at yellow lights, things are getting out of hand. Since our organization opposes new taxes of any kind, we fully support this new source of revenue."

"A 'source of revenue' and a tax are two different things, you know."

For the 2013-14 school year, the traditional five-day week is out the window.

"Instead of 8 a.m. to 3 p.m., Monday through Friday, we're switching to 7 a.m. to 7 p.m. on Mondays, Tuesdays and Thursdays," said N.C. Superintendent July Atkinson. "This will allow the state to spend less money on school lunches, utilities and malt liquor for the teacher's lounges."

For the lunches the state is still responsible for, all school buses will be equipped with a special meat compartment next to the engine block.

"Those engines get pretty hot in the morning, so we're going to use that heat to prepare some warm bologna sandwiches for the kids," Atkinson said. "We'll hand the kids two pieces of bread when they get off the bus; they can have all the meat they want until it runs out."

N.C. Speaker of the House Thom Tillis will be hosting several fundraisers throughout the year that will hopefully bridge gaps left in the state budget.

"Most people don't know this, but Rep. Tillis toured with his cousin Mel Tillis until he figured out there was more money in politics," said the speaker's publicist Mike Torello. "Thom and Mel co-wrote the country hits 'Life Turned Her That Way', 'Commercial Affection', 'Shake The Splenda Tree', 'Your Body Is An Outlaw', and 'Whoomp (There It Is)'."

WOMAN ACCUSED OF STEALING BABY TURTLES
JULY 30, 2013

You've seen them on U.S. 70 on Friday afternoon. Their cars/trucks/lunar excursion modules are loaded down with skis, bicycles, fishing poles and enough Bud Light to fill the Grand Canyon. Where are these lemmings going?

Why the beach, of course.

The beach is a wonderful place. Where else can you do irrevocable damage to your skin, get eaten by a shark, poked by dumped hypodermic needles and get sand lodged in areas where only soap and or the loving hands of a trained physician dare to tread?

Don't forget the $10 parking, the Rhodes Scholars who let their dogs roam the beach without a leash and the family with the 13 children who walks across several acres of wide open sand to set up camp to within a credit card's width of your blanket.

I'm a fan of the ocean air and the sound of the waves crashing against the surf. I used to be a fan of swimming in the ocean until I bumped into something with a large fin on its back a few years ago. It was probably a dolphin, but methinks where they go, their less amiable neighbors go as well. I've eaten some pretty good food in my day, so I'm afraid I'm too delicious for shark infested waters.

My girth has decreased slightly since my last trip to the beach, but I'm still not where I'd like to be. On a positive note, no overzealous marine biology majors tried to push me back into the ocean this time. The Wife wore the same bathing suit she bought on our honeymoon 16 years and two children ago, and she looked great. A well-meaning Carteret County police officer asked her if she was with me of her own free will.

A little early morning tiff over the pronunciation of the word "coupon" (it's coo-pon, not kew-pon) had me worried that The Wife might claim she was abducted to get back at me. Thankfully, she decided to confess she was with me of her own accord, although I don't know why she had to whisper it while pulling her purple cap over her beautiful hazel eyes.

Since there wasn't a military school on the East Coast that would take them, we decided to take Tax Deductions 1 and 2 to the beach. I guess you could say they both deserved a little vacation. TD No. 1 had a good year at school and has been progressing nicely with piano lessons, while TD No. 2 has rounded the corner on potty training and hasn't started a fire in the living room in nearly two months.

The Wife has the beach thing down to a science. Aside from the requisite plastic bucket full of sand toys, everything we need is in one bag. There is nothing more sad than watching a grown man try to carry a cooler, surf board, blanket, TV, volleyball net and air mattress across burning hot sand that doesn't care if said man got drunk the night before and left his flip-flops in an Applebee's bathroom in Portsmouth.

We staked claim to a little square of sand about 2 feet from the point where the tide was hitting the beach. I assumed (wrongly) that no one would come along and try to set up camp the 2-feet of sand between our blanket and the crashing waves.

The TDs loved playing in the ocean. TD No. 2 — the youngest and least afraid of anything — repeatedly tried to run past me and out to the shrimp boats on the horizon. Even though the rolling wall of water dwarfed her, she apparently only saw it as a minor nuisance that stood between her and a career as a mermaid.

A couple of times, I intentionally let a wave bounce her around a little in hope that it would quell her lust for sea exploration. The snout full of salt water did give her pause, but after a few seconds, she corralled a wayward porpoise, hopped on its back like Clayton Moore and asked it to take her to whoever was throwing all the water at her.

TD No. 1 is an avid sea shell collector. I noticed her hands were full of shells, so I offered to keep them in my bathing suit pockets. After a few hours of her bringing her treasures to me, both pockets on my bathing suit were filled with a collection of smooth and jagged sea shells. It looked as if I was trying to smuggle Mickey Mouse out of the country in my shorts.

After an hour or so, I took the TDs for a walk to give The Wife a few minutes to sunbathe in peace. During our walk, I noticed the beach was filled with little girls ranging in age from 4 to 6, each of them squealing at a high pitch whenever a drop of water hit them. It sounded as if everyone on the beach was making tea.

When we returned from the walk, The Wife took the TDs and I was able to stretch out on the blanket and catch a few rays. About two minutes into it, I felt the sun disappear. I looked up to find three people trying to set up in the aforementioned 2-foot area of sand between us and the ocean.

"Would you mind setting up a little to the left, please?" I asked.

"Why?" said a very sturdy woman with leathery skin and a cigarette perched between her drought-reenactment lips.

"Because there's about 70 miles of beach to the left and I don't see why you have to get directly between us and our view of the water that's just 2 feet away," I said. "As much as I'd enjoy watching that beach chair you got with Pall Mall points try to support your ample frame without buckling, I'd rather be able to see my wife and kids play in the water."

"Well, the beach is open to everyone," she said.

"You're right, it is," I replied. "Hey, isn't that Lou Rawls over there?"

While the woman who would be Cannon looked away, I pulled our blanket forward to end this war of eastern aggression.

The sturdy woman was accompanied by what appeared to be her sister and a man who could have been her husband, brother or parole officer. He was a slight man who was obviously just along for the ride.

"Honey, we don't have to sit right in front of them — just move 3 feet to the left and be done with it," he said.

Although she grumbled in some sort of language only parolees understand, she plopped down in her chair. Her skin was already of the burnt, leathery variety. My theory is she was trying to burn out the cancer cells in her epidermis with more sun.

A few hours later as the family and I headed to the car, I noticed the policeman who'd mistaken me for a kidnapper earlier in the day was still on patrol. I waved him over and pointed out the Bride of Ben & Jerry who tried to steal our spot on the beach.

"Officer, you see that Barcalounger over there smoking a cigarette? She's been collecting baby turtles all day and is hiding them in her beach bag," I whispered.

The officer thanked me for the tip, gave me an honorary policeman's badge and went over to investigate.

"She's taken that bag out to her car a few times today," I yelled to him. "You might want to check her car, too."

With that, we headed over to the picnic area and enjoyed a glorious peanut butter and jelly sandwich lunch. As that thing that tried to steal our spot was frisked and her car torn apart by wildlife officials, I decided the beach wasn't such a bad place after all.

DRONE RUNS OUT OF GAS, LANDS IN
WALMART PARKING LOT
AUGUST 1, 2013

Prices and employee benefits weren't the only things falling at the Kinston Walmart on Wednesday.

"I'd stopped at Walmart to pick up a few things," said Amy French of La Grange. "I hadn't been there in at least three hours, so supplies were running low."

As French approached the store's entrance, she was shocked by what she thought was a fast moving storm cloud.

"It was as if someone had erected a tent over half of the parking lot," French said. "The sun just disappeared for a moment."

Within seconds, the sun reappeared and the sound of metal scraping across several parked vehicles alarmed several Walmart shoppers.

"We hit the deck," said Mike Torello, who was visiting Kinston with his wife Julie. "I was a cop in Chicago for 18 years, and my first thought was a plane had crashed in the parking lot — which ticked me off because I'd just waxed the car that morning."

As it turns out, what landed in the Walmart parking lot wasn't a plane.

"It was an unmanned United States government drone," said U.S. Press Secretary Art Carney. "Due to budget cuts, the drones sometimes run low on fuel. The intern in charge of keeping the drone on course was trying to land it at the Murphy Express gas station just across the street from Walmart."

Cell phone photos taken of the drone show what appear to be several bumper stickers on each wing. One wing featured a sticker rendition of the trucker mudflap girl, while the other wing sported a "Hillary 2016" sticker and a "Biden 2017" sticker.

When informed of the drone crash, U.S. House Speaker John Boehner reportedly burst into tears. When Boehner was told there were no injuries, the crying escalated into joyful blubbering. Eventually Boehner collapsed from dehydration and several staffers jumped into action.

"A couple of juice boxes and he'll be fine," a senior aide told the Associated Press. "We learned our lesson during a screening of the last

'Twilight' movie."

When asked why the drone was allowed to run out of gas during flight, Carney again blamed budget cuts.

"This sequester has forced us to turn over the drone program to a staff of unpaid interns," Carney said. "The interns came highly recommended. One of them was employee of the month at a Virginia Kinko's three months in a row before joining the team."

As for the intern in charge of the drone that forcibly added a sunroof to 12 cars on Wednesday, Carney wasn't as complimentary.

"The intern in charge of the drone that suffered a petroleum deficiency has been tough to track down, although his recent postings on social media sights are being investigated," Carney said. "He's been re-Tweeting crowd pictures from the Reggae Sunsplash 2013 Festival in Jamaica but is not answering his phone."

Most of the photos released to the press depict women in various stages of undress, Jimmy Cliff signing autographs, concert-goers smoking large, misshapen cigarettes and eating several bags of Cheetos and Doritos. When asked why the government was flying a drone in Lenoir County airspace, Carney said it was linked to the War on Terror.

"Although Osama Bin Laden is dead, there are many people in the world who are trying to further his efforts," Carney said. "One of those people is his cousin — Leroy Bin Laden — a man known to have ties to the Kinston area. The last time Leroy Bin Laden was on our radar, he threatened to detonate a collard bomb at a Larry The Cable Guy show in Duplin County. We spotted him entering the Kinston Walmart on Wednesday and sent a drone to collect information on his whereabouts."

While in Walmart, Leroy Bin Laden reportedly purchased six heads of cabbage, a container of black pepper, a case of aerosol cheese, a Gerald LeVert CD and a bag of Miracle-Gro.

"Based on these purchases, Bin Laden is either inviting people over for dinner and wants to tidy up his yard," Carney said, "or he's planning a natural gas attack that could singe the nose hairs of every citizen withing a 10-foot radius of the epicenter."

Leroy Bin Laden was last seen walking out of Walmart wearing jeans and a "Jihad-er Done!" T-shirt.

WORLD WAR II VET, FARMER DIES THURSDAY AT 92
AUGUST 15, 2013

Parrott Sutton of Bucklesberry died last week at the age of 92.

He was my granddaddy.

He passed at 4 a.m. on Thursday morning at the wonderful Kitty Askins Hospice Center in Goldsboro. Thankfully, he was able to stay in his home up until four days before his passing. Aside from having both knees replaced and a bout of tuberculosis a few years back, until recent months, he was usually in great health.

Out of his 92 years, he was probably only sick for about nine months total.

How was this guy able to live until 92, only having to give up driving a mere eight months ago? Genetics are no doubt a factor, but work being his hobby probably had a hand in it as well. My daddy recently used the duck analogy to describe Parrott: Calm on the surface, but underneath, those feet were always paddling. A man with a fourth grade education couldn't have gotten as far as he did in life without an above average level of drive.

I worked with him in tobacco from the time I was 5 until the summer after I graduated from college. At 55, he was still working the top tier in a stick tobacco barn. He was still crawling into the hoop and walking the tobacco down well into his 60s, and I think he was still climbing to the top of the grain bin around the age of 70. A good number of people I know couldn't — or wouldn't — have done any of this stuff in their 20s.

Granddaddy was a veteran of World War II, but he wasn't keen on discussing it. He told me just last year of being so thirsty at one point he and his fellow soldiers drank water that had puddled in a cow's hoof print.

A few times, he spoke about having to use his rifle in the war, but he did so without 1 ounce of bravado. It was a hellish situation and he never painted it as anything else.

When he got the news he was finally going home, he slept on the tarmac next to the plane to be sure he didn't miss the flight.

One thing he told me at a young age was the pressure his fellow soldiers put on him to drink, which he didn't do. He said they'd make fun of him and some times even pour booze on his head, but he never gave in.

Whenever I see some talking head prattling on about young people and peer pressure, I want to hit them in the head with a rotary dial telephone.

Many of Parrott's fellow soldiers were from New York City and had no idea how to survive in foxholes and ditches. Having pretty much grown up outside, Granddaddy looked after these guys who were used to sidewalks and paved streets.

Three decades after the war ended, one of the New Yorkers that Granddaddy helped in the war tracked him down. They spoke on the phone for a while, and on top of thanking Parrott for helping him during the war, he told Parrott he'd made a lot of money as a businessman — and that if Parrott ever needed money to just ask and it would be sent immediately.

Granddaddy had done well as a farmer and didn't need any help, but the magnitude of the gesture wasn't lost on him.

Once while we were still using stick tobacco barns, Parrott and I were loading bundles of tobacco sticks into a truck. I picked up a bundle and a snake reared up and snapped at me. Parrott picked up a stick and beat the snake until bumps rose on its head. I was impressed, because the only time I'd seen bumps appear on a noggin that quickly was in a Roadrunner cartoon.

Parrott was always busy, but during tobacco season he was busy and a half. He'd been running so hard one day that when he came in from the field he went in the house and forgot to turn the truck off. It ran all night and the next morning was out of gas.

When tobacco sold good, we'd stop and get a $2 hamburger on the way home. Once during an auction, all of our sheets were taken out of the line and dragged into a corner. We initially thought something was wrong, but it turns out the tobacco looked so good they had to set up a separate auction.

Suffice to say, we got a $4 steak on the way home that day.

Another simple pleasure Parrott enjoyed up until his last couple of months was eating at Ken's Grill in La Grange. Like a favorite pew in church, he had his favorite booth in the corner. I've actually heard of people getting up (without his asking) and letting him have his usual booth. It was pretty much a Southern take on the "Cheers"/Norm Peterson dynamic.

During the summers it wasn't uncommon for he and I to head out to Ken's for an ice cream cone after lighting all the barns. Making this an especially fortuitous endeavor was the fact that my cousin Amy was usually working at night, and she somehow figured out how to get about half a gallon of ice cream onto each cone, bless her heart.

When sitting at Ken's, Parrott loved talking to people. Once during a particularly rainy spell, the Neuse River rose to a few feet above flood stage. I saw Parrott tell a fellow farmer the river had gotten so high you could see under it. He went on to say the mosquitoes in Bucklesberry had gotten so big they were toting chickens off during the night.

Parrott never cared for my long-ish hair, and on the night of his funeral he got his revenge from the other side.

A very sweet woman I've known my entire life came through the receiving line at the funeral to offer her condolences. She is in her 90s and her eyesight isn't quite what it used to be. I was standing next to my cousin Shane, who is about 6-foot-3; I'm about 6-foot even. The sweet lady with the less than perfect eyesight shook Shane's hand, pointed at me and asked Shane the following:

"Is that your wife?"

Granddaddy would have laughed, held up his pocket knife and asked me to lean in for a quick haircut. He did so many times.

For the rest of the weekend, family members young and old ribbed me about the wife question — even my real wife. Just to play along, after I left the family on Friday night, I called back and told Shane to pick up a loaf of bread and a gallon of milk on his way home.

Although he sort of knew about my writing for The Free Press, he never got a handle on the music stuff I do ("What's Jon doing with that music turnout?"). But, I think he knew his family was looking out for him when he got in the short rows, so that's enough.

To everyone who stopped by last week with food and/or a good story about Parrott, it was greatly appreciated. It's telling that a man who outlived most of his contemporaries still had 150 people show up at his funeral. If my funeral cracks a dozen, I'll be lucky.

WHAT HAPPENS WHEN YOUR THROAT LOCKS UP FOR THREE DAYS
AUGUST 20, 2013

Two weekends ago, my throat seized up for an entire weekend. I was unable to eat or drink anything from Friday night through Monday morning.

As long-time sufferers of my column already know, without warning my throat has been known to lock up two or three times a year. Usually these episodes last all of 10 minutes, so I just assumed it was one of those knick knacks life decides to throw your way if it catches you having too long a spell of peace and harmony.

It was an odd time for my body to revolt. In the weeks leading up to the great Anvil In The Esophagus Tour of 2013, I'd switched to drinking water 90 percent of the time, pretty much sworn off fast food and eaten more spinach than Popeye.

Apparently, this new regiment ticked my body off and it decided to revolt. After taking a bite of food equivalent in size to a garden pea that was then masticated into the consistency of sand, my throat seized up tighter than Rush Limbaugh's girdle after a trip to the Sizzler.

(The judges would have also accepted "tighter than Keith Olbermann's hat after reading his fan mail.)

The last time the ol' food pipe went on strike, it was caused by having a drink of cold water, which made me feel incredibly manly. I've observed people in restaurants shovel food into their pie holes with all the finesse of a water buffalo, yet I have to be careful taking a sip of water. Just a few days ago, my 3-yearold daughter took a big gulp of water, winked at me and said, "That's how you do it, big boy."

Once while taking a train trip to New Jersey, I saw a guy eat an entire Egg McMuffin in two bites — while talking on his cell phone. I was conflicted; sure, this guy sounds like the soundtrack to a documentary on animal pornography while he eats, but not only does he not choke, he carries on a rather lively conversation about his fantasy bowling team without missing a beat. Meanwhile, I'm nibbling on a rapidly browning banana that was green as a gourd when I started eating it four hours earlier.

By the time Saturday rolled around, I assumed the throat would've loosened up … but no such luck. I had band rehearsal that day, so I figured the waves of deep bass that would be bouncing around the room would loosen things up. Not only did the throat not loosen up during rehearsal, I developed a case of hiccups with a level of severity unseen since Tennile beat Captain senseless with a saxophone on American Bandstand in 1979.

When I was still unable to even drink anything on Sunday, I started to get a little antsy. Sure, hiccuping like a steam-hammer while unable to eat is a great way to lose a few pounds, but I'd just about had enough of Choking to the Oldies. When the problem showed no signs of improvement on Monday, I had a family member take me to the doctor.

Other than the odd physical for work or life insurance, I'd never been to a doctor. One reason for this is that I've been blessed with good health; also, I have a white-hot terror of anything involving needles or blood.

I did undergo a voluntary procedure that can be filed under family planning a few years ago, and you can read all about that in my book "Making Gravy in Public" (Moodring Publishing, 2011). I won't give too much of the plot away, but let's just say it felt like lighting struck in areas lighting has no business being.

To fix my problem, they were basically going to run a garden hose equipped with a light and a camera down my throat. To do this, they'd need to knock me out, which meant I'd have the wonderful experience of being poked for my first IV. Upon hearing this news, another part of my body tightened up to squeeze-two-nickels-into-a-dime proportions.

The talented, beautiful woman who administered the IV did a wonderful job. She could tell I was no fan of needles since I'd managed to turn my head a full 180-degrees away while she pushed the sharp metal rod into the unsuspecting flesh of the top of my right hand. Since I didn't scream, she told me I'd acted like a big boy.

When they wheeled me back to the procedure room, they asked me to turn on my side. Out of an unnecessary sense of caution, I made sure they knew this was for a throat procedure and not a muffler job. They laughed and assured me they knew which end they were working with.

The anesthesiologist was a genius, because 20 seconds after he started that little drip, I was out of here. When I woke up, I was in the recovery room with no memory whatsoever of the procedure.

Having never been unconscious or even drunk before, I was still feeling the warm, fuzzy feeling of the knockout juice for quite a while. At that moment, if someone had attacked me with a hammer, I don't think it would have bothered me.

Since the procedure, the throat has behaved and I don't have to cut my M&Ms into quarters any more. If all goes well I should be cleared for salad by Christmas.

MASSIVE FOOT ON TINY CHILD A BIG PROBLEM
AUGUST 27, 2013

Over the past few weeks, The Wife has been feverishly trying to find a tennis shoe that will fit Tax Deduction No. 1's canoe of a foot. Honest to goodness, the girl could surf without a board.

Occasionally, a shoe would fit, but it would look like it was cut from the jacket Rodney Dangerfield wore in "Caddy Shack." Flavor Flav would think these shoes were too busy.

I'm a little ashamed to admit it, but this shoe situation was affecting my life. That little tiff between the Israelis and the Palestinians is a parking ticket compared to the pulling of hair and gnashing of teeth generated by this shoe thing.

Thinking if it's not in the local stores it has to be somewhere on the Internet, I sat TD No. 1 beside me and started surfing the web for girl's tennis shoes.

I asked The Wife what size foot TD No. 1 was dragging around, expecting a concise answer such as "4" or — to be more accurate — "9". What I got was an education on the perils of sizing in the women's clothing industry.

Apparently, a Nike size 4 is different from a Converse size 4. After about 30-seconds of a description that was already being dumbed down for me, I started to see little blue dots. I began thinking about how much I loved my long deceased bulldog named Katie, and how she always knew how to show up in the field a few minutes for Nab and Pepsi time.

When I came to, The Wife was saying some nonsense about me not paying attention. I told her she looked cute — which she did — but I'm pretty sure the sentiment wasn't taken in the spirit it was intended.

TD No. 1 and I checked every shoe website between here and Vietnam, and we got close a few times. One shoe was exactly right, except that it was white on the bottom instead of blue. When I asked what the big deal was, TD No. 1 said the white part of the shoe would show dirt too easily.

At this point, I didn't care if the shoes had the Manson family crest on them, but I was happy to see that some of the practicality we've been trying to instill in our little Bigfoot had taken hold.

At this point, I called an emergency family meeting. I assembled The Wife and TD No. 1 in the kitchen; TD No. 2 was climbing a light pole at the time and, frankly, we were enjoying the peace and quiet.

I informed The Wife and TD No. 1 that if this wasn't settled soon, Social Services would show up at the house wondering why our daughter was wearing empty tissue boxes for shoes.

Although we always try to buy local, we had to look outside the county for a solution. A phone call was made to a shoe store in Goldsboro, and some angel named LaToya told us she had the shoe we were looking for.

In an unprecedented display of courtesy, LaToya agreed to hold the shoes for us until the next day. I grabbed the phone from my wife and started telling this woman I'd never met how much I loved her and what a great day this was for my family.

She seemed a little creeped out, but it had to be said.

The next morning, I went around the house beating a frying pan with a wooden spoon. I wanted these people to be at that store the second LaToya put the key in the door. I didn't mean 10 minutes after opening; I wanted my crew there to hold her hand as she walked from her car to the door — just to make sure she didn't trip and injure herself before the store could be opened.

I taught TD No. 2 to walk in front of LaToya and throw rose petals on the ground to make her journey across the parking lot a pleasant one.

I gave everyone a minute to eat their toast, a minute to brush their teeth, and a minute to get dressed. I gave TD No. 1 an extra 30 seconds to deal with those diving boards at the end of her legs. The poor girl's toes are in a different time zone than her ankles.

With everyone fed and brushed, The Wife headed over to Goldsboro with our tax deductions in tow.

I began pacing the hall incessantly. After what seemed like an eternity, I called The Wife to see what was taking so long.

"We just made it to the end of the driveway," she said. "I'm turning off my phone now."

For the next hour, I knew what the staff at NASA felt when they lost contact with Apollo 12 in the winter of 1969. Their crew was somewhere out in space, embarking on an impossible mission — and so was mine.

Finally, my phone rang but I tripped over a dollhouse on my way to answer it. After the swelling and the cursing subsided, I called The Wife back and she gave me the good news: The long national shoe nightmare was over. TD No. 1 and her Barnum and Bailey-esque feet had finally been matched with the right conglomeration of canvas, string, rubber and sweatshop labor.

With the shoes out of the way, the school year and its concurrent nightly hour-long process of putting together the following day's ensemble can commence.

Don't worry about me. If it gets to be too much, I'll just slam a door on my head for 10 or 15 minutes — it works every time.

MEMORIES OF STUCK BUSES, FAT JOKES AND BIG EARS
SEPTEMBER 10, 2013

I believe the children are our future — and the future's so bright, I've gotta wear shades.

Actually, that first sentence was a total fiction. The immediate future will be shaped by (God help us) people from my generation. These people are running the businesses, banks and government agencies that will provide jobs and, eventually, unemployment benefits for our children.

Prior to my senior year of high school, a "friend" of mine talked me into taking advanced algebra II, which ended up being the mathematical equivalent of getting a colonoscopy with a cactus. My teacher applied for and was awarded a grant to pay for the cases of red markers she needed to properly point out the mistakes on my test papers.

Thankfully, I took a few easy electives that year. Whenever my algebra test scores were lower than Lil Wayne's pants, there was an easy A lurking around the corner to even things out.

Judge if you will, but after three years of college prep courses, what brain power I had was spent. Also, here's a little secret: Unless you're one of the few with the gears to be a scientist or an engineer, there is no algebra in the real world. If you don't believe me, see Episode 1 of "Twin Peaks."

Until I was 16, I rode the school bus, which was like "Lord of the Flies" on wheels. It wasn't unusual to find fireworks, knives or livestock on that bus. The route encompassed several dirt roads, and one of them was the dirt road that's now adjacent to Sanderson Farms on U.S. 70.

It had been raining all day, and as the bus was pulling up to the house at the end of the road it got stuck. As I remember it, the house didn't have a phone, so the bus driver asked all of us to get off and push.

I refused on the grounds that if I got mud on my clothes I'd be kicked out of the house. I think a farmer eventually came along with a tractor and pulled us out.

On that same bus, some enterprising truant became obsessed with the size of my ears. Now this guy was a friend of mine, and he weighed around 250 pounds in the third grade. Whenever somebody would start teasing him about his weight, I stood up for him.

You can imagine my dismay when he got everyone on the bus to go along with his thesis that my ears were too big. At the time, there was a popular song called "The Freaks Come Out At Night" by Whodini, and this nudnik changed it to "When The Freaks Come Out At Night, Jon's Ears Get Up and Dance."

For the rest of the year, my nickname was "Ears." I was also a chubby kid, so on top of the teasing about my weight, I had people asking me to fly them around with my giant Dumbo ears.

When I see any of these people today and they act like we're old buddies from way back, the urge to lock them in a bank vault with a starving badger is nearly overpowering.

Years later, my business degree from ECU landed me a prestigious job in administration at KSI at the Du-Pont plant in Kinston. I had an executive office in what used to be a bathroom, with the overrun drain still in the middle of the floor just under my chair.

Wouldn't you know it, but the guy who was obsessed with my ears worked at the same place. I was in charge of payroll, so every time he brought up the good old days with my ears, I'd delete one of his IN punches on the time clock. Whenever he came to my office to correct his time card, I'd pretend my ears were too big to hear him properly.

Near the end of my time with KSI, the ear guy called in sick. I pulled his file in order to document why he was out, and the following is a word-for-word, syllable-for-syllable account of our conversation:

Me: "OK, I have to list a reason for the absence in your file. Did you have to go to the doctor?"

Ear guy: "No; I ate too many ribs last night."

Me: "You cracked a rib?"

Ear guy: "Naw, I ate too many ribs."

Another unfortunate incident linked to the school bus was my one and only experience with the dreaded wedgie.

I guess I'd lived a sheltered life, but I'd never thought of grabbing the top of someone's underwear and trying to pull it up to their shoulders. It happened to me one afternoon and it was not pleasant.

One minute I'm sitting there talking to my buddy about the length of Catherine Bach's shorts on the "Dukes of Hazzard", and the next, it feels as if Satan himself has jumped up through the ground and stabbed me in the tuckus with a pitchfork.

Before the offender let go of my drawers, I turned around and started punching him as hard as I could. The guy's name was Benji, and I ended up busting his lip. The bus driver pulled over and began his investigation. He asked why I punched a guy over a wedgie, and I said because he pulled my drawers up into areas they should not be.

Benji and I were given the option of going to the principal's office or sitting down and letting it go. We opted to let it go, although I was ultra-sensitive to any movement that occurred behind me for several weeks.

Eventually, Benji and I became buddies, and at one point we went into business together selling packs of Now & Later candies (that cost 10 cents) for 25 cents per pack at school and on the bus. The partnership ended when Benji wanted to expand the business into cigarettes. Later in life, I think Benji ended up selling cigarettes that had nothing to do with tobacco.

One good day I had in elementary school was the time a girl named Mindy and I got lost on field day. Our teacher sent us back to the classroom to get something, and when we got back to the football field, the class had disappeared. We walked around looking for them, but not very hard.

Neither one of us had any interest in field day, although several of our classmates bought into it big time. You'd have thought winning the tug of war was the only way to avoid the guillotine. The whole thing was pointless, because our class was competing against a group that included the 250-pound guy who got an entire school bus to obsess on my ears.

"Jon's on their team!" I could hear him yelling from across the field. "Watch out; he'll flap his ears to throw dust in your eyes!"

GOING THROUGH THE BELONGINGS OF A DECEASED LOVED ONE
SEPTEMBER 12, 2013

Going through the belongings of a recently deceased loved one is an odd experience. The amount of things to sift through can be overwhelming — even if the loved one in question wasn't a pack rat.

My granddaddy passed a few weeks back, and after all the condolences and fried chicken faded away, it was time to go through his stuff. He didn't collect anything or have any hobbies. Until age 75, his hobby was work. He liked being home and never understood why anybody would want to go on a vacation.

I tried to explain to him on more than one occasion that most people like to get away from their responsibilities every once in a while, but I think all he heard was the voice of Charlie Brown's teacher.

The closest thing we found to a collection was a plastic bag containing eight old watches. These weren't antiques or anything, just run-of-the-mill Timex fare. The older ones were covered in scratches as they were worn during his working years. The only digital watch in the bag was there because he spotted it in a ditch while driving a tractor. He put me in charge of getting a battery for it, as he suspected that's all that was wrong with it.

Sure enough, it fired right up when the new battery was installed, although when its alarm started beeping at midnight, my grandparents initially thought the fire alarm was going off.

Getting a song on the radio or a column in the paper was never that big of a deal, but when I was able to make the watch stop beeping, you'd have thought I'd cured dandruff. Suffice to say, I ended up with the alarming watch.

In his storage room, there was a glass pitcher full of nuts, bolts, nails, springs and various ephemera. He was occasionally given a hard time for keeping that pitcher of "junk" around, but it had a purpose. At least 10 times during my tenure with the administration, I was sent to the house to retrieve that pitcher when something either broke down or needed to be invented.

One time a winch motor was acting up and I was sent after The

Pitcher. The winch itself was probably built sometime in the mid-1980s, while I doubt anything in The Pitcher was any manufactured past 1968. Nevertheless, something was pulled out of The Pitcher and screwed/hammered into the winch that fixed the problem.

When I found out The Pitcher was probably going to be jettisoned, I immediately requested it. I don't have the mechanical acumen to fix anything more complicated than a sandwich, but I didn't want it to disappear.

Anyone who stuck their hand in The Pitcher was usually mutilated by all the sharp edges therein, so it could be a valuable DNA source if the need were ever to arise.

Another oddity I requested was a wedge pillow that had a home on his couch for I'm guessing a couple of decades. In the days when we were still working in wood stick tobacco barns, we'd come in for dinner around noon. The food lovingly prepared by my grandma would usually be inhaled so we could fit in a 15-minute nap.

Granddaddy sat in a recliner (covered with a series of towels) and I got the couch (covered with a series of towels). The wedge pillow seemed to have ether in it, and I would sometimes get emotional when I had to leave it and go back to the field.

I also ended up with the apron he wore when chopping up barbecue, a pair of his overalls and his remaining dress hats. Even with a shaved head, my noggin is too big to wear any of his hats, so right now they're sitting in a chair next to a framed tobacco leaf. The pillow aside, I have no idea what I'll do with any of this stuff.

These items may end up in a box that'll sit on a shelf in a closet, but I'll feel better knowing they're there.

SMARTPHONE BLAMED IN BUGGY ACCIDENT, NO EVIDENCE AT SCENE
SEPTEMBER 24, 2013

The telephone was first patented by Alexander Graham Bell in 1876 — only six months prior to Fred Thompson patenting the telemarketing call in 1877.

To paraphrase Tim Wilson, I believe if Mr. Bell had known the telephone would evolve into the smart-phone, he would have scrapped it and just fixed the toaster like his wife had asked him to. Bell is also credited with inventing the metal detector, the hula hoop and the Cross Your Heart bra.

I'm no Luddite, but the whole phone thing has gotten way out of hand. At concerts, people are on their phones texting about the show instead of watching it. In movie theaters these days, there are so many phones lit up it looks like ET's family reunion.

Just this weekend, I saw a guy trying to text while operating a leaf blower.

So far, I've avoided the whole smart-phone revolution. Until recently, I clung to my basic cell phone with the grip of a rustic watchdog on a revenuer's ankle. That beautiful, out-of-date phone was about half the size of a Mr. Goodbar but twice as sweet. On one full charge, I could make it through a five-day work week.

As for my cellphone plan, I kept it pretty basic: Phone.

Long-suffering readers of this space know how much guff I took for having an old TV in my living room, but it was nothing in comparison to the grief I had to endure over my phone.

"Do you have to put a quarter in it?" "Do you have to wind it up?" "Did you win it as a prize from a gumball machine?"

Phone elitists, tech-no-snobs and all-out dunderpates scoffed at my phone as if it were responsible for canceling "Seinfeld." I've seen people stand up in court to address those convicted of heinous crimes have better dispositions than those who talked so ugly about my tattered but dependable little phone. That little sucker rang if I had a call, and that's all I needed it to do.

This abhorrence of smartphones has nothing to do with age but rather a belief that some things have been perfected, such as bikinis, DVD players and pizza. I'm not a drinker, but it turns out we're still trying to build a better alcohol delivery device. Apparently, beer cans now come equipped with an extra opening that will facilitate a quicker transfer of beer into your pie hole.

My prediction: Each 12-pack of brewski will come equipped with its own funnel and fake ID card by January.

For years, I owned a VCR, but when DVD players came along, I realized they were an improvement. Now, all of a sudden, we have Blu-ray players, which supposedly have enough clarity to make the pores on Christian Bale's nose viewable from outer space. If you're really into movies loaded with special effects, I can see where a Bluray player might be a good investment.

Conversely, if you're into Wes Anderson movies, the need to see Bill Murray's beard hairs in state-of-the-art clarity really isn't there.

As for the bikini, that's been a champion product for many decades now, so let's forego any further R&D on what I think we can all agree is a home run.

You lunatics at the corporate level of pizza companies, just stop it right now. There is enough cheese on the pizza without injecting more of it into the crust, the napkins and the soda.

Some of us leave those bits of plain crust behind so we can tell ourselves, "Well, at least I didn't eat the whole thing." If you squirt cheese into the part of the crust none of us eat, we're going to end up eating it and that's going to be a major blow to our self-esteem, which will in turn make us eat more pizza.

Oh, I see what you guys did there — touché.

I owned a smart-phone briefly a few years ago. At work, we were issued Samsung Moment phones by our former owners, and never has a product been more aptly named.

At full battery power, those phones needed a cigarette and a nap after three calls and a text message. I once tried to send a photo while it was plugged in and it still shut down. I used the phone's GPS app once while trying to find an address in Raleigh.

I realized it wasn't very reliable when I T-boned a horse and buggy up around Pennsylvania.

Thankfully the Amish don't believe in photography — so evidence, schmevidence.

LA GRANGE MAN CHARGED WITH OPERATING FAIR WITHOUT PERMIT
SEPTEMBER 26, 2013

A La Grange man has been arrested for operating a fair in a vacant field behind his house.

According to an incident report obtained from the La Grange Police Department, Cedric Lombard, 48, of 7244 Prairie Ave., operated several concession stands and amusement rides without the proper permits from Sept. 20-23.

"What do I need a permit for?" Lombard asked on Wednesday. "I have a permit for this land, which in turn should permit me to do what I want to do with it."

Law enforcement officials shut down Lombard's fair after receiving reports of fraud and counterfeit sauerkraut.

"Finances are tight, so to save money we took our two boys to Mr. Lombard's fair," said Trudy Joplin, 47, of Kinston. "It only cost $3 per person, so we figured a cheap fair would be better than no fair at all. The hot dogs were OK, but the petting zoo was nothing more than a collection of stray dogs fighting over a trash can lid full of Ol' Roy mixed with malt liquor."

Other attractions that raised eyebrows at Lombard's fair included The Maze of Old Car Batteries, The Bearded Uncle, The Hall of Busted Mirrors, Muffler Jousting, Bobbing for Brisket, Spot the Weave, Lawn Mower Derby and a Wet Sock contest.

"(Lombard) threw a water hose on top of his house and called it a water slide," said Ira Stone, 42, of Snow Hill. "They'd slide off the roof and land into a pile of mattresses he'd picked out of the landfill."

Lombard said the parents were out of line to accuse of him of creating an unsafe environment.

"This all plays into the nanny state mentality that's ruining this country," Lombard said. "Just because trace elements of rickets and Texas Pete were found on those mattresses, everybody went crazy.

"Helmets, vaccinations and toothbrushes are making these children wimps!"

If some patrons were willing to cast a blind eye to Lombard's unusual fair activities, none of them could ignore his menu.

"We had hot sewer trout sandwiches, squirrel on a stick, boiled pennies, fried Snickers, worm spaghetti, pocket lint gumbo and cabbage splits," Lombard said. "And our cotton candy wasn't that fake stuff that's all sugar; ours was made from real cotton."

This is not Lombard's first brush with the law. A background check revealed Lombard was arrested twice in Miami for running an illegal Girl Scout fighting ring in 1985. In 1991, he pleaded no contest to one count of soliciting prostitution at the San Diego Zoo, and in 2004, he served four months in jail for crimes against origami.

Lombard is currently being held in the Lenoir County Jail under a $2,000 secured bond. His first court date is scheduled for Sept. 31.

LONG TIME EDITOR NANCY SAUNDERS
LEAVING THE FREE PRESS
OCTOBER 1, 2013

Free Press Assistant Managing Editor Nancy Saunders has ridden off into the sunset.

As I type this on Monday, a meal is being planned at Free Press HQ to honor the many years of service Nancy Saunders has given The Free Press. Although a memo has been sent out to discourage it, many malnourished reporters have already started lining their pockets with Ziploc bags and aluminum foil.

Some have blamed past luncheon larcenies as a symptom of low pay, while others refer to it as a built-in anti-obesity safeguard — which actually counts as a health benefit with the new Obamacare law kicking into effect today.

Nancy has been with The Free Press since 1999; rumor has it she was the inspiration for Prince's hit song "1999." Lending credence to the rumor is the fact Nancy lived only three blocks away from Prince's Paisley Park Studios during her stint as Minnesota Vikings cheerleader from 1980-82.

In an interview on the Free Press Radio Show in 2012, Saunders said the split with Prince stemmed from an argument over a blouse. Saunders also said the song "Raspberry Beret" was inspired by a jelly mishap during a visit to the Golden Corral breakfast buffet.

Although her job title at the Free Press is Assistant Managing Editor, Nancy deals with many issues well outside of her purview. Largely consumed with community events over the years, Nancy has also served as an unpaid counselor to Free Press staffers young and old.

"This job can be stressful but Nancy has a lot of practice talking people down from ledges," said Free Press Chief Photographer Janet Carter. "A few months after I started here, I began to feel overwhelmed. Nancy took me out to lunch and I poured my heart out to her."

Janet continued, "The next day, she went up to the reporter who kept forgetting to post his photo assignments in a timely manner and caught him with a left hook and a two good rabbit punches. From that day forward, all photo assignments were posted at least 24-hours in advance, and my stress just melted away.

"Every few months she would give him a shot to the ribs to just keep him in check; that's called being thorough."

Nancy is also superb when it comes to interacting with the public. Whether it's the civic group chairperson who calls at 4:58 p.m. to alert Nancy about an event that's happening at 5 p.m., or the person wishing to place a wedding announcement with a photo that makes the infamous photo of the Loch Ness monster look like an Olan Mills portrait, she knows how to navigate those waters.

I once witnessed a man with a tattoo of Mickey Gilley on his forehead give Nancy a recent photo and ask if she could airbrush the tattoo away. Wanting to give top notch customer service at all times, Nancy spent her entire lunch hour touching up the photo with a packet of Hellmann's mayonnaise that had been in the Free Press break room since the Ford administration.

"I was able to conceal the Mickey Gilley tattoo, but the photo still looked odd. It was as if he'd come back from another dimension but bits of him were still stuck on the other side," Saunders said as she opened a gift of No. 2 pencils and Kinston Centennial mouse pad at her going-away party on Monday.

Even though Nancy's commitment to customer service is unparalleled, even she would occasionally get on someone's bad side.

"I was going over the text for a family reunion announcement with a customer back in 2002, and I suggested we conjugate a few verbs to make the announcement more readable," Saunders said. "The next thing I know, my boss receives an irate phone call from someone who's upset that I offered to conjugate with them."

Saunders said after the angry customer was told what conjugate actually meant, it only made things worse.

Although Nancy is leaving The Free Press, she is not retiring. Plans to spend more time with her children and family abound, but she's also beginning a new career.

"I'll be playing the role of Dorothy in the touring version of 'Summer of 42' starting in October," she said. "They've narrowed the role of Hermie down to either Shia LaBeouf or Jon Dawson."

SCHOOLS, UTILITIES AND LAW ENFORCEMENT HIT HARD BY SHUTDOWN
OCTOBER 3, 2013

In lieu of a column, I've decided to use this space to alert the public to local services that will be affected by the latest government shutdown.

TRANSPORTATION:

Motorists in Lenoir, Greene, Jones and Duplin counties will be operating with partial stoplight service for the foreseeable future. In order to save money on electricity and LED light maintenance, all yellow lights will cease to function as of midnight on Friday.

Green and red lights will still function as normal from 7 a.m. until 7 p.m. After 7 p.m., all traffic lights will be shut down. Drivers are encouraged to use caution and courtesy while driving during non-peak hours.

Drivers in the aforementioned communities will also be seeing fewer STOP and YIELD signs if the government shutdown expands into next week. Emergency personnel have confirmed that crews will be dismantling traffic signs Monday.

"Metal from traffic signs, manhole covers and storm grates can be sold for scrap," said Jack Nance of the N.C. Department of Energy. "The wood posts used to hold up signs in the rural areas will be beneficial as the temperatures drop over the next few weeks. Many local government buildings still have active wood-burning furnaces, so if funds for heating government buildings are depleted we'll be prepared."

Nance said funds raised from selling the traffic signs for scrap would be used to fund an independent study of the effectiveness of road signs, manhole covers and storm grates.

UTILITIES:

In order to conserve energy for essential services such as law enforcement and health care, all residential electrical service will be shut down between the hours of 11 p.m. and 5 a.m. Anyone working third shift is advised to stock up on flashlights, batteries and Vienna sausages.

If purchasing flashlights is not an option, the federal government will be providing one candle per household free of charge. To receive your free candle, visit www.house.gov and click on the "Leadership" tab for instructions. Your candle should be mailed out within four to six weeks after processing.

Matches will be issued by state and local governments on a first-come/first-serve basis. If the match supply is depleted before you receive yours, the feds suggest you rub two sticks together and hope for the best.

Capturing fireflies in old mayonnaise jars is also an option.

LAW ENFORCEMENT:

Federal and local authorities are asking all citizens to refrain from breaking any laws during the government shutdown. Without crimes to respond to, police and sheriff's offices will save thousands of dollars on fuel and vehicle maintenance.

If a crime does occur, citizens are encouraged to handle the situation themselves, be it through persuasive conversation or through the use of baseball bats or stun guns. Anyone feeling the need to take the law into their own hands is asked to subdue and secure the suspects and leave them on the curb to be picked up with the morning trash.

At this very moment, city utility workers are being deputized and equipped with handcuffs and night sticks.

SCHOOLS:

Since schools are already struggling financially, the shutdown is going to hit them the hardest. As of today, there will be no more money in the budget for chalk, so teachers will be holding classes outside in order to draw lessons in the sand with sticks. Curriculum changes known as "Survivalist Core" are also to be enacted immediately.

There will be less of a focus on foreign languages and more time spent on teaching children how to hunt and prepare wild game. Grocery stores and anything associated with an actual society are beginning to fade, so teaching the youth of today how to survive with a bow and arrow is essential.

When the dollar finally collapses, the younger generation will most likely develop its own monetary system based around shiny rocks or those little silver tabs used to open a can of Pepsi. Youngsters who only know how to communicate via social media or texting will be given a grace period to adapt to a world without the Internet.

"After 90 days, children caught rolling their eyes and huffing when an adult asks them a simple question will be paddled with an old phone book," said Walter White of the N.C. Center for Education. "The parents who raised these snotty children will also receive the same punishment — unless of course they like that sort of thing, which would defeat the whole purpose."

CONTROVERSY SURROUNDS KINSTON MEDICAL PRACTICE
OCTOBER 17, 2013

When Robert Smigel decided to start his own medical practice in Kinston, he had no idea what he was in for.

"I'm an ear, nose and throat man," Smigel said. "To me, that's as American as apple pie and French fries. Apparently some people around here don't agree with me."

Smigel, 46, is originally from Boston. His parents, Frances and Ira, ran a chain of funeral parlors in Massachusetts until they retired four years ago. After high school, Robert Smigel admits he was adrift.

"I was always a hard worker, but at 18, I was directionless," Smigel said. "My parents offered to bring me into the family business, so I accepted. After a few years working at the funeral home I realized I wanted to become a doctor."

Although his parents were supportive, they were initially skeptical.

"I thought it would be bad for our funeral home business," Frances Smigel said from her home in Boston. "People were already starting to eat healthier and exercise, which really affected our bottom line. The way we saw it, our son becoming a doctor was going to hurt our bottom line."

The training Robert Smigel received while working at his parent's funeral home gave him a leg up in medical school.

"My fellow students were dreading the day we'd start working with cadavers," Smigel said. "It actually reminded me of home."

After a stint as an emergency room doctor in Detroit, Smigel decided it was time for a change.

"I have family in Kinston and they suggested it would be a good place to start a practice," Smigel said. "When I started checking out office space in the area, I realized all of the available buildings were too big for a medical office, so I decided to use the extra space for a second business."

That second business? A funeral home.

"Being trained as a physician and a mortician, I decided to open the world's first doctor's office/funeral home," Smigel said. "It would be convenient for customers who'd stopped buying ripe bananas, and if a

314

patient were to need a new elbow or thumb, I'd have a fresh inventory right next door.

"To sweeten the deal, if we use your dearly departed Uncle Mortimer's body for spare parts, we'll knock 10 percent off the price of the funeral."

Storm clouds on the horizon struggled to match the intensity on the faces of protesters outside Smigel's office on Monday. Emily Watts, 33, of Jenny Lind, yelled insults at Dr. Smigel while a group of 13 cheered her on.

"It is a conflict of interest to portray yourself as a healer while running a funeral home in the same building," Watts told the crowd. "One-stop shopping is one thing, but this is ridiculous."

Undeterred by the protesters, Smigel says there are benefits to having a funeral home adjacent to a medical practice.

"Sometimes when I tell a patient they need to alter their diet or stop drinking, I get the feeling they're not taking me seriously," Smigel said. "Now, I can walk them over to the morgue and ask them to have a look at the fellow behind door No. 3. You've never seen somebody slim down so fast; sometimes before they even make it out of the room."

Dr. Smigel's Healatorium is located on 1419 Countrybrook Drive, Kinston. Two-for-one specials are available every Tuesday in November.

PARENT SEEKS RELIGIOUS EXEMPTION FROM MATH HOMEWORK
OCTOBER 22, 2013

Age supposedly brings wisdom, but that's not been my experience. The number of things that perplex me has risen exponentially with my age. To this day, I'll never understand why Shelly Long left "Cheers," why Kanye West has a career or why a quarterly magazine doesn't cost 25 cents.

Our oldest tax deduction is a third grader now, and with that comes a giant leap forward in the volume and difficulty of homework. Traditionally, The Wife has helped with math homework and I usually handle the word stuff.

Over the last few weeks, however, I've had no choice but to go back on a promise I made to myself and God many years ago: I've done math.

I do believe the children are our future, and frankly it scares the supper out of me. If they're depending on me and my ilk to help them with anything above basic algebra or geometry, I see crooked buildings and cattywampus bridges in our future. Computers will be nothing more than cigar boxes with flashlights taped to them and the only thing you'll be able to do with a cell phone is make a phone call.

The first dyspeptic episode I remember experiencing came immediately after reading my very first word problem in middle school. It was so terrifying that I remember it even to this day:

"Train A leaves Milwaukee at 7 a.m. traveling at 48 mph. Train B leaves St. Louis at 7:13 a.m. traveling 53 mph. Both trains are heading to New York City. Train A is carrying 4 tons of coal, while Train B is carrying 5 tons of confetti. Although train B is traveling at a faster rate of speed, the conductor of Train A just learned his wife has been fooling around with the milkman. If the conductor of Train A flies into a blind rage and maxes the train's speed out at 87 mph, which train will arrive in New York City first?"

I believed thinking about that question for more than 30 seconds would cause my brain stem to knot up in a most unappealing way. The following was my answer:

"Trains never arrive on time anyway, so the question is moot."

The teacher laughed out loud at my answer but still drew a big red X through it large enough to cover Ruben Studdard and three of his cousins.

This math homework Tax Deduction No. 1 brought home was in my mind intellectually vulgar. Imagine if you will a square divided into nine smaller squares. In the bottom right hand square is the number 2,551. Your task is to glean which numbers — when arranged horizontally and vertically — will add up to both 2,551 and the numbers in the right column that are subtracted from a larger number to arrive at that same number.

My first response was to go out and buy a dog so it would eat this infernal math worksheet. I then considered simply burning the house down with the homework still in it. Knowing my luck as of late all the furniture, Mr. T figurines and family photos would be destroyed while this demonic homework would survive.

Sensing there was no way out, I hunkered down in an attempt to find out how eight numbers that didn't exist might result in another number that does exist. The first couple of scenarios I tried failed so miserably the smoke alarms went off. Somehow, the third try yielded the results we were looking for.

I hadn't been that happy since Daisy Duke started driving a Jeep with no doors on it.

Historically, when we help TD No. 1 with her homework, we'll show her how we came to the answer and then erase it so she'll have to go through the steps herself. In this case, however, I had no idea how I came upon the correct answers. I know I added something to the one number they gave us which resulted in a larger number, but beyond that it was just a miracle.

I kept expecting three wise men to show up with gifts.

It took longer to figure out how I got the right answer than it did to get the right answer. After piecing it together, I ran through it with TD No.1 a few times until she either comprehended what I was trying to say or figured out how far you could get in this life by simply smiling and nodding.

I handed her a blank sheet of paper, a fresh quill and a bottle of ink and after a few minutes she recreated the math miracle. No wise men showed up but that commercial with the talking camel did pop up on the telly a few minutes later.

With homework squared away, I now had time to tackle the 10 other things I needed to get done. Sadly, I didn't have the will. Any vestige of ambition left in my tank was devoured by math homework. Yes, math is a silent killer.

My gut tells me we haven't seen the last of this math turnout. Word on the street is they'll keep sending it home from now until she finishes college.

Right now I'm leafing through every piece of Methodist doctrine I can get my hands on. If the love of money is the root of all evil, then math is bound to be somewhere between the root and the trunk.

Religious exemption here we come.

RICH NEIGHBORHOODS TARGETED BY
MASKED GROUPS
OCTOBER 24, 2013

Young children and maladjusted adults everywhere are making Halloween plans like there's no tomorrow. In a related story, the U.S. government is threatening to cancel Fridays altogether to save money.

Nadine Hurley, 46, of Hookerton won't be dressing up this year, but she is busy making Halloween plans for her two children.

"I've been doing some research and I've mapped out where the higher income families live in Lenoir, Greene and Jones counties," Hurley said. "The current itinerary I have mapped out is a 58-mile loop that I believe will take around three hours. Based on the property taxes, these people are paying, they should be handing out your higher-end candies such as Snicker's, Baby Ruth and Kit Kat."

Hurley is not alone in her quest to acquire the most expensive carbohydrates this year. The P.U. Research Center estimates that roughly 43 percent of all families that participate in Halloween actively target richer neighborhoods.

Laura Palmer of Jenny Lind is an attorney who has seen the number of trick-or-treaters creep into triple digit numbers over the last few years.

"When I was a kid, my parents would take me to the homes of people we knew; it was totally out of the question to take food from a stranger," Palmer said. "Nowadays, these kids are organized. Last year, a group from Goldsboro rented a bus and shook down the entire neighborhood in about 10 minutes. By the end of the night, I was giving out leftover meatloaf."

Dr. Lawrence Jacoby is one of Palmer's neighbors who have decided to fight back.

"I didn't work my way through eight years of medical school to just give away everything I own," Jacoby said. "To combat Halloween— which is the Latin term for socialism — I've drafted a seven-page candy application form that all trick-or-treaters must fill out before receiving any of my hard-earned candy."

He continued: "I'm also going to require three forms of identification, fingerprints and a canceled check. And you teenagers who are already old enough to shave need not come around here looking for free candy. If you're willing to rake a few leaves or wash my car, then we'll talk about a Reece's cup.

"Also, I'm in no mood for any smart alecs who just look depressed and say 'my costume is misery'. If you TP my house, be forewarned: I'm a doctor; I know where all the important stuff is."

Many residents of affluent neighborhoods have resorted to posting "No Trespassing" signs on their property on Halloween night. Others have decided to turn what has traditionally been a night of fun into a learning experience.

"We only hand out nutritional treats on Halloween," said Shelley Johnson of Maysville. "My husband Leo and I make cucumber, celery and mint smoothies for the kids. If their Halloween masks prevent them from being able to drink, we'll also have a large supply of rutabaga jerky and asparagus fritters on hand."

On the other side of the tracks, families who are barely making ends meet are doing their best to take part in the Halloween tradition.

"We're giving out M&Ms, but just one at a time," said Robert Briggs of Seven Springs. "I work at a barbecue restaurant, so if we run out of candy, we'll switch over to hushpuppies to finish out the night."

While many people will be turning out the lights and hiding in the basement on Oct. 31, one resident of a well-to-do Kinston community has no problem with the disproportionate amount of foot traffic his neighborhood attracts.

"There is nothing better than handing out sugary treats to large groups of children," said Dale Cooper, a local dentist. "I've already flown in cases of soft drinks from Mexico that are made with real sugar. My wife and I have already prepared 300 goody bags that include six-packs of sodas and boxes of Goobers, Junior Mints and Skittles.

"We've also got candy bars in there — Butterfinger, Mr. Goodbar — and I don't mean the dopey 'fun size' either; these suckers are the size of license plates."

LOCAL PRISONS TO WELCOME TRICK-OR-TREATERS
OCTOBER 29, 2013

In an effort to close an ever widening budgetary gap, several North Carolina prisons will be hosting haunted houses during the Halloween season.

"We're running out of money," said Strother Martin, director of the N.C. Dept. of Corrections. "There's talk of doing away with free legal counsel, and the recreation budget has already been cut to nearly nothing."

Just last week a group of inmates over in Rutherford County staged a production of "Joseph and the Amazing Technicolor Dream-coat" without a coat. It's pretty hard for me to rehabilitate a guy doing 15 years for taking a pipe wrench to his anger management instructor while asking him to pretend he's wearing a coat that isn't there."

Martin said anyone who disagrees with him should look at the numbers.

"The N.C. Department of Corrections is currently housing 37,000 inmates at an average cost of $76/ day," Martin said. "Multiply 37,000 by 76 and you've got— carry the one — I'm not exactly sure what you've got, but it's a lot of money."

In an effort to refill the prison system's spacious coffers, Martin brought in Christopher St. Clair of The Guffman Group. St. Clair was named "America's Top Prison Fundraiser" six years in a row by Better Jails and Penitentiaries Magazine.

"My first idea was to let the parents of children with behavioral issues pay a fee that would allow them to bring their little brats to the prison for trick-or-treating," St. Claire said. "That idea was met with trepidation by some of the more conservative prison officials, so that's when I pitched the idea of turning the prison into a haunted house for Halloween."

While haunted houses have been staged in abandoned prisons across the country, North Carolina is the first to allow an active prison to do so.

"People are always complaining about the lameness of most haunted houses," St. Claire said. "They'll have a guy rev a chain saw a few times and hang a few plastic spiders from a tree, but it's so amateur. We've got people in these prisons who are experts when it comes to slinging chains, bats and gats. If you can find a more authentic house of horrors this Halloween I'll eat my beret."

St. Claire has spent the last few months traveling to prisons all over the state in preparation for Halloween week.

"We've been scouting the inmate population for just the right people to play homicidal maniacs," St. Claire said. "It's been tough bringing some of these guys at the grey bar hotel out of their shells. You'd think a guy who tried to take out an entire Denny's with a flame thrower would be able to summon a little intensity."

While the idea of arming convicted felons with machetes, hammers and torches has stirred more controversy than Duke University's recent decision to hire Al Sharpton as their new lacrosse coach, St. Clarie wears the tumult like a snug turtleneck.

"This isn't the first time the people of North Carolina have gotten all knotted up over one of St. Claire's ideas," said Dennis Weaver of Seven Springs. "St. Claire advised me on an adult-themed haunted house I operate every year just off N.C. 55. He helped me come up with stuff that would scare any adult, like 'The Hall of Mortgages,' 'The Tunnel of Taxes,' 'The Visiting In-Laws,' 'The Pren-up Cleanup,' 'The Husband Who Thinks Bodily Noises Are Endearing,' 'The Wife Who Doesn't Recognize 'Yes' or 'No' As An Acceptable Answer,' 'The Enlarged Prostate,' 'The Audit Room,' 'The Political Zombie Who Thinks His Candidate Is Somehow Better Than The Other Guy,' and the ghastly "Radio That Plays 'Wagon Wheel 24hrs A Day.'""

Admission to all prison-hosted haunted houses is $5. Soft drinks, hot dogs and semi-automatic weapons will be available for purchase at concession stands.

KINSTON MAN CAUSES HAVOC ON CRUISE LINER
OCTOBER 31, 2013

Free Press Editor Bryan Hanks has been out of town since last Friday. The lucky dog has been on a cruise with his better half, a woman who to this day still gets calls from Amnesty International asking if she is being held against her will.

If you know Hanks, you know he loves social media. He lives for Twitter, has a vendetta against Face-book (although it's just Twitter with pictures) and has lately been obsessed with Vine. Even though Hanks turned 68 last month, he has the social media prowess of an 18-year-old. Sometimes his obsession with Twitter gets him in trouble — like the time he got caught up in a Twitter war with Dick Vitale during a briss.

The plus side of Hanks' love of Twitter is that if you love the man like we do, it's easy to keep up with him. Just the other day I was feeling a bit down, but all of that changed when I saw a photo Hanks posted of himself in the water somewhere near the Cayman Islands. It made me happy to see our leader having a good time, but after a while jealousy set in and I spent the rest of the day duct-taping his computer to the ceiling of his office.

Aquatic respites aside, all is not well on the Bryan Hanks Caribbean Tour 2013. According to Tweets and Facebook postings, what was supposed to be a well-deserved, restful vacation has turned into a series of international incidents.

By all accounts, there have been a few issues with the buffet. Anyone who has ever been on a cruise knows the food is incredible and plentiful. While most passengers seemed happy with the food on the ship, Hanks apparently complained so vociferously about the lack of Cheetos on the buffet, the ship's captain made an unscheduled stop in West Bay to purchase cheese doodles from a Walmart. Hanks appreciated the effort, but was incensed that the captain bought the soft, poofy kind instead of crunchy.

Although details are sketchy, a fellow passenger Tweeted a photo of Hanks being removed from the main dining room on Tuesday night. After drinking two Shirley Temples, Hanks allegedly proceeded to mold an entire bowl of potato salad in the image of Virginia basketball legend Ralph

Sampson. A press release posted on the website of Affondamento Cruise Lines stated the buffet was immediately shut down, although Bryan Hanks refused to return to his cabin without his cheese doodles.

Hanks has reportedly also had a run-in with the band that plays in the ship's ballroom. To accommodate the tastes of thousands of passengers, the band historically plays a cross-section of pop, r&b and rock hits. While most passengers seemed happy with the band's repertoire, Bryan Hanks reportedly stormed the stage during the middle of "Wagon Wheel" and demanded the band play only Barry Manilow songs for the rest of the night.

Thinking if they played just one Manilow song it would diffuse the situation, the band launched into a spirited version of "Copacabana" with Hanks on lead vocals. By all accounts Hanks gave a spot-on performance, even bringing the band down in the middle of the song to deliver a Bono-style spoken word section about ending world dandruff.

"It's been an experience having Mr. Hanks on the ship," said Capt. Murray Slaughter. "I thought asking members of the crew to sign his speedo was a bit much, but luckily there was only so much room."

During a costume party on Monday Hanks mistook a party-goer for an actual pirate. In a panic he threw his fiance' at the would-be pirate and jumped overboard to escape. A few hours later a shrimp boat crew found Hanks clinging to a bag of cheese doodles just off the coast of Georgetown. Upon returning to the ship, Hanks assured the captain he would calm down and relax by the pool. He relaxed so much the ship's staff had to quadruple the pool's chlorine levels.

Late Wednesday Hanks donned a "King of the World" t-shirt and duct-taped himself to the front of the ship, where crew members plan to leave him until the ship returns to Miami on Saturday.

Copy Desk Chief Richard Clark has been filling in for the vacationing Bryan Hanks this week. When asked to comment on Hanks' exploits on the open sea, Clark seemed to take it all in stride.

"I've been using Bryan's office all week — which has been a challenge with all the New Kids On The Block posters on the wall," Clark said. "I'm three days in and I'm still scared to open any of the drawers at his desk."

LOCAL REACTION TO AFFORDABLE CARE ACT MIXED
NOVEMBER 5, 2013

With all the controversy swirling around the malfunction of the HealthCare.gov website, it's taken a few days for local business owners to fully digest how they will be affected by the Affordable Care Act.

"We haven't been able to afford pretzels for the break room since 2004," said Terry Jones of Chilton Rental Properties in Kinston. "Right now, our company health care plan is a bottle of store-brand aspirin and half a box of kids-size Scooby Doo Band Aids under the sink. I've yet to take a month off of work to read up on the Affordable Care Act, but if it means we can get big-boy Band Aids, then I'm willing to give it a shot."

While Jones contemplates the ability to purchase adhesive bandages that do not prominently feature an animated talking dog and its dope smoking dirty-hippie owner, another local business owner is contemplating shutting down completely.

"You won't hear this on the TV, but did you know that according to the Affordable Care Act, I have to allow each of my employees to take a 30-minute nap after lunch?" said Graham Chapman, Owner/operator of Ramrod Equipment Rental in Snow Hill. "It's not a big deal for the younger guys on the crew, but you get a 48-year-old man in a deep sleep in the middle of the day and he's pretty much furniture for the rest of the day."

Chapman added, "If that's not enough, most of our guys snore at a semi-pro level. It's going to be tough maintaining a business-like atmosphere in our lobby when it sounds like the local clown college is giving a balloon animal class down the hall."

Bucklesberry native and Applebee's table maintenance coordinator Michael Palin thinks the Affordable Care Act is a great idea that is long overdue.

"Thanks to the ACA, I'll have health insurance as an adult for the first time," Pal-in said. "I've spent most of my life worrying about my health; I've avoided sugar, caffeine and cholesterol for the past 20 years but that's about to change. As soon as my insurance kicks in, I plan on eating nothing but Ben & Jerry's Ted Nougat Crunch and triple bacon cheeseburgers from here on out.

"I'll swing by the doctor's office every few thousand miles to have all the pipes flushed, but otherwise it's Cinco De Mayonaise all day, every day. I'm also interested in this meth I've been hearing so much about."

As of this writing, improvements to the Health-Care.gov website were beginning to speed up the insurance purchasing process for consumers.

"Listen, we realize Health-Care.gov was riddled with problems when it was unveiled but that's all in the past now," said Secretary of Health and Human Services Kathy Sybilius. "Over the past 24 hours, over 27 Americans have been able to successfully navigate the website and purchase health insurance."

While Sybilius's numbers were accurate, FactCheck.org reports that three of 27 customers were stoned college students buying health insurance for their bongs.